"On the evening of November 16, 1957, visito   rm-house-not in the backwoods New England but in rural Wisconsin. Hanging in an adjacent shed was the nude, butchered body of a woman. She had been suspended by the heels and decapitated, then disemboweled like a steer. In the kitchen next to the shed, fire flickered in an old-fashioned potbellied stove. A pan set on top of it contained a human heart.

But amidst the accumulated debris of years in the three tenanted rooms, the searchers found:

Two shin bones;
A pair of human lips;
Four human noses;
Bracelets of human skin
Four chairs, their woven; cane seats replaced by strips of human skin;
A quart can, converted into a tom-tom by skin stretched over both top and bottom;
A bowl made from the inverted half of a human skull;
A purse with a handle made of skin;
Four "death masks"-the well preserved skin from the faces of women-mounted at eye-level on the walls;
Five more such "masks" in plastic bags, stowed in a closet;
Ten female human heads, the tops of which had been sawed off above the eyebrows;
A pair of leggins, fashioned from skin from human legs;
A vest made from the skin stripped from a woman's torso.

The bodies of 15 different women had been mutliated to provide these trophies. The number of hearts and other organs which had been cooked on the stove or stored in the refrigerator will never be known."

From *The Shambles of Ed Gein* by Robert Bloch.

THE ED GEIN FILE

A Psycho's Confession and Case Documents

Produced and Edited By John Borowski

Waterfront Productions

THE ED GEIN FILE: A PSYCHO'S CONFESSION AND CASE DOCUMENTS

Cover Illustration by Erica Kauffman - atomicotton.com

Published By:
Waterfront Productions
P.O. Box 607085
Chicago, IL 60660
U.S.A.

ISBN
978-0-9976140-0-8

OTHER FILMS BY FILMMAKER JOHN BOROWSKI

serialkillerculture.com

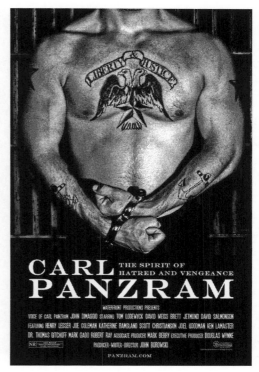

panzram.com

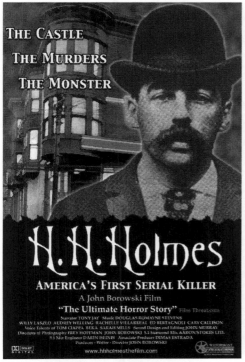

hhholmesthefilm.com

albertfishfilm.com

OTHER BOOKS BY AUTHOR JOHN BOROWSKI

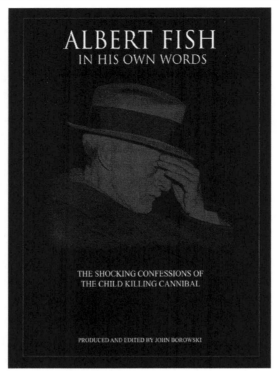

albertfishfilm.com

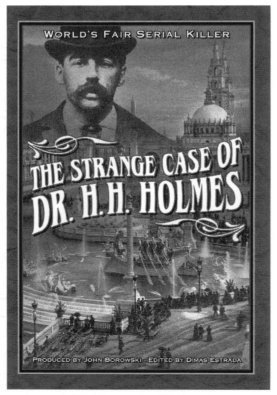

hhholmesthefilm.com

Plainfield Butcher's Story!
Admits Murder, Robbing Graves

Girard Gets Suspended 3-Year Term

MALEBA-HI, Japan, Nov. 19 (Tuesday) (P) A Japanese court Tuesday convicted G.I. William S. Girard of killing a woman brass warmonger on a "rubbish when" and gave him a suspended sentence of three years.

The suspension provides for four years good behavior...

A-Project Cancelation Headed Off

...

ED GEIN (FOREGROUND) AND SHERIFF ART SCHLEY LEAVING FOR MURDER SCENE

Killer Tells How He 'Deer-Dressed' Widow at Farm

By Journal Staff Writer

WAUTOMA, Wis., Nov. 19—A timid 51-year-old bachelor handyman, his hands trembling as he shielded his face, ended for the first time bloody details of the butchery of a Plainfield widow and his farmhouse "deathhouse" where her body and 10 other human skulls were found.

Edward Gein, longtime solitary occupant of a farm 10 miles northwest of here, ended a 30-hour silence with a statement to Waushara County District Atty. Earl Kileen in which:

• Gein admitted transporting the body of Mrs. Bernice Worden, 58, from her hardware store in the hamlet of Plainfield by truck and car to his woodshed at his farm home, where he butchered her.

• He maintained that the 10 other skulls and portions of female bodies discovered on the farm came from local cemeteries in a series of grave robberies he committed over an undetermined number of years.

Gein to Face Lie Detector Test

Kileen released portions of Gein's confession before and after the man described his confession to a typical lawyer. Magistrate...was arraigned before County Judge Boyd Clark at the Courthouse here.

He was charged with robbery and was placed under $10,000 bond. From the Kileen said a murder charge would be filed against him as soon as all investigating agencies have completed their investigations.

The district attorney had requested bail of only $5,000 but the court set the higher figure, explaining that if other charges should follow, the bond should be adequate.

Kileen said he was satisfied Gein was telling the truth when he claimed the 10 human skulls at his gruesome collection came away from the graves of already deceased women, and not as previously speculated from victims abducted and slaughtered.

However, Kileen said Gein will be taken to Madison to undergo a lie detector test in the offices of the State Crime Laboratory.

Explanations Branded Vague

The request was made by Crime Lab investigators on the scene, determined to use all scientific means available to get answers on one of the most shocking crimes in Wisconsin history.

The answers provided by Gein himself in his initial statement to the district attorney's office provided only the vaguest and most in...coated explanations for his...

State Farmer Groups Agree

Neighbors Now Remember Gein as 'a Strange One'

(Courtesy of Renick Wooly.)

CONTENTS

FOREWARD

Whenever most people think of the Hitchcock classic, *Psycho*, I assume the shower scene when Norman stabs poor Janet Leigh to death is what comes to mind. And for good reason... it's an iconic, shocking, visceral moment in American horror. In American film, in fact. Still, my memory of this terrifying story is a different one. My fascination with the study of serial murderers and extreme killers is grounded in the intersection of abnormal psychology and pure horror. When Norman's mother is turned around in her chair to reveal her rotting corpse, dressed and wearing a wig on top of her open-mouthed skull, and the moviegoers come to the realization of the depth of insanity and depravity in which Norman is immersed, that moment stands still in time. Norman Bates and his mother were of course, heavily influenced by the very real story out of Plainfield Wisconsin; that of Edward Gein. I've always believed the most terrifying figures are the ones with which you believe you could actually cross paths. Ed Gein's story and his influence in American horror, on more than one occasion, is possibly unmatched. So the story of Ed Gein is one that needs to be told, and told well. As a person who respects the genre and cares about how it's presented, I'm pleased this story is being told by John Borowski, whose reputation for immersing himself in the history of a subject and "wearing" it, (much like Ed would) is the way it should be done. The value of such a compilation of documents, interviews, profiles and the like is difficult to overstate. Anyone who is familiar with the literature of the topic of serial and famous murderers could tell you of the case study and second-hand recounts usually encountered. While there's nothing wrong with most of these resources, the availability of transcripts of actual conversations, rather than someone else's summary and interpretation, is invaluable. As I pored through the interviews of "Eddie" by investigators and doctors, I was most struck first by the gentle hand they took with him. It's easy to think law enforcement officers and even mental health professionals in 1957 could be less than empathetic with the crazy man who'd murdered a couple of locals and performed bizarre acts of grave robbing and body part collection. When you read these pages and find yourself involved in the conversations, you see the value in the soft, friendly approach and insight that allowed interviewers to ask Ed the most difficult of questions, and elicit, eventually, some pretty honest and graphic responses. This was due in no small part by the interviewers' abilities to make Ed feel like they were able to understand what it was like to be there, an empathetic skill difficult to find to this day. I also was taken by Ed's journey of conversation, from his denials to his "self-serving amnesia or vagueness," as a doctor put it, to his eventual admissions and very clear descriptions of events. Eddie sometimes used wording like "I didn't kill her that I know of," or "I might have done something but not to my knowledge." This verbal qualifying seems to belie his immaturity, his attempt to obfuscate his responsibility, not as someone who would eventually be found insane by the State of Wisconsin, but by a child who was caught taking money from his mother's purse. Without reading these real-time raw documents, all you remember about Gein is his crazed behavior and being found schizophrenic and legally insane by the doctors who analyzed him and the courts who judged him. Putting yourself in the room where Ed-

1

ward Gein said, "it will show my mental imbalance," gives the reader another view, a context of a man very aware of his status as a person with a mental disturbance and that value as a criminal defense. His continuous references to blackouts and headaches might have been sincere, but the more you read, the more you question. One last thing I took from those pages is Ed Gein's label as a serial murderer. This is debated by scholars, because Ed "only" killed 2 victims, Bernice Worden and Mary Hogan. He's easily dismissed as an insane grave robber obsessed with his mother's memory. I agree with the theory that numbers are irrelevant in determining the serial killer mindset. The fact is, Ed Gein's actions, and his future intent for creating the "dolls" that brought him comfort, is clear by his words and were only ceased by his arrest. Gein was a serial murderer every bit as much as his fellow Wisconsin resident Jeffrey Dahmer. And while I'll always remember and appreciate Gein's influence in films such as *Psycho*, reading these interviews added a new memory for me: the scene from *Silence of the Lambs* when Buffalo Bill pranced in front of the mirror, "adjusting" himself to physically appear as a woman... and the admission that Ed Gein had actually preceded this behavior in real life. Just a bit more graphically. I am confident in the new perspectives and context John's book and presentation will bring you.

Stephen J Giannangelo
Author, *Real-Life Monsters: A Psychological Examination of the Serial Murderer*

Portrait of Ed Gein. (Lou Rusconi)

1. FULL NAME OF CHILD

2. COLOR

3. SEX

4. NAMES OF OTHER ISSUE LIVING

5. FULL NAME OF FATHER

6. OCCUPATION OF FATHER

7. FULL MAIDEN NAME OF MOTHER

8. DATE OF BIRTH

9. PLACE OF BIRTH

10. BIRTHPLACE OF FATHER

11. BIRTHPLACE OF MOTHER

12. NAME: ATTENDANT SIGNING CERTIFICATE

13. RESIDENCE OF SUCH PERSON

14. DATE OF CERTIFICATE

15. NAME OF HEALTH OFFICER OR CLERK

16. RESIDENCE

17. DATE OF REGISTRATION

18. ANY ADDITIONAL CIRCUMSTANCES

Ed Gein's Birth Certificate.

U. S. BUREAU OF INVESTIGATION, DEPARTMENT OF JUSTICE
WASHINGTON, D. C.

Record from: __Waushara County Sheriff's Office__ (Address) __Wautoma, Wis.__

On the above line please state whether Police Department, Sheriff's Office, or County Jail

Date of arrest __11-16-57__

Charge __Murder__

Disposition of case __Committed State Hosp. Waupun, Wis. for 30 days obs.__

Residence __Plainfield, Wis.__

Place of birth __8-28-06, La Crosse, Wis.__

Nationality __U.S.__

Criminal specialty ....

Age __51__ Build .... brown,

Height __5'6-3/4"__ Comp. .... Hair __greying__

Weight __146__ Eyes __blue (right eye__

Scars and marks .... __partially blind)__

PLEASE PASTE PHOTO HERE

11-18-57

CRIMINAL HISTORY

NAME	NUMBER	CITY OR INSTITUTION	DATE	CHARGE	DISPOSITION OR SENTENCE

(Please furnish all additional criminal history and police record on separate sheet)

I-7-66

HX U   B.

6

35

Name Gein, Edward Theodore

Alias none

Class.

No.   Color W   Sex M   Ref.

RIGHT HAND

1. Thumb	2. Index Finger	3. Middle Finger	4. Ring Finger	5. Little Finger

LEFT HAND

6. Thumb	7. Index Finger	8. Middle Finger	9. Ring Finger	10. Little Finger

Classified_____ Assembled _____	Note Amputations	Prisoner's Signature
Searched _____ Verified _____	None	*Edward Gein*
Index Card_____ _____ Answered _____		

Four Fingers Taken Simultaneously				Four Fingers Taken Simultaneously
Left Hand	L. Thumb	R. Thumb	Right Hand	

Ed Gein's Fingerprint Chart.

AUTOPSY REPORT OF BERNICE WORDEN

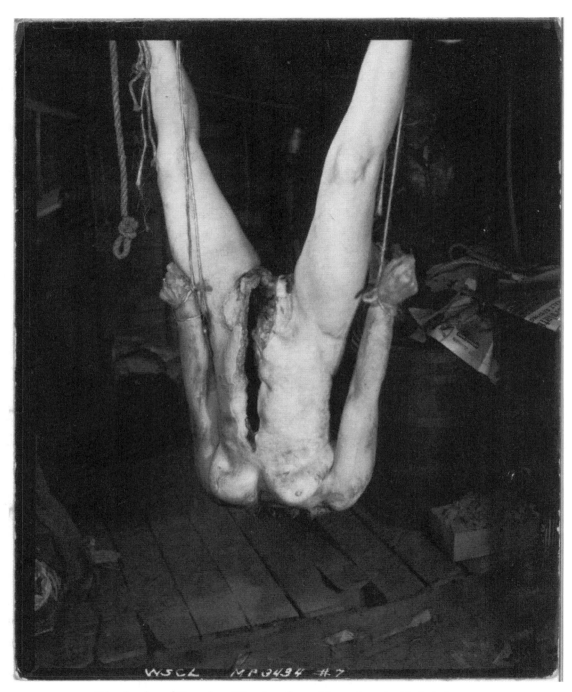

The body of Bernice Worden found hanging in Gein's barn.

Sheboygan Memorial Hospital

INCORPORATED
Sheboygan, Wisconsin

R E P O R T   O N   P O S T   M O R T E M   E X A M I N A T I O N

Body of Mrs. Bernice Worden, Plainfield, Wisconsin
Requested by Wisconsin State Crime Laborabory
Performed in Goult's Funderal Home, Plainfield, Wisconsin
Assisting: Mr. Allan Wilimovsky, Firearms Identification Specialist
            Mr. James E. Halligan, Jr., Micro-analyst

13A

General information:

    The body of a murdered and mutilated woman, Mrs. Bernice Worden, had been found in the woodshed of the old Gein farmhouse near Plainfield, Wisconsin. Investigation which had led to this discovery had been started in the hardware store owned and operated by Mrs. Worden, where an incompletely wiped pool of blood had been found. Further observation had led to the belief that the body had been dragged through the store, loaded upon a truck, then transferred to a private car in which the body had allegedly been brought to the place where it was discovered. The body had been found hanging by the heels from the roof bars--decapitated and eviscerated. Head and viscera had been found in the same location, the vulva in a box, and the heart in a plastic bag. Before performing the autopsy the above mentioned locations were visited.

Autopsy

Inspection:

    The body was that of an over middle aged, allegedly 58 year old woman, well shaped, and in a good state of nutrition. It had been decapitated at shoulder level by a smooth circular cut which severed skin, all the soft structures and the intervertebral cartilage between the 6th and 7th cervical vertebrae had been cut with a sharp instrument. There was no evidence of jagged edges indicating that no axe or similar implement had been used.

    The body had been opened by a median incision from the manubrium sterni

11

WSCL MF3434 #4

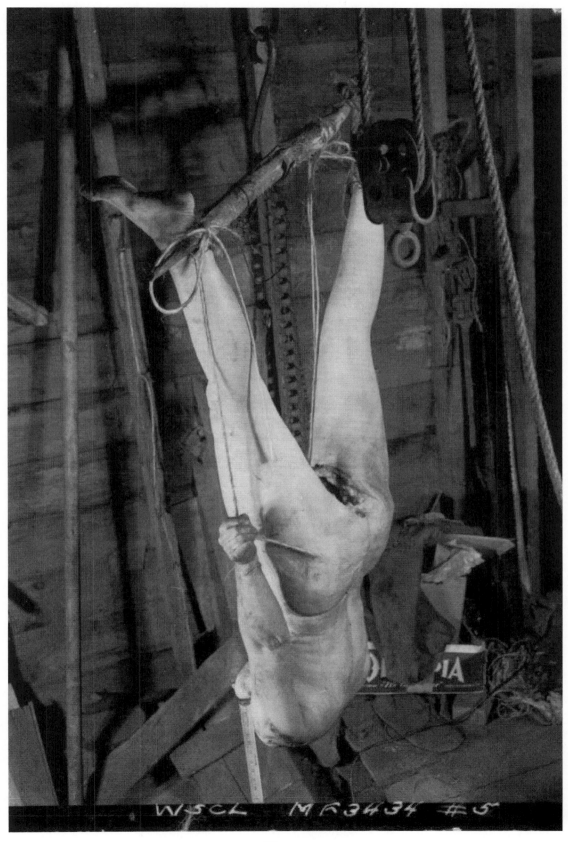

Sheboygan Memorial Hospital
INCORPORATED
Sheboygan, Wisconsin

PAGE 2
REPORT ON POST MORTEM EXAMINATION CONTD.
R$_e$: Body of Mrs. Bernice Worden

and extending in the midline to the area just above the mons veneris. Here

the cut circled around the external genitalia for the complete removal of

the vulva, lower vagina, and the anus with the lowest portion of the rectum.

To accomplish this, the symphysis pubis had been split and the pubic bones

widely separated. From the appearance of the cut for evisceration it was

concluded that the cut was started from the lower end and terminated above

the stomach pit. The reason for this was the somewhat jagged appearance of

the cut skin hear the chest indicating hesitation in terminating the knife cut.

The vulva and adjoining structures that had been removed were presented

in a carton box together with preserved and dried other specimens of the same

type. The freshly removed vulva fitted well into the tissue defect of the

body. Only few pubic hairs had remained on both sides of the removed organs

and a portion of this hairy skin was removed for purpose of identification.

Examination of the outer genitalia revealed no evidence of trauma and no

conclusion could be reached whether or not sexual intercourse had taken place.

The body cavities had been completely eviscerated together with most of

the diaphragm. Inspection of the trunk and extremities revealed how the body

had been hoisted by the heels.

There was a deep cut above the Achilles tendon of the right leg and a

pointed crossbar made of a rough wooden stick covered by bark had been forced

underneath the tendon. The other side of the crossbar had been tied to a cord

which was tightly fastened to a cut of the leg above the heel. This cut had

severed the Achilles tendon and had necessitated the tying with cord to hold

PAGE 3
REPORT ON POST MORTEM EXAMINATION CONTD.
Re: Body of Mrs. Bernice Worden

the body securely to the crossbar. The length of the crossbar was estimated as about three feet. Both wrists had been tied with longer hemp ropes to the corresponding ends of the crossbar attached to the feet, thus holding the arms firmly when the body had been suspended by the heels.

Inspection of the skin surface of the body revealed dirt covering of the shoulders, mostly the upper dorsal area, and the dirt resembled dry mud in thin scaly crusts. The skin of the back, both arms and legs, less of chest and abdomen was somewhat discolored by dust which showed irregular smudgy areas of heavier covering. Rather striking was the amount of black dust covering both plantar surfaces, dust which appeared somewhat "rubbed in", as if from walking barefooted on a dirty, dusty floor.

Both breasts appeared good sized and, for her age, well formed. They felt medium firm, mostly because the adipose tissue had hardened from the exposure to cold. The right nipple appeared normal, the left was somewhat inverted. Both breasts appeared to lean upward, apparently due to the long suspension by the heels. There was no evidence of mutilation of the breasts.

Inspection of the body (trunk and extremities) revealed no evidence of ante mortem trauma. The exsanquination was complete, only finger nails showed moderate cyanosis. On the left ring finger was a cameo ring. The empty body cavities were glistening and free from blood, appeared as if they had been washed. No fractures of the trunk or extremities were found. The 7th cervical vertebra was removed for further examination by the Wisconsin State Crime Laboratory.

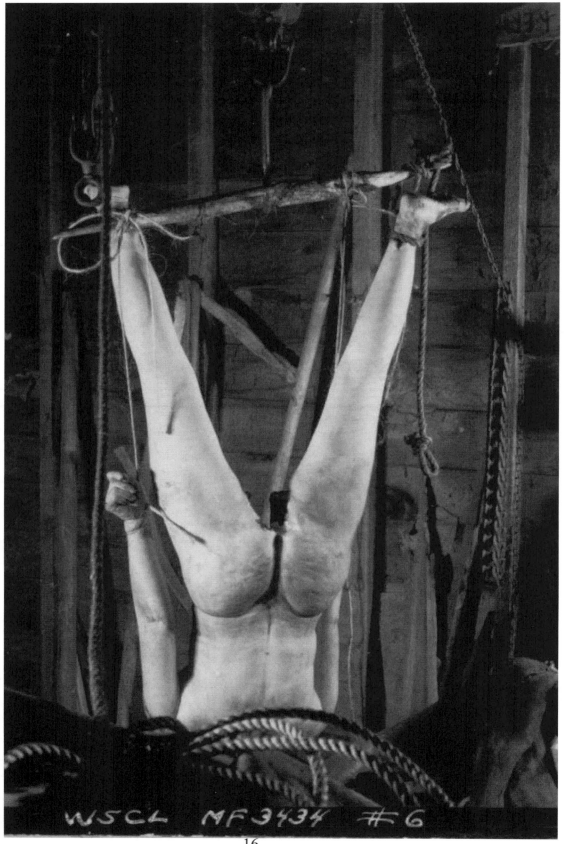

WSCL MF3434 #6

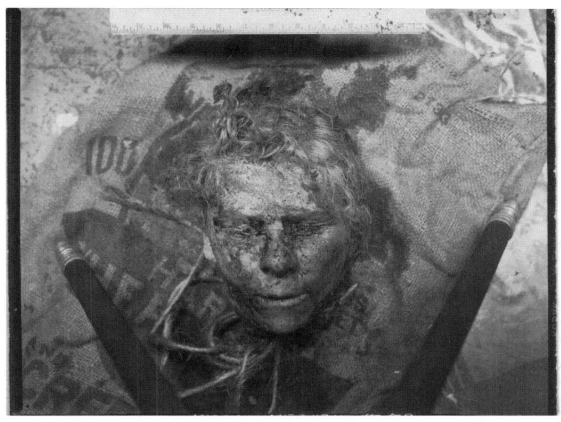

Bernice Worden's head.

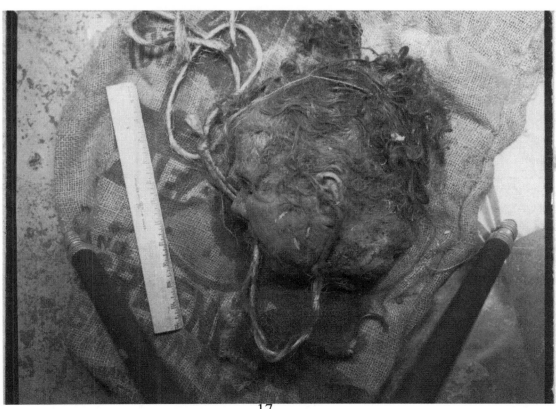

Sheboygan Memorial Hospital

INCORPORATED

Sheboygan, Wisconsin

PAGE 4
REPORT ON POST MORTEM EXAMINATION CONTD.
Re: Body of Mrs. Bernice Worden

Visceral organs:

The thoracic and abdominal viscera had been separately kept, wrapped in newspaper, and hidden in a bundle of old clothing. These viscera consisted of both lungs with the trachea, the aorta from the base to the abdominal bifurcation, the esophagus, stomach, small and large intestines with mesentary and omentum to the lower rectum. En bloc with this were removed: The spleen, pancreas, adrenals, kidneys with the ureters, upper half of the urine bladder, and internal genital organs. Separately removed had been:

1. Heart, (without the pericardium) and this had been kept in a plastic bag.
2. Liver.

EXAMINATION OF THE VISCERAL ORGANS:

Lungs:

Trachea and large bronchi contained some aspirated blood. The mediastinal lymphnodes were normal, all lobes were crepitant, showed no passive congestion and the cut surfaces appeared normal.

Heart:

Size and anatomical configuration were normal. The valves showed no pathological changes. TV measured 9, PV 6.5, MV 10, and AV 6.5 cm. The base of the aorta showed a minimal degree of atheromatosis, both coronary ostia were patent, and the coronary vessels appeared thinwalled, without evidence of sclerosis. The heart muscle was firm, reddish brown, the greatest thickness of the left ventricular wall was 1.2 cm., of the right 0.3 cm. There was no evidence of any traumatic lesion.

Esophagus:

contained no blood or vomitus.

18

Sheboygan Memorial Hospital

INCORPORATED

Sheboygan, Wisconsin

PAGE 5
REPORT ON POST MORTEM EXAMINATION CONTD.
Re: Body of Mrs. Bernice Worden

Stomach:
The stomach was almost empty, showed no pathological changes.

Intestines:
Small and large intestines appeared normal.

Pancreas:
Size and appearance were normal.

Liver:
The size was within normal limits, the surface smooth and glistening, the cut surface reddish brown with normal architectural markings. The gall-bladder had been separated from the liver with a wedge-shaped segment of parenchyma, apparently by cutting. The lumen of the gallbladder contained liquid green bile, no stones.

Spleen:
Size and color appeared normal. The capsule was somewhat wrinkled.

Adrenals:
The left adrenal had been torn in the process of evisceration, appeared otherwise normal, same the right adrenal.

Kidneys:
Both kidneys were normal in size, the capsules stripped easily leaving a smooth red surface. Cut surfaces revealed no abnormal findings. Ureters and bladder were normal.

The examination of the viscera revealed no evidence of ante mortem trauma.

Head:
The head with the neck was submitted in a separate cardboard box. It fitted with the trunk of the body. The hair was medium short cut, somewhat curly, and appeared soiled with dust and smeared with blood. The color of the hair was dark, showing considerable graying. Examination of the scalp revealed

PAGE 6
REPORT ON POST MORTEM EXAMINATION CONTD.
Re: Body of Mrs. Bernice Worden

a longitudinal laceration 2 x 1 cm. with ragged edges 3.5 cm. to the right
of the midline over the occipital bone, 8 cm. above the neck hairline, 4 cm.
laterally and above the protuberantia occipitalis externa. A roundish hole
of the scalp which was difficult to find on outer inspection, measured, when
moderately stretched 0.76 cm. in diameter. The edge of the defect revealed
a narrow marginal abrasion. There was no tear in the contour of the opening
and no evidence of burn, nor could any powder particles be grossly visualized.
This skin defect suggesting the entrance wound of a bullet was located to the
left of the midline and about 6 cm. above the neck hairline, 3.5 cm. laterally and 2 cm. above the outer occipital protuberantia.

The face appeared covered with dust in irregular distribution. There
was no evidence of external trauma to the face. Both eyes were closed. The
pupils appeared moderately dilated, equal, measuring about 0.6 cm. in diameter.
There was no evidence of hematoma in the facial area. The nose appeared
intact on palpation, but there was blood in both nostrils. The left ear had
a hooked spike inserted, the tip of which was at the time of examination 2 cm.
deep in the external ear canal. There were slight, apparently post mortem
excoriations, on the outer border of the ear canal. Blood oozed from this
ear in larger quantities than the excoriations indicated.

Tied to the head of the hooked spike was a cord to which another hooked
spike of the same size had been attached. This right spike was at the time
of examination not inserted in the right ear canal. No excoriation and no
blood could be found in the right ear.

The neck revealed no evidence of applied force, like from strangling,

PAGE 7
REPORT ON POST MORTEM EXAMINATION CONTD.
Re: Body of Mrs. Bernice Worden

no finger or nail imprints, nor scratches. The trachea and larynx appeared normal. The portion of the lower medulla oblongata and the upper cervical spine had been ripped out. This portion of the spinal cord was not found.

ANATOMICAL EXAMINATION OF THE HEAD:

After removal of the scalp there were two hemorrhagic areas found, the larger of which, 7 cm. in diameter, corresponded to the above dexcribed laceration of the right posterior inferior area of the head, the smaller, 3 cm. in diameter, to the bullet hole on the left lower portion of the head. No actual hematoma was present, but the blood must have circulated at the time both traumas had occurred. There was no evidence of contusion in the remaining tissues of the scalp. The bony skull revealed two defects. The one on the right posterior inferior area located as described above consisted of a chipped angular defect, the one on the left side appeared as a round hole characteristic for the entrance effect of a bullet. This measured 0.8 x 0.76 cm. in diameter on the tabula externa, was somewhat inverted funnel-shaped with a larger bony defect on the tabula interna 0.9 x 0.8 cm. The removed convexity of the skull showed no evidence of fracture, while there were long irregular fracture lines of the right basal cranial bones involving the sphenoidal, temporal, parietal, and occipital bones. The sell turica was completely crushed and the pituitary gland was destroyed (smashed). The ala magna of the sphenoidal bone forming the roof over the right orbit showed numerous fracture lines and splintering. The fracture line extended from the corpus of the sphenoidal bone through the pyramis of the right temporal bone through the squamous portion, a short distance through the right posterior

21

PAGE 8
REPORT ON POST MORTEM EXAMINATION CONTD.
Re: Body of Mrs. Bernice Worden

lower parietal bone, and part of the right side of the occipital bone. The defect of the latter occurred at the intersection of fracture and sawcut and was probably an artefact. The dura was under slight tension, showed a slit-like opening corresponding to the bullet hole in the occipital bone. The subarachnoid space contained some blood in the area of the left temporal lobe.

There was no evidence of subarachnoid hemorrhage nor brain injury beneath the right injury of the head.

Dissection of the brain showed hemorrhages in all ventricular spaces. The actual bullet track through the brain was difficult to visualize. It was evident that the bullet had traversed the brain beneath the corpus callosum passing partway through the ventricles, and struck the sphenoid bone causing the mentioned fractures. To facilitate the localization of the bullet as there was no exit defect, X-ray pictures were taken and the bullet, apparently of a 22 calibre, was located and found within the right orbita beneath the median portion of its roof without destruction to the eyeball. (Bullet turned over to the Wisconsin State Crime Laboratory). The extensive basal skull fracture had been the cause for the bleedings from the nose and the right ear canal.

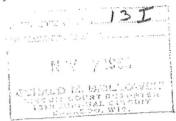

PAGE 9
REPORT ON POST MORTEM EXAMINATION CONTD.
Re: Body of Mrs. Bernice Worden

MICROSCOPIC EXAMINATION:

Brain:
Sections from the left temporal cortical area show subarachnoid hemorrhage, while the cortical layers reveal no significant changes. One section taken from the area of the basal ganglia near the third ventricle shows traumatic crushing of brain substance, hemorrhage, but no reactive exudative changes.

Lungs:
Some areas reveal localized engorgement of blood vessels apparently hypostatic.

Heart:
The myocardium appears normal, same endo- and pericardium.

Liver:
normal histological pattern.

Spleen:
normal histological pattern.

Kidneys:
normal histological pattern.

SUMMARY AND CONCLUSION:
Examination of the decapitated and eviscerated body of Mrs. Bernice Worden revealed as the only cause of death a bullet shot wound in the head which had been fired in the back of the head. The bullet had penetrated the brain anteriorly causing destruction of vital areas and inter-ventricular hemorrhage as well as extensive skull fractures and some subarachnoid hemorrhage. The bullet had lodged in the left orbit. It had apparently not been a contact nor a very close shot. The other head trauma had occurred

Sheboygan Memorial Hospital

INCORPORATED
Sheboygan, Wisconsin

PAGE 10
REPORT ON POST MORTEM EXAMINATION CONTD.
Re: Body of Mrs. Bernice Worden

while the blood had still circulated. Death had apparently occurred very

shortly (seconds or minutes) after the shot had been fired. All the other

mutilations of the body had been carried out after death.

F. Eigenberger, M. D.
Pathologist

WISCONSIN STATE BOARD OF HEALTH
ORIGINAL CERTIFICATE OF DEATH

State Filing Date

1. PLACE OF DEATH
   a. COUNTY **Waushara**
   b. CITY (If outside corporate limits, write RURAL and give township) or TOWN **Plainfield** b. LENGTH OF STAY (in this place)
   c. FULL NAME OF HOSPITAL OR INSTITUTION (If not in hospital or institution, give street address or location)

2. USUAL RESIDENCE (Where deceased lived. If institution, residence before admission)
   a. STATE **Wisconsin** b. COUNTY **Waushara**
   c. CITY (If outside corporate limits, write RURAL and give township) or TOWN **Plainfield**
   d. STREET ADDRESS (If rural, give location)

3. NAME OF DECEASED (Type or Print)
   a. (First) **Bernice** b. (Middle) **Conover** c. (Last) **Worden**

4. DATE OF DEATH (Month) **11** (Day) **16** (Year) **1957**

5. SEX **Female** 6. COLOR OR RACE **White** 7. MARRIED NEVER MARRIED WIDOWED DIVORCED (Specify) **Widowed**

8. DATE OF BIRTH **May 9, 1899** 9. AGE (In years) **58** If under 24 hrs. Hours / Min. **6 2**

10a. USUAL OCCUPATION (Give kind of work done during most of working life, even if retired) **Proprietor** 10b. KIND OF BUSINESS OR INDUSTRY **Hardware**

11. BIRTHPLACE (State or foreign country) **Canton, Illinois**

12. CITIZEN of WHAT COUNTRY? **U.S.A.**

13. FATHER'S NAME **Frank Conover**

14. MOTHER'S MAIDEN NAME **Agnes Putman**

15. WAS DECEASED EVER IN U.S. ARMED FORCES? (Yes, no, or unknown) (If yes, give war or dates of service) **No**

16. SOCIAL SECURITY **393-14-8814**

17. INFORMANT **Frank Worden**

MEDICAL CERTIFICATION

18. CAUSE OF DEATH
   I. DISEASE OR CONDITION DIRECTLY LEADING TO DEATH (a) **Bullet wound, penetrating, skull with hemorrhage into the ventricles.**
   ANTECEDENT CAUSES
   Morbid conditions, if any, giving rise to the above cause (a) stating the underlying cause last.
   DUE TO (b)
   DUE TO (c)
   INA L. McCOMB, CLERK
   II. OTHER SIGNIFICANT CONDITIONS
   Conditions contributing to the death but not related to the disease or condition causing death

19b. MAJOR FINDINGS OF OPERATION

19a. DATE OF OPERATION

20. AUTOPSY? Yes ☒ No ☐

Interval Between Onset and Death **10 min.**

21. ACCIDENT SUICIDE HOMICIDE **Homicide**

21a. (Specify)

21b. PLACE OF INJURY (e.g., in or about home, farm, factory, street, office bldg., etc.) **in her store**

21c. (CITY, TOWN, OR TOWNSHIP) **Village, Plainfield** (COUNTY) **Waushara Wis.** (STATE)

21d. TIME OF INJURY (Month) (Day) (Year) **11-16-57** (Hour) **OAM**

21e. INJURY OCCURRED While at Work ☐ Not While at Work ☒

21f. HOW DID INJURY OCCUR **shot by thief.**

Reserved for coding
Hospital
Residence
Co.
Place
Local—Cause of death

Worden's Hardware Store.

The bloody floor of Worden's Hardware Store.

ED GEIN PHYSICAL AND PSYCHOLOGICAL REPORT

December 19, 1957

CIRCUIT COURT
WAUSHARA CO., W
FILED

JAN 8 1958

IRA T. BUCNER, CLI

The Honorable Herbert A. Bunde
7th Circuit Court, Waushara County
Wisconsin Rapids, Wisconsin

Dear Sir:

Re: Edward Gein

I am sending you a copy of the records in the case of Edward
Gein. Mr. Gein was seen by a board of doctors at Central State Hospital
on December 18, 1957. This board consisted of me, Dr. R. Warmington,
Chief of Medical Services; Dr. O. Larimore, Psychiatrist; Dr. O. Goetsch,
Physician; Dr. L. J. Ganser, Superintendent of the Diagnostic Center;
and Dr. H. J. Colgan, Clinical Director of the Winnebago State Hospital.
In addition to this group of doctors, Mr. Robert Ellsworth, Psychologist,
and Mr. Kenneth Colwell, Social Worker, also attended the meeting and
took part in the proceedings.

The staffing of Mr. Gein took several hours and consisted of
questions by the members, with the object of obtaining an opinion of
Mr. Gein's thinking and reactions. It was determined that Mr. Gein has
been suffering from a schizophrenic process for an undetermined number
of years and that this schizophrenic process is made apparent by what
is delusional thinking. He stated that his activities were the result
of some outside force acting upon him and that he had been chosen as
an instrument of God to carry out activities which were ordained to
happen. He also presented numerous somatic complaints for which there
is no physical basis and which must be considered in the nature of
somatic delusions. There have been at least several incidents of
olfactory, auditory and perhaps visual hallucinations in the last
twelve years.

The patient showed himself to be an extremely suggestible
individual who, without question, was inordinately emotionally attached
to his mother, and it was from her that his very strict moralistic
attitudes in regard to sex and drinking were obtained. It is not clear
what his motives were in violating the graves, since he claims at this
time that this activity was the result of an evil spirit influencing
him to engage in this activity. It seems probable that this activity
was the result of his desire to re-create the existence of his own mother.
After the death of his mother, he felt that he had a special power where-
by he could raise the dead to life by an act of his will power; and when
he found that this was not successful, his emotional needs influenced
him to attempt the re-creation of his mother by using the parts of bodies
from other graves.

- 1 -

The Honorable Herbert A. Bunde   December 19, 1957
7th Circuit Court, Waushara County
Wisconsin Rapids, Wisconsin

Re: Edward Gein (concluded)

        His opinion of Mrs. Worden was that she was a very loose and
disreputable woman who deserved to die; and, although he now claims
that her death was accidental, if such should be the case, his actions
in bringing about her death were then unconsciously determined because
of his judgment that she deserved this fate.

        Although Mr. Gein might voice knowledge of the difference
between right and wrong, his ability to make such judgment would be
and is influenced by the existent mental illness. He would not be
capable of fully realizing the consequence of any act because he would
not be a free agent to determine either the nature or the consequence
of acts which resulted from disturbed and abnormal thinking, which is
part of his mental illness. Because of his extreme suggestibility and
the nature of his mental illness, he is not completely or fully capable
of acting in his own behalf in consultation with his attorney. Because
of these findings, I must recommend his commitment to Central State
Hospital as insane.

        The 30-day observation period is up on the 22nd of December.
I realize that no court action will be feasible because of the holidays.
His confinement at Central State Hospital would certainly be acceptable
to me; however, I would request your indulgence in sending me a statement
indicating your desires in the matter.

                                Respectfully,

                                E. F. Schubert, M. D.
                                Superintendent

EFS:mcl

Enclosures

                                - 2 -

State of Wisconsin

CENTRAL STATE HOSPITAL

Continued Notes

Name GEIN, Edward   1   Consecutive Number   2753

November 25, 1957 by Dr. Warmington

This patient was admitted on 11-23-57 for a 30 day observation period upon order of the Circuit Court of Waushara County after he had been arrested and charged with the crime of Murder, 1st Degree.

Physical inspection disclosed a well developed, well nourished, middle-aged, white male that was ambulant and not in any apparent distress. A right inguinal hernia was noted and he asked about an abnormality in the left supraclavicular fossa that may be a lymph node overlying an arterial vessel with resultant pulsation transmission. Mentally he was found to be in contact with his surroundings, carried on a coherent conversation and verbalized without difficulty while speaking in a rather quiet, well modulated voice. He gave an adequate account of his past life and spoke some of the offense but no attempt was made to explore this in greater detail at this writing. He seemed to be fairly well at ease but mentioned being under strain and failing to sleep while under investigation prior to admission here. History indicates he has been closer to the mother than the father possibly since the father drank and was somewhat irritable on occasions. Mention was also made by him that he never married, has never had sexual relations and the impression was gained that he has been rather limited in his social contacts. At this time he also seems to recognize this as for example he thinks that it might have been better if he had been drafted into the service and afforded more opportunities for maturation through socialization. He was assigned to ward J1.

December 8, 1957 by Dr. Bayley

Interpretation of chest x-ray taken on 11-26-57 is as follows:

No significant pathology of the heart, lungs or bony thorax.

December 3, 1957 by Dr. Bayley

Interpretation of GI Series done on 12-3-57 is as follows:

No significant involvement of the esophagus, stomach or duodenum. Normal gastrointestinal motility without gastric residue at the 4 hour period. Gall bladder studies are suggested.

November 26, 1957 by Dr. St[?]le, Wisconsin Diagnostic Center

EEG No. 57-34; Age: 51; Referring Physician E. F. Schubert, M. D.;
Taken by C. Disterhoft, R.N.; Date of EEG Study November 26, 1957.

INTERPRETATION

Characteristics: Awake and drowsy record. Seconal gr. 1½ was given but
            did not induce sleep. Record is primarily a tension
record. Basic frequency of 9-11/sec. No seizure discharges; no focus;
no asymmetry. Normal response to hyperventilation.

Impression: Normal awake and drowsy record from the accessible cortex.
            A sleep record would be necessary for complete EEG
evaluation.

December 5, 1957 by Dr. Stehle, Wisconsin Diagnostic Center.

EEG No. 57-35; Date of EEG Study December 5, 1957; Age 51; Referring
Physician E. F. Schubert, M. D.; Taken by C. Disterhoft, R.N.

INTERPRETATION

Characteristics: Record is a Seconal (gr. 3) induced drowsy and sleep
            record. Normal sleep frequencies. No seizure
discharges; no focus; no asymmetry.

Impression: Normal drowsy and sleep record from the accessible cortex.
            This record and awake and drowsy record of 11-26-57 give
no EEG evidence of cerebral dysrhythmia or epileptic discharges.

December 9, 1957 by Dr. Cook

Interpretation of skull x-ray taken 12-7-57 is as follows:

    Boney tables are of normal thickness and density. There is no
evidence of old or recent fracture. There is no abnormal calcification
or vascularity. The pineal gland is not calcified. The sella turcica
and petrous ridges are normal. Impression normal skull.

December 9, 1957, by Dr. Schubert

    Mr. Gein was interviewed on this date. He was oriented as to
place; however, he was not completely oriented as to time. He stated
that it was sometime in December of 1957 and gave as his excuse for not
knowing the particular day of the month, that he had no calendar and
had no newspapers from which to obtain the date. He stated that he
had seen me before and correctly indicated that such contact with me
had been on Ward J-1.

    He immediately began speaking about the difficulty which brought
him to the institution. He rather vehemently stated that none of this
would have happened if his neighbors had shown some interest in him
and would have visited him. He stated that the only time the neighbors
came to his home was when they wanted to borrow things. He complained
about the neighbors playing "dirty deals." He applied this phrase to

34

December 9, 1957. by Dr. Schubert (continued)

business dealings that he had had with one particular neighbor who had rented a field from him some years ago for $10.00 a year. This neighbor paid the rent for the first year but neglected to pay the rent for subsequent years. He claims that about five of his neighbors were constantly taking advantage of him and that they all owed him money. He denied that he had any difficulty with the people in Plainfield, although he said that many of them didn't appreciate the things that he did for them.

He complained of memory deficits and more specifically with regard to the crimes he is accused of committing. He stated that he is unable to recall any of the details of the murder of Mrs. Hogan and said that some of the things that they claim he said in Madison at the Crime Laboratory were not true. He said that he is unable to figure out how he could have had time to do everything that they have accused him of doing. He also claims that he is not clear on many of the details involved in the murder of Mrs. Worden. He vaguely remembers putting a cartridge, which he found in his pocket, in a rifle which he took from a rack in the Worden Store, but he feels that her death was an accident because the gun must have discharged accidentally. He states that he does not remember putting the body in his truck and driving it to his home, although he admits that he must have been the one who did this.

His opinion of Mrs. Worden is that she was a rather disreputable woman who was known to have a bad reputation. To illustrate this opinion, he stated that, prior to the marriage of Mr. and Mrs. Worden, Mr. Worden was keeping company with the daughter of a dentist and that Mrs. Worden stole her future husband from this other woman, and that this woman subsequently killed herself with chloroform because of this. He denies that he blames Mrs. Worden for the girl's death, but he also stated that he feels Mrs. Worden received her just desert when her husband died of some blood dyscrasia and feels that this was in the nature of a punishment for her.

Much of the interview was spent in discussing his feelings about his mother. His mother was a very religious woman and his only description of her was that "she was good in every way." His mother suffered two strokes, and much of his time was spent in caring for his mother after the first stroke. He began to cry when he described his mother's infirmities and stated that "she didn't deserve all of her suffering." His mother's second stroke followed an argument that a neighbor by the name of Smith had with his wife and daughter. This man Smith was "an evil man" who brought a married woman to live with him on the farm neighboring the Gein property. This man would have temper tantrums and, upon one occasion, killed a puppy because the dog irritated him. The patient's mother suffered her second stroke shortly after an argument which this man had with his wife and

December 9, 1957, by Dr. Schubert (concluded)

daughter, and the patient feels that this man was, therefore, responsible for his mother's death.

His feelings for his father are completely negative. He stated that his father drank excessively and would abuse both him and his brother.

Following the death of his mother in 1945, he was very depressed for about two years and it was during this time that the farm fell into disrepair. He states that he "has had spells of the blues," and that he wanted to sell the farm because of all of the unpleasant memories connected with this farm. Apparently he made some half-hearted attempts to sell this farm and stated that he planned to visit some of his relatives and eventually to settle down in the southern part of the United States with the money obtained from the sale of the farm.

With respect to his claims of memory deficits, he says that his lapses of memory started after the death of his mother. While discussing much of his symptomatology, he becomes tangential and irrelevant. When asked specifically about his interests since the death of his mother, his only answer was that he wished he could have had more contact with other people. He stated that since the death of his mother he has had feelings that things around him were unreal and at one time, shortly after the death of the mother, he felt that he could raise people from the dead by will power. He also stated that he heard his mother talking to him on several occasions for about a year after she died. His mother's voice was heard while he was falling asleep and, apparently, this is in the nature of a hypnagogic hallucinatory phenomenon. He has also had dreams that his mother was with him upon occasion. He mentioned one unusual experience occurring two or three years ago in which he saw a forest with the tops of the trees missing and vultures sitting in the trees; he feels that this was more in the nature of a dream.

He feels that the death of Mrs. Worden was justified because she deserved to die, and he goes on to explain that he is actually fatalistic and that this whole sequence of events was ordained to happen.

E. F. Schubert

December 11, 1957, by Dr. Cerny

History: Patient has been aware of tumor in the left outer angle since infancy. The left vision has apparently also been poor since infancy, and this was first definitely determined by an army examination. No accidents, surgery, or other eye diseases are recalled. During the past eight years the patient has suffered from periodic headaches, at first frontal, then unilateral (usually left), accompanied by nausea and vomiting, and being relieved after the acute phase. No definite eye symptoms are noted during these attacks, aside from an additional difficulty in reading. Patient also states that he usually has some difficulty reading smaller print.

36

December 11, 1957, by Dr. Cerny (concluded)

EXAMINATION:

RV 20/20 correctible to 20/15 - 2   (-.25)
LV 20/200 correctible to 20/70 - (fleetingly) (-1.00 + 75 c 90°)
     central scotoma is evident, and left vision
     is slightly eccentric.

In the left outer canthus is a soft grey-pink mass, easily
visible on "eyes right". A small subcutaneous fullness is noted
at this outer angle also.
Lids and conjunctivae otherwise normal. Lacrimal apparatus neg.
E.O.M. full and parallel, in all planes, with no evidence of paresis.
Rt. pupil 4 mm. regular and active.
Left pupil 4 x 3.5 mm. slightly irregular, but active.
Cornea and anterior chamber clear.
Media clear.   Tactile Tension normal.

Fundi: Normal. No edema. Discs clear and healthy. No vascular
       sclerosis or other changes. No hemorrhage, congestion,
       deposits, etc. Maculae very normal.

Confrontation fields full.

Diagnosis: Amblyopia, left eye, congenital.
          Compound myopic astigmatism, left eye.
          Myopia, slight, right eye.
          Presbyopia.
          Lipoma or dermo-lipoma, left lateral orbit.

F. J. Cerny M.D.

December 12, 1957, by Dr. Schubert

     The patient was interviewed on this date. He again denied any
knowledge about the death of Mrs. Hogan and stated that he had admitted this crime because this was what the investigators wished him
to do. It was impossible to obtain a chronological series of events
with regard to the death of Mrs. Worden. He specifically denied
remembering the evisceration of the body. He stated that he had
violated nine graves and when questioned as to his reasons for doing
this, he stated that he thought it was because he wanted a remembrance of his mother. He denied any sexual relations with any of
these bodies and gave as his reason for this, that " they smelled
too bad." He again admitted that, for a period of time after his
mother's death, he felt that he could arouse the dead by an act of
will power. He claimed to have tried to arouse his dead mother by
an act of will power and was disappointed when he was unsuccessful.
He also admitted that he had attempted this sort of thing with

<u>December 12, 1957</u>, by Dr. Schubert (concluded)

some of the bodies which he had exhumed.

Questioning this man requires a great deal of tact because he
is extremely suggestible and will almost invariably agree to any
leading questions.

At the present time, he is in contact with his surroundings and
co-operates as completely as possible. His knowledge of current
events is intact and his memory for past events, with the exception
of details involved in the evisceration of Mrs. Worden and the death
of Mrs. Hogan, is also intact. He denies any hallucinatory phenomena
at this time. There is ample reason to believe that his violation of
the graves was in response to the demands of his fantasy life, which
was motivated by his abnormally magnified attachment to the mother.

F. Schubert

<u>December 13, 1957</u> by Dr. Warmington

MENTAL EXAMINATION

Personal and Family History: This patient was admitted to this insti-
                              tution on November 23, 1957 for a 30 day
observation period under W.S.S. 957.27 (3) after he had been arrested
and charged with the crime of Murder, 1st Degree. The offense occurred
at Plainfield, Wisconsin on or about November 16, 1957 and involved the
shooting of a woman, one Mrs. Worden, by the patient. Gein had entered
a hardware store which the victim operated sometime during the morning
of November 16th (?), looked over the guns, took one from a rack,
found he had a .22 caliber bullet in his pocket, placed it in the gun
and shot the woman in the head. The bullet apparently struck her
obliquely and passed through the skull. He then walked over to her
and pulled the body into a back room where it would not be visible from
the street. At this time he declares he was nervous, agitated and did
not think clearly but put the body in her truck which was standing
in back of the store, drove it some distance, abandoned the truck, walked
back to the town of Plainfield, got his car, drove to the truck and
put the body in his own car. The body was then taken by him to his
home and according to reports was strung up by the feet, disembowelled
and mutilated. Toward evening he was taken into custody as a suspect
since people had seen his car earlier in the day parked in front of
the hardware store and had also seen him driving the truck. It appears
that he confessed to the homicide and investigation of his house revealed
several so-called human masks, the use of human skin as upholstery
material for a chair and other remains of human anatomy. These findings
prompted a further search of the property and several human bones and
dismembered parts were excavated. According to the records, the subject confessed to the murder and admitted exhuming several whole bodies
and parts of others, particularly the head and neck. Before coming here
he was subjected to interrogation by authorities, was given lie detector
tests and revealed his actions. Personal history reveals that the
patient was born on August 8, 1906 at La Crosse, Wisconsin, spent a short

December 13, 1957 continued

time there with his parents and then moved to the Plainfield area
where they lived on a farm. In addition to the patient there was
one other male child in the family who lost his life in a fire in
1944. Edward attended a country school, attained the 8th grade
and did odd jobs, farm work and baby sitting after leaving school.
He had no technical education but describes himself as being interested in study and read considerably. Since childhood his attachment was closer to the mother than the father as the latter drank
in earlier years and seems to have been a threat to both the
mother and the patient at times. The father preceded the mother in
death and at the time of arrest Gein was living alone as the mother
had died in a hospital from a second stroke. The first stroke
occurred sometime previously and resulted in her incapacitation
and the patient's occupation with her nursing needs. He believes
that the stroke may have been precipatated by witnessing of neighbor argumentation and disturbances particularly in connection
with the first stroke and in his mind she suffered a further set-
back after the death of her elder son. In recent years he has been
a lonely individual that occasionally had some visitors to his home
and did baby sitting in the area but did not have the ordinary
social outlets.

Personality Makeup: The subject is an introverted, odd, withdrawn
personality that has had difficulty relating
closely to other people. He also has shown some paranoid trends
but on the other hand may have been duped and unfairly used on
some occasions as he speaks of doing work for other farmers and
failing to be paid for his labor. He is passive, inhibited and somewhat evasive when questioned about the offense and may harbor deep
seated feelings of hostility. He denies ever having had sexual
experience and declares that in this connection he was taught
the moral code by his mother that sexual experience before marriage
was wrong--"If a woman is good enough for intercourse, she is good
enough for marriage". In his general reaction immaturity and shy-
ness are noted, however, a certain cleverness and ability to plan
are present. A belief in spirits is also expressed by him and he
tends to be superstitious.

Mental Status: Since coming here the patient has been very tract-
able, cooperative and readily abides by the institution
rules. During sessions he sat quietly and displayed no belligerency
but information was volunteered and he discussed his case but when
interrogated for details became cloudy, cried or gave indication
that the subject was distasteful. He has been clean in personal
habits and shows no particular mannerisms or stereotypy of speech
or action. He has slept considerable and relates this to his
inability to procure uninterrupted rest prior to his hospitalization

Robs Graves For Heads

* * * * *

Home Found Filled With Human Heads— Finally Butchers Woman In House

(Dion Henderson)

Wautoma, Wis, Nov 19 (AP)—A diffident little man who admitted in puzzled tones yesterday that he had opened fresh graves over a period of years to collect human heads and finally butchered a neighbor woman — "while in a daze-like" — faces a polygraph test of his story.

EDWARD GEIN, a 51-year-old Plainfield bachelor handyman, is scheduled to go to Madison today for a lie detector test at the state crime laboratory.

He is being held under $10,000 bond for the armed robbery of Mrs Bernice Worden last Saturday.

DIST ATTY Earl Kileen said the filing of a murder charge in the death of the 58-year-old widow, whose disemboweled corpse was found hanging like a deer carcass in Gein's woodshed Saturday night awaits only a complete sifting of the gruesome remnants found on his secluded farm, about 120 miles northwest of Milwaukee.

Tere are some of the questions the lie detector test may answer:

DID GEIN mould hideous death masks from the faces of new-buried dead?

Did he fabricate upholstery for furniture in his cluttered farm house from human skin?

DID HE intend to eat the one victim he admits killing, the one of whom he said, almost apologetically, "I am not too sure that I killed her"?

"That is what I can't remember," Gein said in a question-and-answer session with Waushara County officers.

A "DAZE," he said, came on him when he did such things as dig up the graves from which he took at least 10 heads.

Once, he said, the daze left him while he was digging in a burial mound.

"I quit then," he said.

INVESTIGATORS, who found Mrs Worden's decapitated corpse, discovered the heads of four other persons in Gein's house Sunday and found six more there yesterday. Some were packaged neatly in plastic bags, others were tossed under furniture.

IN A SIGNED statement, Gein said he had not "collected any for two or three years."

Kileen said Gein took him to cemeteries he had visited.

AT MADISON last night, Charles Wilson, state crime laboratory director, said that when all the human segments had been collected from Gein's farm, technicians would study them in an effort to identify the victims of the grave robberies.

Gein said he had followed death notices published in the local newspaper and then opened the graves from 1944 to 1952. He indicated that on other occasions he snapped out of his "daze" and went home without violating a grave.

IN HIS STATEMENT, Gein recalled visiting the Worden hardware store Saturday morning and paying 99 cents for some antifreeze. He also remembered transporting Mrs Worden's body to his farm home.

Asked whether he remembered killing her, he said, "No, that is what I can't remember; my memory is a little vague."

GEIN SAID he did remember hanging the body from its heels in the shed and butchering it "because I thought I was dressing out a deer."

In the statement, he said, "That is as close as I can remember. I was in a regular daze-like and I can't swear to it."

<u>December 13, 1957</u> continued

here. Consciousness is clear, there is no history of epileptic seizures, orientation is correct in all fields and the train of thought is coherent and relevant but sometimes somewhat illogical. Faces have been seen by him in leaves and he spoke of hearing his mother's voice while in a twilight sleep zone but it is uncertain if these should be designated as overt hallucinations. No delusional material has been elicited but his behavior has been very unusual as he admits to excavating several bodies as mentioned above. In this connection he is not always clear in his statements and at times holds his head and declares he is not sure of his actions. During interviews he talked of using a rod to determine the nature of the rough box by its sound upon tapping and also knew some of the exhumed people in life. They were all women of varying ages. The bodies were removed from three cemeteries--Plainfield, Spiritland and Hancock, but some were returned after a short time as he became remorseful. In other instances he made the so-called masks from the head by removing the skin and separating it from the bones. The tissue in the back of the neck was cut and the cavity stuffed with paper or sawdust. One of these was placed in a cellophane bag but others were kept throughout the house. The unused parts of bodies were burned or buried and eating is denied. He has also denied having sex relations with the bodies or parts of them as he declares the odor was offensive. His memory is intact for most subjects but when emotionally charged situations are encountered there is a suggestion of a self-serving amnesia or vagueness. Denial or inability to recall shooting Mrs. Hogan is made and there is an intimation that the most recent homicide may have been accidental. At times the remark was made---"It seems like a dream, impossible". Since the death of his mother he had feelings that things were unreal, he felt that he could raise people from the dead by will power and some ambiguity was noted in his account of the happenings. Mrs. Worden on one interview was described as being short, inconsiderate and brusque but during a later interview was declared to be a friendly, pleasant woman. Physical attraction for either woman was not admitted and he denied seriously attempting to escort Mrs. Worden to a roller skating rink. Mrs. Hogan was a tavern operator and it is gathered that she was regarded by the patient as being a rather poor representative of womankind and he could have felt justified in shooting her because of his self-righteous, rigid attitude.

<u>Criminal Motivation Factors and Psychodynamics</u>: The motivation is elusive and uncertain but several factors come to mind--hostility; sex; and a desire for a substitute for his mother in the form of a replica or body that could be kept indefinitely. He has spoken of the bodies as being like dolls and a certain comfort was received from their presence although ambivalent feelings in this regard probably occurred. When questioned regarding the reason for his bizarre conduct, no explanation is given but sex relations with the bodies has been denied several times. This does not seem to check with heresay in which he admitted having sex activities with the cadavers. He has been a lonely man particularly since the death of his mother and some drive, uncertain at this time, may have arisen in this area to account for his misconduct. Review of the life of this individual indicates poor ego structure, excessive self-consciousness and deep seated feelings of insecurity in his social

Farmer Gets Lie Test for Horror Story

WAUTOMA, Wis. (AP)—A diffident little man who admitted in puzzled tones Monday that he had opened fresh graves over a period of years to collect human heads and finally butchered a neighbor woman—"while in a daze-like"— faces a polygraph test of his story.

Edward Gein, a 51-year-old Plainfield bachelor handyman, is scheduled to go to Madison for a lie detector test at the state crime laboratory.

He is being held under $10,000 bond for the armed robbery of Mrs. Bernice Worden last Saturday.

Dist. Atty. Earl Kileen said the filing of a murder charge in the death of the 58-year-old widow, whose disemboweled corpse was found hanging like a deer carcass in Gein's woodshed Saturday night, awaits only a complete sifting of the gruesome remnants found on his secluded farm, about 120 miles northwest of Milwaukee.

Here are some of the questions the lie detector test may answer:

Did Gein mould hideous death masks from the faces of new-buried dead?

Did he fabricate upholstery for furniture in his cluttered farm house from human skin?

Did he intend to eat the one victim he admits killing, the one of whom he said, almost apologetically, "I am not too sure that I killer her"?

"That is what I can't remember," Gein said in a question-and-answer session with Waushara County officers.

A "daze," he said, came on him when he did such things as dig up the graves from which he took at least 10 heads.

A portrait of Ed. (Charles D. Moisant, silverphoenix.net)

December 13, 1957 continued

contacts. The source of the poor ego strength is problematic but could be related to psychologic traumatization suffered at the hands of the father, over-identification with the mother and morphologic factors of small stature and an eye defect.

Summary: This is the case of a 51 year old, single, well developed, well nourished, white male that was admitted to this institution on November 23, 1957 for a 30 day observation period upon order of the Circuit Court of Waushara County after he had been arrested and charged with the crime of Murder, 1st Degree. He has been involved in morbid, ghoulish behavior with exhumation of several bodies and the fashioning of masks from the heads. He has also admitted to commission of the homicide in the case of Mrs. Worden but intimates that this may have been accidental and now is uncertain about his connection with another homicide that occurred a few years ago in which he has also been implicated. Longitudinal history discloses that this individual has been withdrawn, limited in his contacts over a period of years and failed to develop emotionally in a normal manner. He was overly attached to the mother and developed a diffident, non-assertive personality with consequent feelings of frustration and some hostility. Most likely particularly disturbed were sexual emotions but he is also unstable, cries easily and displays some feminine characteristics. He is intellectually adequate as shown by an I.Q. of 99 and has an average fund of school and general knowledge. Consciousness is clear, orientation is satisfactory and his verbalizations are coherent but he makes remarks suggesting a simple or primitive belief in spirits. He also probably fantasies excessively and may have been hallucinated on some occasions. His judgment has manifestly been poor and insight is faulty. Physical examination and laboratory studies are non-contributory except as related in a general sense to his personality structure.

R. Warmington   M.D.

Chief of Medical Services

December 18, 1957, by Staff

The members of the staff were Dr. E. F. Schubert, Dr. R. Warmington, Dr. O. Larimore, Dr. O. Goetsch, Dr. L. J. Ganser, Dr. H. J. Colgan; Mr. K. Colwell, Social Worker; and Mr. R. Ellsworth, Psychologist.

The patient was seen by the staff on this date for diagnosis. A lengthy period of questioning was conducted in which each of the staff members took part. It was determined through this questioning that the patient had been living a withdrawn and solitary existence for a number of years and, since the death of his mother in 1945, has

December 18, 1957, by Staff (continued)

had little social contact with the people in his community. His
description of his mother was that she was as good a woman as it
was possible for anyone to be, and through her teachings he developed a rigid moralistic attitude regarding women and the use of
alcoholic beverages. He claimed to have been instructed by his
mother that women in general were tainted with evil and should be
shunned as much as possible. His attitude towards the drinking
of alcoholic beverages was determined by his unpleasant experiences
with an alcoholic father.

There was a very marked sexual pre-occupation throughout most
of his answers to questions. When asked what was responsible for
his activities, he stated that it was all due to "a force built up
in me." He feels that this force was in the nature of an evil
spirit which influenced him to dig up graves.

With respect to the charge which brought him to the institution,
namely, the death of Mrs. Worden, he stated that he had been chosen
as an instrument of God in carrying out what fate had ordained
should happen to this woman. He stated that it would not have
happened if events had not fallen into place the way they did.
He placed the ultimate blame for everything that occurred on an
outside force which is conceived of by him as God.

There were numerous complaints of physical illness. He complained of headaches, sore throat, chest pain, abdominal distress,
and constipation. It was felt by the staff that this symptomatology could best be classified as a pseudoneurotic schizophrenic
process.

He readily admitted that he had heard his mother's voice telling
him to be good several years after her death and that, on one occasion, he had experienced what was probably an olfactory hallucina-
tion, in that he smelled what he thought was decaying flesh in the
surrounding environment of his property. Upon occasion, he stated
that he has seen faces in piles of leaves. It could not be determined whether this was actually hallucinatory phenomena or an
illusion.

It was the consensus of the staff's opinion that this man is
best diagnosed as a "schizophrenic reaction of the chronic undif-
ferentiated type" and that this has been a process going on for an
undetermined number of years. Because his judgment is so influenced
by his envelopment in a world of fantasy, he is not considered to
know the difference between right and wrong. His concept of the
nature of his acts is markedly influenced by the existence of the
delusional material concerned in particular with the idea that
outside forces are responsible for what occurred. Because of his

State of Wisconsin

CENTRAL STATE HOSPITAL

Continued Notes

Name GEIN, Edward   – 11 –   *Consecutive Number* 2753

December 18, 1957, by Staff (concluded)

extreme suggestibility, he is not completely or fully capable of acting in his own behalf or in consultation with his attorney. This man, in the opinion of the staff, is legally insane and not competent to stand trial at this time. His commitment to Central State Hospital under Section 957.13 of the Wisconsin statutes is recommended.

E. F. Schubert, M. D.
E. F. Schubert, M. D.
Superintendent

R. Warmington, M. D.
R. Warmington, M. D.
Chief of Medical Services

O. M. Larimore M. D.
O. M. Larimore, M. D.
Psychiatrist

O. F. Goetsch, M. D.
O. Goetsch, M. D.
Physician

Lutheran Religion-never confirmed   Claims Scotch-German descent

Patient is on no specific medic~~State of Wisconsin~~-only symptomatic;asp and
catharsis-at time of   **CENTRAL STATE HOSPITAL**
physical examination.   **PHYSICAL EXAMINATION**

CIRCUIT COURT
WAUSHARA CO., WIS.
FILED   By O. M. Larimore

JAN 8 1958

Name Edward Gein   **No.** 2753   **Age** 51   **Date** 11-29-57
INA T. McCOMB, CLERK   (on Aug 28, 1957)
Color White male   **Height** 66"   **Weight (without clothing)** 141 1/4 lbs
· ideal calculated weight 129-139
State of nutrition fair-muscles soft and   Posture sl round shouldered-erect
flabby
Temperature 98.4F   **Pulse** 100   **Rate of Respiration** 24
(full minute)

small **HEAD:** normal in size-shape-outline and contour. No bruits-no depr
essions felt-no undue prominence of the bossae. No areas of tenderness
  A. Scalp freely movable-no parasites or vermin found.
Eyes are blue-E.O.M. well performed-no apparent opthalmoplegias-pupils
are   B. Eye concentric-round-regular-the left larger than the right-
the right reacts sluggishly to 1 but ok to a....the left does not react
to 1 but l. Uncorrected R reacts to a. Patient alleges diplopia on occassion.
the outer canthus of the left eye and the left eyelid appear full and puff
y -and to casual observation there is a fleshy growth at or in the outer
canthus of the left eye-whitish in color-soft in consistency-which appear
s to be modified skin-that gives the left eye a ptotic look--intraoccular
pressure n C. Ears (manual method)-alleges dimness of vision left eye-
ears-are not dystrophic-no tophi-canals patient-some wax-drums intact-
Hearing normal to clinical methods of testing-Rinne positive. Weber
not referred--no obstruction to breathing spaces-septum deviated-
  E. Teeth missing teeth-carious teeth-gums good condition-has sufficie
nt masticatory surfaces
    F. Tongue lesion-midtongue lateral border-left-abrasive-due to recent
"bite"-soft-thot traumatic. Protrudes midline-no tremor-movements normal
    G. Pharynx pink-a bit dry-smooth-no excess lymphadenoid tissue-
no lesions seen
    H. Tonsils visible-not inflamed-cryptic-but no pus expressed-not enl
No strum normal to inspection-short-movements complete-no nucchal rigidi
ty-discrete, palpable adenopathy posterior triangle left.no tracheal tug
  III. CHEST: no gross deformities-expansion only fair-but symmetrical-
pn note dulled over backs-booming and hyperresonant over fronts-VF norma
lly transmitted. BS diminished-dry insp and exp rales left base-posterior
ly that disappear on coughing.
    B. Heart sounds indistinctly heard-no murmurs-shocks-thrills-no precor
dial bulging-sl enl to 1 and downward to p. No arrythmias found. pulse
feels mildly Blood Pressure Corrigan-in-character-vw thickened-
      BP rt arm 124/74   left arm 128/72-pulses syncronous
  IV. ABDOMEN: flabby-scaphoid-no masses or viscera palpated-no signs
free fluid-umbilicus intact-peristalsis heard-reflexes diminished-
    V. INGUINAL REGION right ing inal hernia(complete-truss worn--left ing
ring is intact. No C-V-A tenderness-neither midney felt
  VI. GENITALIA well developed. Male in type-foreskin reducible-2ndry sexu
al characteristics male in type and farily well eeveloped
      VII. RECTUM
Scrotum and contents normal to insp and p. Testicles moderate sized and
soft to palpation. pain ellicited by pressure.
Rectum: sphincter of good tone-contract and relax on request-no piles
seen or felt. Prostate is normal in size, shape-and consistency. Median
fissure well felt. No tenderness or bogginess. No masses--no blood on
gloved finger-rectum is empty.

47

General attitude: Patient difficult to examine by this examiner—he seems to have a sort of cringing attitude—complains constantly & & bitterly of a "headach -e"...places left hand over . ft eye and then both hands over eyes—and holds his head..sometimes closing or folding his hands behind his back"funny how this help -s.". Moves slowly and either fears or resents contact and touch by examiner— but mostly of all just quits and has to sit down or lay down—and says he feels sick at his tomach and thinks he will have to go back to ward in a wheel chair— feels like he is going to throw up—sick at stomach,etc,etc;—movements seem
P.E. continued: slower nd more retarded than is usual
Gait: awkward & constrained —not free +/or easy. (omf)
Glandular system: Positive findings.
                    No general glandular enlargement. In the left supraclavic -ular area there is a discrete-hard-nontender mass....of woddy hardness— fixed to deeper structures-nonpulsating. to palpation.,over which the skin is freely movable. This is thot to be an enalrged lymph gland-and its consistency and feel speaks for either chronic inflammatory reaction or malignancy(metastatic)-apparently of a year or two's duration.
      There are several small-discrete-palpably enlarged-nontender-hard lymph nodes palpable in the left axillary area-high up. These glands feel to be of the same consistency as the mass in the supraclavicular area.
      Shotty-discrete nodules(glands,) also palpable in the posterior triangle of the neck on the left side.
      No other findings indicative of a generalized lymphadenopathy found at this examination.
Since this adenopathy is of unknown etiology and because of the possibility of malignancy----biopsy of at least two glands-the mass in the left supraclav icular region and one or two of the palpably enlarged nodules in the left axillary area is advised. Two glands because of the possibility of the axill ary ones -geing of different etiology than the mas in the neck-that is-two different etiologies being present.

Tongue-left lateral border of the tongue-midway back-presents a lesion that patient says is due to a recent "biting of his tongue"...and in proxima tion thereto are some missing and sharp teeth-making this feasible-seen by tw -o physicians this lesions appears superficial-with scratch-like marks about 1/4" long-that could well be abrasive tooth marks-it does not feel indurated and is not accompanied by regional lymphadenopathy-except for a mildly enlarged slaivary gland-not tender-and bilateral in enlargement
Suggested examinations and consultations:
1. Complete blood count,to include differential leucocyte count,
   Sedimentation rate r b s determination-
2. Complete urinalysis-to include microscopical examination
Blood chemistry-blood sugar-npn
3. Neurological consultation-eyeground examinations and visual acuity tests
4. G-I Series and gastric analysis(fasting)
5. X-ray chest
6. Biopsy-mass in left supraclavicular area and also biopsy lymphadenopathy
7. in left axilla-AP and Lateral and stereo,if feasible.
    X-rays of skull-
8. Ophthalmological consultation.   O.M.L.
                                        ᴼᵀᴴ ᑯ.

48

cars: 1. left upper arm–white linear–"barbed wire injury?"–
      2. white, linear–narrow–middle finger left hand doesent remember etiol.
      3. vaccination scar–left upper arm–healed–
      4. Lesion,recent–red–indurated–left upper arm–site of recent vacc for
      smallpox–apparently a "take."
Two dark–black and clue areas–sacroiliac areas–symmetrically placed–apparently
ue to trauma of wearing a truss.for right inguinal hernia

~~s areas of depigmentation or excessive pigmentation seen.~~
VIII. SKIN: smooth–moist–warm–scattered disappearing–red papular lesions over
iest and back–probably impetigo–or acne(so called) no dermatographia
  IX EXTREMITIES:no gross deformities–no excess or limitation of motionsof any
f the joints–no abnormal swellings or abnormal crepitus found. Movements all
iolnta–back–pelvis–well performed.
X. LABORATORY:

   A. Urinalysis: 1. 11–26–57
              2. 12–5–57
   Specific gravity 1. 1.030 .... Color Straw .... Sugar Neg.
            2. 1.028   Straw   Neg.
   Albumin .... Neg. .... Casts .... Reaction Acid
             Neg.   Acid
   Other pathological findings .... 2. Micro. negative ....

   B. Wassermann: 11–27–57

     1. Blood Non–reactive

     2. Spinal fluid Gold Sol., 0000000000; Total Protein,32 mgs. %.;
                        VDRL Test, Non–reactive.
      Blood Chemistry Analysis   Blood Count

Date	Sugar	N.P.N.	U. Ac.	U. N.	Crea.
11–27–57	106	– –	– –	– –	– –
12–6–57		37	– –	– –	– –

Date	11–26–57	
H.B.	86% Spencer	
Color Index		
R.B.C.	4,680,000	
W.B.C.	8,400	
Neutro		
Eosin		
Baso		

S.F.C.C. 3
S.F.P. 20 mm Hg)11–25–57
Smallpox Vacc. 11–26–57

Edward Gein

Gastric Analysis: Free   Total

Fasting   50°   60°

After test meal   70°   85°

In view of the discrepancy in pupils-and p or vision -left-patient
should have an Opthalmological consultation(especially in view of alledge
-d "headaches". Eyeground examination especially. alledges "diplopia on
occasion.

NEUROLOGICAL EXAMINATION

Smell says smells bad odors at   Opthalmoscopic exam not done
times-"smells like flesh"
         Outline   Size   Reaction to light   Acc.   Cons.   Symp.
see under eyes and Opthalmologists findings-   etiology?
    Right
Pupils: Visual acuity test-Snelling chart?- 20/200 left   20/60 right

    Left

Eyelids and muscles deformity left eyelid-probably due to fleshy growth
outer canthus left eye......lacks convergence --alleges "diplopia"
Facial symmetry, nasolabial fold lacks mimatic expression-appears washed out-but
nasolabial folds are intact
Mastication adequate masticatory surface Speech no dysarthria-speech fluent
                                              voice thot effeminate
Tongue: Movements normal-complete Position midline   Tremor none

Tast accurate(history)   Swallowing no dysphagia

Vertig equivocal   Headach alleges   Crisis denies   Localized pain head
         long standing headaches
Knee jerks: Right diminished Left diminished Babinski neg   Romberg fair

Ankle clonus none found Biceps decreased Triceps decreased Wrist diminished Achilles absent

Plantar normal   Abdominal diminished Intercostal decreased   Scrotal present
   response   superficial reflexes decreased
Sensation: Heat identifies Cold identifies Touch identifies Pain identifies

    Position sense good   Stereognostic perception accurate(coin)

Extremities: Spasticity none found   Palsy none found
deep tendon reflexes diminished-Achilles absent-
Note:

Missing teeth, carious teeth right inguinal hernia,complete. Tumor-left
eyelid-benign-Acne vulgaris,mild chest and back,Lesion tongue(traumatic.)
abnormal reflexes(probably congenital),Cicatrices(as per examination).
Adenopathy-as described body of physical-etiology unknown
 Diagnosis: (Based upon Neurological examination)
abnormal reflexes as described

Further impressions +
diagnoses deferred until   Ogilvie M Larimore, M.D.
after requested exams + consultations (OML)

50

<u>December 4, 1957</u>, by Mr. Ellsworth

  The patient is a shy, 51-year-old, white male. He is a rather short person of wiry build and has short, greying hair and pale blue eyes. In the interviews and test situations, he was friendly and co-operated to the best of his ability. His speech was spontaneous, which, on occasions, became rambling in nature. He verbalized several physical complaints, such as double and blurred vision, dizziness, headaches, shooting pains in his neck, stomach trouble, and pressure like a tight band around his head. The patient talks of "forces" which were uncontrollable, that made him do the things he did over the past several years. He also gives the heart attacks suffered by his mother and his mother's death a peculiar twist: first, he blames himself for letting her into situations which caused the attacks; and second, he blames the people's actions at those times for bringing on the attacks. His reasoning here is not too realistic. There is also reference to visions, but it is difficult to obtain a clear explanation.

  The patient's manner is calm with occasional jesting. At the present time, he is oriented as to place and person but has some difficulty in giving the date. His recent memory is good. His remote memory is also good except for facts surrounding some of the offenses. Here it seems that the patient has difficulty and becomes confused in separating and remembering data from that which has been presented to him in the past few months. His insight into his problems is rather superficial. He has shown poor judgment in dealing with his conflicts in the past.

TEST RESULTS

<u>Wechsler Adult Intelligence Scale:</u> Verbal I.Q., 106; Performance
            I.Q., 89; Full Scale I.Q., 99.

  There is a large difference between the verbal and performance levels along with a large degree of variance among the subtests themselves, which would indicate emotional disturbance. However, with all of the visual motor subtest rather low, organicity should be considered. This possibility is weakened by the fact that he is able to complete the tasks providing he is allowed to exceed the time limit.

  There are temporary inefficiences--not knowing the number of weeks in a year or Washington's birthday but getting more difficult items. Also, peculiar verbalizations are occasionally present along with poor planning and poor organizing ability.

  His display of a fair amount of general information, good

51

<u>December 4, 1957</u>, by Mr. Ellsworth (continued)

vocabulary, and ability to reason abstractly points toward a higher intellectual potential, near the "bright normal" level, rather than the indicated "low average" at which he is functioning now.

In general, the impairments would indicate a strong emotional disturbance which would be psychotic in nature.

<u>Bender-Gestalt:</u> In view of possible organicity, this test was given to the patient. His reproductions here gave no indication of organic disturbance in the visual-motor area. This strengthens the hypothesis that the disturbance is functional rather than organic.

<u>Rorschach:</u> This test was started once but the subject's complaints of a severe headache discontinued the test until he felt better. On second testing, it was completed.

There are indications that subject is better than average intelligence, but here again is shown inefficient functioning. His productivity is not in keeping with his intellect and his thinking may be tangential and alogical at times. This is especially true when confronted with emotionally charged stimuli. His contact with reality is within range of adequacy but is probably kept there through an effort that takes much out of him. He is capable of recognizing the common events of existence but finds it difficult to accept and see the world in the same terms as others do, often discarding conforming views for less adequate ones.

The patient is a suggestible person who is colorless and emotionally dull. Yet, he is not too predictable and an undercurrent of aggressiveness that is present may be expressed by inappropriate reactions, followed by remorse and mild mannerness. He is also an immature and self-doubting person who is fearful in social contacts, letting others take the initiative.

In defense against the surfacing of conflicts and impulses, he uses withdrawal and repression. An inner tension is created by his strong effort to inhibit impulses. As shown by the history, his defenses weaken, at which time he deviates from the normal. At these times, he may have an exaggerated percept of himself and act accordingly.

The over-all picture is not that of a well person but of one with insufficient ego, immaturity, conflict concerning identification and possibly the presence of alogical thought processes.

<u>Figure Drawing:</u> The drawings give evidence of his being withdrawn and having a rather expansive fantasy life centering

<u>December 4, 1957</u>, by Mr. Ellsworth (continued)

around himself. He attempts to control drives and concern over bodily functions by intellectual inhibition. Sexual conflicts are present and appear to be centered around guilt feelings, identification, and voyeurism. There is evidence of some hostility, which he finds difficult to express.

<u>T.A.T. and M.A.P.S.:</u> In the more structured T.A.T., two of his stories centered around young girls and their boy friends, which is a peculiar twist for a man his age and background. Aggressive themes appear but are soon toned down or not carried out at all. It is also felt that feminine identification is present along with wishful thinking.

Going into the less structured M.A.P.S. where figures have to be placed on the background, the patient's initial comment upon seeing the figures was, "Oh, even ghosts." In setting up the situation, he showed poor organization and the figures he used were not in keeping with what has to date been found in the average person. The stories ended usually with a moral or with a warning about lack of temperance. One story displayed a rather morbid sense of humor. In some of the stories, peculiarities were present. They would suggest odd and possibly bizarre religious beliefs and project the blame for evil on alcohol or some other person. As found in other tests, there were conflicts concerning aggressiveness and identification. The M.A.P.S., in general, has a schizophrenic bend to it.

<u>Rosenzweig P.F.:</u> On this test we find an ego-defensive person who probably has various shortcomings and guilt feelings. He, therefore, attempts to project the blame mostly onto others or objects. On this test, he gave several very aggressive responses.

<u>Blacky Pictures:</u> Sexually, the subject is functioning at the pre-genital stage of development. He is an orally dependent person who has guilt feelings concerning sexual activity. It is evident that he was quite close to his mother and probably felt rejected by the father.

<u>M.M.P.I.:</u> Records showing similar profiles as produced by the patient were those with complaints of headaches, pains in the back, and pains in the eyes. Any internal pains appeared to be precordial in location. The patient has expressed similar complaints on various occasions.

In spot checking some of his replies, he has very little faith or trust in people, difficulty concentrating, disturbed sleep, blank periods, and feelings of wanting to smash things at times. He also relates experiencing unusual events and visions, but gives an unclear

December 4, 1957; by Mr. Ellsworth (concluded)

explanation of what is meant.

General Conclusions: On superficial contact, this 51-year-old, white male appears fairly well intact; however, closer observation and test results indicate otherwise. His speech on occasions is rambling and his thinking is rather difficult to follow at times. No strong evidence of hallucinations and delusions were brought out in talking with him, since his explanations were rather vague. Concerning visions, his explanation referred to periods before he was born and had a rather bizarre trend to it. Physical complaints that were verbalized are mentioned previously. This shows some hysteroid components and tests gave some evidence of compulsion and phobic reactions.

The patient is a very suggestible person who appears emotionally dull. Beneath this lies aggressiveness that may be expressed by inappropriate reactions that are followed by remorse and mild mannerness. He is an immature person who withdraws and finds forming relationships with others difficult. He has rather rigid moral concepts which he expects others to follow. He is suspicious of others and tends to project blame for his own inadequacies onto others. His fantasy life is immature in nature, possibly pictures himself as a much more adequate and bigger man than he is.

Sexually, he is a conflicted individual and is functioning on an immature level. Guilt feelings are great and repression is put into use quite frequently in this area.

In general, it appears that this is basically a schizophrenic personality with several neurotic manifestations. At the present time, he is confused and has difficulty in looking at his situation realistically.

Robert E. Ellsworth
Psychologist

State of Wisconsin

CENTRAL STATE HOSPITAL

SOCIAL SERVICE

Name GEIN, Edward   1   Number 2753

December 16, 1957 by Mr. Colwell

JAN 8 1958

SOCIAL HISTORY T. McCOMB, CLERK

Identifying Information: This 51 year old patient was admitted to Central State Hospital for 30 days observation under Statute 957.27(3) by order of Waushara County Circuit Court following a charge of Murder, First Degree.

Informants: The information in this report was obtained from the patient and other sources. The patient expressed a desire to be cooperative, indicating that this "was a job which must be done". The patient talks freely in a low voice, frequently with his head in his hands. He described incidents in his life with continuity, but on occasion would respond to a specific question by relating other aspects of his life history. He expressed appreciation for his treatment here and apparently viewed the Staff's professional approach as an acceptance of him personally that he has not experienced in his home community in many years. Patient appears to respond to suggestion, making questioning difficult. He professes confusion, partial loss of memory as well as trouble distinguishing between what he remembers and what he was told. He attributed difficulties in responding to not feeling well and to extensive interrogation both here and prior to admission here.

Present Offense: The patient's conversation indicated an acceptance of responsibility for the death of two women, but he denied prior motivation. He described an inability to recall significant details of the acts which he viewed as accidental. His recall of the grave robbing incidents was more complete.

Previous Offenses: The patient denied any previous criminal offenses or arrests.

Personal History: The patient's father, George Gein, died in 1940 at the age of 65 of a heart condition. He was born in Coon Valley, Wisconsin and was an orphan who had little opportunity for education. During the patient's early life, while in LaCrosse, the father worked in a tannery as a carpenter for the railroad and for the LaCrosse City Power Plant. When the patient was eight years old, the family moved to the farm in Plainfield which now belongs to the patient. The father was described as a heavy drinker who would become easily angered when inebriated. He "did not like to work" and on occasion the mother found jobs for him. The father drank less in later years and was a semi-invalid for sometime prior to his death.

<u>December 16, 1957</u> continued

The patient's mother, <u>Augusta nee Loehrke</u>, died in 1945 at the age of 64. She was described as the dominate parent who handled family decisions and, at times, managed the farm work. She was of German extraction and very thrifty, hard working and moralistic. The patient was closely identified with her, accepting her guidance and her demands. He described her courageousness even while bed ridden, stating that she never complained, but was able to "enjoy fun and make other people feel better".

The patient's brother, <u>Henry</u>, who was five years older, died in 1944. Both were treated equally well by the parents and adjusted well to each other except "for the usual arguments that brothers always have". The brother worked away from the farm much of the time and on one occasion was a foreman for a farmer who hired Jamaicans. "He was the only man in the area who could handle those guys". His death occurred when a marsh fire got out of control. The patient got one side of the fire under control and went to help his brother, but could not find him. He states that he got a search party and "when we returned, I went right to where he was". "Funny how that works". The patient assumes that the brother was either overcome by smoke or had a heart attack.

The patient describes his childhood as not happy due to the family's poor financial situation occasioned by the father's drinking and difficult job adjustments. The father was abusive when drunk and the mother had stated that she would have left the father except for the children. The family moved to the farm at Plainfield because the father wished to be independent. It would appear that the mother's moralistic preachings were not well accepted by the neighbors and the patient indicated that they were envious of the farm which was always neat and well cared for. It is probable that the family did not accept the habits of their neighbors and quite a point was made of the fact that Geins did not work on Sundays. He also stated that when "we came there the neighbors did not cooperate and tell us how to work the sandy soil".

The patient completed the eighth grade of school and got along well with his classmates, joining them in recreational and social activities when time could be spared from the farm work. After the completion of school he remained on the family farm, assuming more responsibility after the father's death. With the death of the brother, and the mother's invalidism, he was unable to operate the farm as efficiently. Following the mother's death he kept

<u>December 16, 1957</u> continued

stock on the farm for a time, but began working out on a day to
day basis with the neighbors. Later he sold the stock and the
farm gradually deteriorated. He stated that he preferred to let
it reseed itself to wood land. He had hoped to sell the farm,
visit relatives throughout the country for a time and then settle
down in some other part of the country. He felt that he was not
accepted in the neighborhood and states "people would come to
visit me, but I would soon find that they only came to borrow
things or to ask for my help." He added that "we had always
tried to be good neighbors but people took advantage of us". With
the exception of a couple of families, he was not invited into
other homes although "the women were kinder in this regard than
the men folks."

For recreation the patient has skied most of his life and
also practiced archery. He enjoyed watching basketball games and
other sports events. He is interested in music and plays the
violin, the accordian and the mouth organ. He enjoyed listening
to music, preferring old time music to modern. He lost his
interest in music after the mother's death. He frequently attended
movies preferring adventure and western stories to love stories.
He and the brother frequently attended dances but "we were too
self-conscious to dance". He did, however, enjoy square dancing,
for a time.

Sexual History: Patient's early sexual information was given by the
mother who impressed upon him the need for sexual
abstinence prior to marriage. He indicated that she was not as
strong in her admonitions against masturbation. He obtained
additional information in a more uncouth manner from his classmates.
He views not marrying, in part, as a family trait saying that his
brother did not marry, nor did two of his mother's brothers.
The patient gave more thought to marriage after the death of the
mother and felt he would have married if he could have found "the
right girl". He rejected one girl after he learned that she could
not get along with her mother and "I couldn't straighten her out
on that. I almost fell in love with another girl, but found that
she had had many affairs with other men. Morality is pretty low
in Plainfield."

The patient also described the moral standards of his two
victims. The first, "was a dirty talker, operated a tavern and
people said that she was in some crooked business". He states
that the second victim wooed her husband away from another girl
and married him shortly after the other girl committed suicide.

<u>December 16, 1957</u> continued

(He became tearful when describing his sorrow for the other girl.)
He went on to describe the husband's death as his just punishment
and then relates that his victim broke up another marriage. His
comments have a strong religious connotation.

The patient received religious training from his mother
whose strict teachings were unusual in the community but were not
viewed as excessive by the patient. He did not attend church
frequently because there was no Lutheran church in Plainfield.
After the mother's death he "turned away from God because he did
not feel it was right that his mother should have suffered so
much". Later he decided that "God knows best", and now feels that
the Bible gives him hope for the future.

He indicated that he would not have gotten into his present
difficulty if he had married, if the neighbors had treated him
better, or if he had been able to sell his farm and travel. He
stated that prior to the first grave robbing incident, he had
been reading adventure stories of head hunters and cannibals. He
related in detail one story of a man who had murdered a man,
acquired his yacht and was later captured and killed by head
hunters. He learned about shrunken heads, death masks, etc., from
other similar stories.

He admitted to feelings of excitement during the grave
robberies and describes periods when he felt he should return the
bodies. There were also feelings that the bodies should be
preserved and that he should care for them. When asked about the
sexual aspects of this activity he commented on the great
variations in age of the bodies. When it was pointed out that
he was interested only in the bodies of women, he stated that the
articles he read indicated that these heads were more valuable
because of their longer hair. Relative to the murders, he
recalled the sequence of events up to the act itself which
in the latter case he described as accidental, but had no recall
for his activity following the acts.

Kenneth Colwell

WISCONSIN STATE CRIME LABORATORY

Re: Unidentified Human Remains - Waushara County, Wisconsin, Laboratory N.F. 3437

The nature of the fabrics and styling of most of the clothing and wearing apparel is such as
to suggest clothing very old and of no interest to us and has little or no intrinsic value.
It is now stored in Waushara County. Group V was selected to reflect more modern styling
and fabrics and will be retained in Madison.

I. CLOTHING
    Men's and women's stockings   60 paired and odd pieces
    Gloves and mittens   40   ditto
    Men's and women's shoes   30
    Men's and women's hats   15
    Neckties   13
    Men's handkerchiefs   11
    Women's handkerchiefs   7
    Women's clothing: blouses, skirts, dresses,
                      coats, underwear, aprons   50
    Men's clothing: dress clothes, work clothes, underwear   100
    Boy's clothing   10

The bulk of the above items were used, soiled, eaten by animals, torn and/or repaired. Only
the handkerchiefs, some of the women's clothing, and the 10 recovered items were reasonably
clean and whole. Most of the clothing was of an old style (ankle-length skirts, boned cor-
sets, velvet collars, button-fly trousers, etc.), and none bore visible identifying marks
except the following:

    1 Man's handkerchief   initial "G"
    1 Woman's handkerchief   initial "M"
    1 Woman's handkerchief   initial "A"
    1 Man's jacket, fleece lined   initials "W" "G"
    1 Man's overcoat   cardboard tag: "Gein, George, Annex B, 3-20-40"
    1 Woman's dress, dark blue cotton   small cloth tag: "253"
    1 Woman's dress, white floral on   small yellow & blue enamel button: "American
      green (Item IAU, recovered)   Legion Auxiliary"

II. FABRIC, RAGS, ETC.
     Burlap sacks   Torn garments (rag-like pieces)   Quilts
     Feed and flour sacks Towels   Bedspreads
     Rags   Cotton batting   Rugs
     Pieces of fabric   Mattresses   Pillows
     Table cloths   Blankets

III. MISCELLANEOUS HARD MATERIAL   String
      Trunk   Umbrellas   Pails
      Suitcase   Papers   Nuts and seeds
      Books   Boxes   Animal skins

IV. The following listed items of clothing were found to be in fair condition and could
     conceivably be considered as saleable (possible value $5.00 to $7.00).

         2 Men's three quarter length heavy cotton jackets, fleece lined, large
         1 Pair rubber overshoes, with buckles, size 9-9½

V. A group of what appears to be reasonably modern styling and fabrics (six women's pairs
    articles and four men's) which were recovered and transported to Madison. The intrin-
    sic value represented, if any, is very small.

WISCONSIN STATE CRIME LABORATORY

March 15, 1958

Re: Bernice Worden - Death Investigation
    Waushara County, Wisconsin
    Laboratory No. W. F. [illegible]

The following items were recovered in course of the investigation of the above-captioned case and which were reportedly the property of either Mrs. Bernice Worden or Mr. Frank Worden:

GROUP I - Items remaining in possession of W.S.C.

```
                                          CIRCUIT COURT
                                       WAUSHARA CO., WIS.
                                           F I L E D
                                            MAY 7 1958
                                       INA T. McCOMB, CLERK
```

Item	Description	Approx. Value
AAU	One button pad	$ ---
ANU-1	One brown leather belt	.25
ANU-2	One brown flower patterned scarf	.25
ANU-3	One brown corduroy jacket	1.00
ANU-4	One blue corduroy jacket	1.00
AOU	One brown checked overcoat with a pair of black gloves	5.00
BNU	One reddish white girdle	2.00
DNU	One pair of woman's eyeglasses	.25
EXU-1-2	Two boxes of Remington .22 cal. short ammunition	1.00
GSU	One Speed Queen color illustrated poster	---
GTU	One red and silver colored earring	.25
GUU	One sample of rope, 6" in length	---
GXU	One pair of brown cotton gloves	.10
GZU	One small jar containing sample of anti-freeze	---
GMU	One burlap bag	---
HTU	One blue denim apron	---
HPU	One pair of woman's black rubbers	---
M	One 11" x 14" brown envelope containing an empty Scotch tape can	---
IBU	One silver dollar - 1922	1.00
ICU	One pair of woman's brown shoes	1.00
P	One original sales slip for anti-freeze	---
IXU	One original sales slip for length of stovepipe	---
FWU	One Remington .22 cal. Fieldmaster, Mod. 121, Serial #149009	14.00

GROUP II - Items returned to Frank Worden

Item	Description	Date
AHU	One cash register - K. C. Allen	19 Feb. 1958
FUU	One Remington .22 cal. Mod. 514 Bolt Action Rifle	19 Feb. 1958
FTU	One Remington .22 cal. Mod. 550 Bolt Action Rifle	19 Feb. 1958
GNU	One steering wheel from Worden truck	22 Feb. 1958
FZU	One glass cover (ammunition display case)	19 Feb. 1958
GLU	One Winchester brand single bit axe head	*
--	One mop handle (replacement for Item C)	*
X	One lady's wristwatch - Hampton brand - 6¼ ligne 17 Jewel, in 14k gold case with 2 white stones on each side	*

(*) To be returned under court order.

ED GEIN SUMMARY REPORT

This is the original transcript of the confession of Edward Gein. He was
questioned several different times in the first few days after his arrest
November 16, 1957. The questioning was done by Joseph Wilimovsky of
the Wisconsin State Crime Lab. Originally, this was taped on reel to reel
audio tape, then would be transcribed from these recordings. It is not
known what ever became of these recordings. The dialogue can be hard
to follow at times, as the transcriber could not understand what was
being said. Also, Mr. Gein seemed to be somewhat incoherent
throughout the questioning, and many of his answers don't seem to make
sense; they seem to ramble on. Overall, it is quite interesting material
and sheds light on many facts not readily known by most.

Disc No. 1	2 sides	28 pages
2	2	25
3	2	21
4	2 — 2 – 3	19
5	2 1, 2, 3 (4 5) 4, 5 (6) (8)	16
6	2	22
7	2	11
1A	2	24
2A	2	26
3A	1	14
4A	2	21
5A	1	10

9, 10 11, 12 13

Gein, during the course of his interrogation at the jail, was generally cooperative, nevertheless, the majority of his replies to relevant questions were calculated, guarded and evasive.

Gein denied undisclosed knowledge, participation and/or commission of the crime in instant case. From the inception of his interrogation, he suggested the following of his own volition to the interrogator: "Give me a lie detector test, it will show my mental unbalance."

Gein readily admitted that on Saturday morning, November 16, 1957, after completing his breakfast at home, he drove in his car to Plainfield to purchase some automobile anti-freeze and kerosene. Gein set the time of his departure from his farm at some time after 9:00 a.m., that it had stopped raining shortly before.

Gein declared that he drove his automobile, a Ford, to Plainfield, Wis., at the Ellis Gas Station he purchased a jug of kerosene, and then he went to the Worden Store to buy some anti-freeze. Gein stated that he and Mrs. Worden were the only persons in the store. He purchased a half gallon of permanent type anti-freeze in a glass gallon jug he had brought along for the purpose. He gave her a dollar and alleged that Mrs. Worden gave him one cent in change.

Gein said that he conversed with Mrs. Worden and that the discussion was primarily about the "deer check station" across from her store.

Gein claimed that the last recollection he had of being with Mrs. Worden in her store at the time in question was that Mrs. Worden was standing and facing close to one of the front windows looking out towards the deer check station, and that he, Gein, was standing many (unestimated) feet to the rear of Mrs. Worden, that from that point on he had a "blackout", i.e., could not remember events from that point on.

The Suspect Gein alleged his first recollection was driving home in his car, and that later that afternoon he worked on his truck, that in the later afternoon he went to the Lester Hill farm and had supper consisting of one porkchop, some macaroni, a cooky and coffee. He explained he had gone to the Hill's to install a battery for them.

During Gein's interrogation, he was repeatedly asked whether or not he killed and cut up the body of Mrs. Worden. Gein never replied or gave a direct denial, but did give some of the following representative answers:

"I didn't kill anyone that I know of."

"To my knowledge, I didn't do it."

"In a way, I can't remember about it, I might have done something, but not to my knowledge."

"The evidence (interrogator previously informed Gein that a bloody palmprint (pretext) discovered at the Worden Store had been identified as his and further that Mrs. Worden's body was found in his shed) you say points to it, but, it is hard for me to believe that I would do anything. I don't remember that."

Gein persisted in giving implied tacit admissions of his guilt as outlined above, although in the concluding phase of the interrogation at the Waushara County jail he alleged he was able to sufficiently refresh his memory to the extent that he did recall seeing Mrs. Worden suspended from the chain hoist in his shed but disclaiming knowledge or commission of the act other than reported by his implied admissions.

Gein further admitted that he recalled putting her "vagina" (vulva) in a box that contained other (3)(?) vulvas, but denied knowledge or recollection of its removal from Mrs. Worden's body.

In reference to the other physical evidence of human origin discovered up to the time at the crime scene, Gein originally and emphatically insisted that the preserved human female head found in a plastic (freezer) bag was a dried head that he paid a dollar for that he ordered through a magazine. Later Gein amended his representations reference to the preserved human female head, the vulvas, the four human skull caps and the other sections of human skin.

Gein admitted that he had disinterred bodies from the Plainfield Cemetery and that the above-described physical evidence in this paragraph originally came from nine or ten bodies that he had disinterred from graves.

Gein claimed that the first body he disinterred from a grave was from the Plainfield Cemetery, that this was a woman whose last name was Shermen, that he disinterred approximately nine to ten bodies during the period of 1950 to 1954.

Interrogation of Gein was concluded at this point and arrangements were made to make Gein available for resuming this interrogation and examination by means of the Polygraph (Lie Detector) Technique at the Wisconsin State Crime Laboratory on Tuesday, November 19, 1957.

Gein agreed to submit to a physical examination, to submit to having his fingernails scraped and also to provide samples of his head and pubic hair.

Dr. Friedrich Eigenberger, Pathologist of Sheboygan, Wis. examined Gein at approximately 6:30 p.m., Sunday, November 19, 1957 at the Waushara County jail. The fingernail scrapings and hair were recovered by Laboratory Technician James Halligan in the presence of Dr. Eigenberger and the undersigned.

On November 19, 1957 at approximately 2:00 p.m., Edward T. Gein was made available at this Laboratory. Gein's interrogation was resumed.

As previously reported regarding his interrogation that occurred on Sunday November 17th at the Waushara County jail, Gein again on this date continued in his evasiveness and persistence in his denial of any direct knowledge of his involvement and/or commission in instant case.

On this date, he did furnish and elaborate on names and information of persons whose bodies he had removed from graves. Further, he admitted that the graves he had disturbed involved three cemeteries instead of one as he originally contended. In addition to the Plainfield Cemetery, he named the Hancock Cemetery and Spirit Land Cemetery.

Gein stated that to the best of his knowledge he removed the following bodies of women from graves in the Plainfield Cemetery: Shorman, Bergstrom, Adams, Everson, Sparks, Mother of Henry Woodward, an unknown woman; from the Hancock Cemetery: Foster; from the Spirit Land Cemetery: Beggs.

Gein was also examined by means of the Polygraph (Lie Detector) Technique on this date at this Laboratory. Results of his examination revealed deception to the answers he gave to relevant questions pertaining to his representation and knowledge in the Bernice Worden investigation.

At the conclusion of Gein's interrogation and examination at this Laboratory on November 19, the undersigned and special deputy Leon Murty accompanied Gein to the Madison Police Department jail.

At the Madison P. D. women's detention ward where arrangements were made for Gein to be confined over night; while waiting for Gein's bed to be prepared by the jail orderlies, the undersigned had private conversation with Gein in another room. The undersigned told Gein, "Ed, you have known from the beginning when I first spoke with you at Waushara last Sunday that I have known all along what you did to Bernice. Now, Ed, please tell me the truth."

Gein then admitted to the undersigned that he did kill Bernice Worden. Gein was asked by the undersigned why he waited until now to make this admission and Gein replied, "I wanted to see how long this would go on." After this admission was made, Sheriff Schley, Special Deputy Murty and C. M. Wilson were called into the room by the undersigned where Gein repeated his admission to them.

This Summary Report is submitted by Jos. C. Wilimovsky, Jr.

C. M. Wilson
Superintendent

111/kb

Woman's Body, Bones of 7 Found in House

Farmer Admits 'Killing for Seven Years'; Latest Victim, 58, Disappeared Saturday

Ed Gein's farmhouse.

ED GEIN'S FULL CONFESSION

Q   Sit down, please. How've you been since I saw you last? This is hot.

Be careful. Feel pretty good?

A   Not too good.

Q   A headache? Those headaches you've been telling me about.

A   That's right.

Q   Eddie, will you please talk loud because I'm hard of hearing. One thing

that I'd like to ask you is I read in the newspaper that you asked for a lawyer

yesterday.

A   Yes, sir.

Q   Who was the first one that gave you the idea and told you that you should

have a lawyer?

A   The judge.

Q   No, no, who told you before that - who told you on Sunday? Do you

remember my telling you that?

A   No. That's right I did read it, too.

Q   No. I was the first one. Isthat correct?

A   That's right.

Q   And told you that you should get a lawyer and if you didn't have money

that the judge would arrange so that you could get - and - have you selected your

attorney already?

A   Yes.

Q   Who is he?   (Some indistinguishable)

A   Belter - I don't think I'll find it - see, he's right there in Wautoma.

Q   Have you known Mr. Belter before?

A   I've seen him.

Q   How do you like your new clothes?

A   They could be a little bit tighter at the waist. They should give me a little bit more to eat.

Q   Why, were you hungry? Would you like something more to eat?

A   No, I've had a good meal now.

Q   You can thank Sheriff Schley for the clothes. You remember Erb (?) also, don't you?

A   Yes, sir.

Q   Well, I understand that you've been able to refresh your memory to some extent.

A   Yes.

Q   Eddie, I know this particular point — you know that I've been levelling with you all along. There were some things that I didn't know about, remember when you became a little upset when I asked you where you had hidden the intestines and the head, and then when I got the message that the head was found I didn't know exactly where it was found. Then, of course, you began to tell me well if you tell me where it was found in effect, I'll tell you whether or not you are right or wrong. Remember that? Because I didn't know, you and I were together, we' were many miles from your place. Now, Eddie, there were other things that I told you -- that I didn't withhold from you at all. Did you know on your way down here, did you meet my brother Allen, the young fellow with the trench coat? (Gein made some answer) - got in the car? Well, anyway, you will recognize him when you see him later on. The rifle from Bernice's store - has your middle finger of the left hand been finger printed?

A   Oh, I can explain that.

Q   You can?

A   You know - and I believe ? - well, of course, he's upset. I don't know if he remembers or not. You know when I bought them rifle shells, you know when we was talking about deer-hunting -

A   Yes.

Q   He told me - well, he told when the deer season would end. And I walked over there to see if they had any rifles, deer rifles - and there wasn't any there.

Q   Frankly, I will tell you, Eddie, I haven't been at the Worden's place. I was outside, but I never was inside.

A   There was just some 410 shotguns and 22 rifles - that's all I remember. And then there was some of these light action rifles.

Q   Yes, um-m-m.

A   And I hadn't seen any of them of that style, and I looked them over there especially, oh, I can't say just for sure.

Q   Would you like to take your rubbers off so that your feet don't get too warm and sweat? Did you get a chance to take a bath or wash up?

A   Yes, I did, only he said he'd get a razor, or something like that

(indistinguishable)

Q   Oh, Eddie, do you have any recollection at all of picking off one of the 22 calibre rifles in the rack at Worden's, loading it, and firing it? Do you remember when you went to Bernice's, did you have any ammunition, any 22 shorts with
At least,
you then? Even if you had but one -

74

A   I don't believe so. Even if I did - if I'd been hunting squirrel or

something -

Q   You might --

A   I might have had, but -

Q   I know on occasions I find ammunition in my pocket - even in my dress

clothes. I know I'll put a handful of cartridges in my pockets and then remove

'em later on and miss one, and I'll find it later on stuck in the corner of my

pocket. I was wondering whether or not that could have occurred - that you had

found one in your pocket - in your trousers or in your jacket.

A   Where was that ? - do you know?

Q   Yes, on the barrel.

A   There was no other finger prints on the stock in back there?

Q   Yes, there was, but this particular one is the only one up to this time

that has been identified or compared, do you understand what I mean?

A   Oh, there is others -

Q   See, there were others and the main thing was to determine whether or

not at least one of the prints could be yours or someone else's. At least one

of them is known to be yours.

A   Because I'm pretty sure that would be on the barrel when I looked that

over.

Q   But here's the other thing, too, that I'd like to tell you, Eddie, and

that is of all the rifles in the store this one with your finger print is the

only one that had powder residue in the barrel indicating that it had been fired.

Now, the Sheriff let me read the statement that you had given to him, and I

75

think you made the remark that you possibly – that you thought that you possibly

could have hit(the guns)with the jug. Is that correct?
              Berniece

A   Yes, that's right. That's only the once in ??   of my having the jug.

Q   You remember Sunday that I also told you that the doctor found a bullet

in her head? You remember my telling you that, don't you?

A   That's right.

Q   So that you know, and in addition to being struck or being hit with an

object she also was shot, and I am wondering whether or not you have refreshed your

memory any further to see if you can't come up with some definite answer to whether

or not you know now that you shot her at her store.

A   Well, see, I couldn't swear to that – – – you know that ain't clear to
              the way
me -- except that it has been told that there was blood there –

Q   Yes, but you were –   (Gein talked at same time – indistinguishable)

A   Frankly, I don't know.

        (Gein, more not understandable)

Q   That's right. But there was blood in your truck. I know about that.

A   In the car?

Q   In the truck. Do you remember, Eddie, of placing the body in the truck,

in her truck, or the Worden's truck?

A   Well, – – –? – no. It seems like I do; whether it's just that we've been

talking about it – in my mind just the way I told --? – or whether it's that I

remember, you know –

Q   Yes, there have been so many things told to you that sometimes a person

begins to feel that he knew it of his own knowledge beforehand. That's understandable, and that was some of the things that we covered when I had conversation with you on Sunday.

A   I ~~think~~ believe you also told me about when they tell you this and they tell you that, but if the wall is black and it ~~im~~ isn't black, you know, a person shouldn't really believe that.

Q   That's right, you've got to make up your own mind, speak out the truth about things as best you remember them.

A   That's where I think I made my mistakes. I made it harder for everybody because they tell me this and they tell me that –

Q   They confuse you.

A   –– but they either didn't know or jump to conclusions. They wasn't right and that got everything mixed up.

Q   Eddie, tell me this. As we discussed together on Sunday – is there this possibility that since you were not too much concerned about taking the bodies from the graves that you felt that it wasn't a serious crime or offense. Then went on and told me that you knew that killing a person was a serious offense. You also explained – and I ask you the question now – do you know the difference between right and wrong?

A   That's right.

Q   And you explained it to me earlier on Sunday, too. – Is it – as a result of the fact that you realize that you did something which was wrong that it prevents you from speaking out the truth for fear that you might not be understood as to why you did this?

A   Well, no, not exactly. There's two other things. Just like putting the body in the truck and stuff - that's hazy - but whether that's from just talking

about it, I asked many questions - everything they told me - - - and where the

truck was and everything - that might have registered on my mind, but I think it

was that I done it, you know, or else I didn't remember - - - but there's other

                                        what
things that they told me, and if it's so/they told me - then, as I say, if I could

believe -   it's just as blank as -

Q   Have you found anything that has been told to you, whether or not it was

by myself or Art Schley, your Sheriff, or Herb Wansersky from Stevens Point - have

we lied to you about anything that you know up to this time?

A   No, not intentionally.

Q   Well, do you recall any instance where I lied to you?

A   No, I don't even remember who it was, you know, still I'm in a kind of

haze -- everything happening - -

Q   No, I said that - let me explain this to you. I wasn't lying to you.

I was basing that on the fact that ordinarily a saw must be used whether or not

in slaughtering cattle or in doctors examining a dead body. But I have since

learned, after I saw you last, that Bernice, that the only instrument that was

used on her was a knife.

A   I asked the doctor that - -

Q   Yes, and he told you that, sure. Now, Eddie, I also had discussion with

you regarding Mary Hogan, and remember you told me that in addition to Bernice

that you were hazy about Mary Hogan. Do you feel at this time that there is any

possibility that you could have done the same thing to her? Now, your gun from

under your pillow - remember my telling you about being the same type - is in the

78

process of being checked. I don't know if it can be accomplished while we are

having conversation here or not. But I would like for you to tell me whether or not

you have any recollection or xxxxxxxxxxxxxxxxx thought of doing the same thing to

Mary Hogan.

A   I've been faced with so much of that. The way I remembers about going to

Bancroft - that's all - that I couldn't just swear to - - the day after that

happened or if it was two days after.

Q   Well, remember the answer that you gave me, Eddie, when I spoke to you

about this little girl Mary Jean Weckler, you said "Positively not." And I asked

you whether or not you knew about Evelyn Hartley; you says, yes you read about her,

but you absolutely know in your own conscience that you had nothing to do with her

disappearnce.

A   You see why I knew that was because I hadn't even been anywheres around

there up in that country. Never been there.

Q   What do you think is the greatest distance that you have ever left home?

A   Well, there's been two. The greatest distance, let's see, that would be

(doggone it, I'm losing my mind again) I remember it was - towards LaCrosse -

there was one - two - three - four - we wanted to look at a car. Were they people

from Plainfield?

Q   That's right. What's that one - Mauston?

A   Mauston, there's Mauston.

Q   That's the town - we visited - -

A   That's not too far from the Rapids, Mauston, from Wisconsin Rapids.

Q   Is Mauston where they keep them hounds, them bloodhounds?

A   I don't know.

Q   The way I remember now - I asked "Is this the place where they keep bloodhounds?"

X Q   Well, they keep bloodhounds at Fond du Lac, I know. Of course, that's in the opposite direction. They used to keep bloodhounds at LaCrosse. You told me that you had or have relatives in LaCrosse, so I imagine that if you had gone to look at a car in LaCrosse you probably would have looked up your relatives.

X A   That's right.

Q   The Lerkys?

A   That's right.

Q   Gus, isn't it?

A   That's right.

Q   Did you tell about Gus Lerky to these detectives who spoke to you. They're from LaCrosse, I think it was Mr. Weber probably - Vern Weber, big fellow -

A   That's right.

Q   He's very nice, too.

A   Yes - I know that myself - - I wish I could have been - -

Q   It's too bad that they didn't bring the field unit - we have a big truck that's picking up the majority of stuff from your place. I still haven't seen the dress. Remember I told you about the girl's dress. I understand that it's of cotton material and it's about that big.

A   That must be a baby dress of either my brother or me - seems to me I remember.

Q   Something your mother probably saved for you?

A   That's right.

Q   Do you recall telling me and to Herb on Sunday that you sort of didn't care, that you became moody or sad or depressed after your mother passed away?

A   Well, naturally, I was upset but after about two years I believed it was God's will that way. Of course, a person naturally would think -- my mother was real good to me -

Q   Did you idolize her like a son should?

A   That's right, and after that when she was trying to get well -

Q   Yes, Eddie (I wouldn't say that this is an unfair question, I have been asked this question many times) would you say that your love was equally divided for your mother and father or did you have greater love for your mother -

A   I believe I did.

Q   - Ordinarily, that's the way it is. Was she ill a long time?

A   Yes, she had two strokes. After that first stroke, you know, she was worried - learning to walk (sobbing) - I'd help her and she wanted me to tell - she wanted to surprise them.

Q   Eddie, I assume, and I don't want to hurt your feelings, that as a result of my short visit at your home, that you sort of began to slip after your mother passed away because you must admit that your house is not in the best order.

A   That's right.

Q   I was wondering whether or not as a result of the appearance of your home, whether or not there were many occasions when you lived or slept elsewhere.

A   No. I don't know if I mentioned it to you. It might have been to these

81

from LaCrosse, from Chicago - - - You know, there is a neighbor, Earl Hines(?) - that's the only time I was away from home, when his wife was sick, had to take her to the hospital. She had a large tumor and they had to operate. I stayed there then because there were so many - -

Q   Don't rub your eye because it will irritate, especially with the kleenex. Any time you want to go to the bathroom or any time you want anything to drink or to eat, just let me know and we'll take care of it.

A   I appreciate that.

Q   Eddie, it's been hard for you. So many people have been having conversation with you. I mean, you mentioned Chicago. They want to know whether or not you were responsible for the girl being cut up and put in the oil - - -. LaCrosse talked to you, and then I explained to you on Sunday along with Herb, every disappearance is indirectly being pointed at you.

A   That's right.

Q   And I think you believed this on Sunday, sometimes you got a little irritated at me because I couldn't tell you the specific details because I myself didn't know but as fast as we found these things out I'd make 'em known to you, no matter how much or how little I learned. Do you think and do you believe in you think and do you believe in your own conscience that Mrs. Worden was the only woman whose life you took?

A   That's true. I believe that, and you know, like you say - - -

Q   Is there any remote possibility about Mary Hogan?

A   Well, like I've said, I can't really - that my mind is this way now, I couldn't really swear to anything.

82

Q   Is there a possibility that it could have happened - I don't want to put

words in your mouth. Is there a possibility that you could have done that to

Mary Hogan?

A   It possibly could be, but it seems almost impossible because you know when

I went there with that fellow to Bancroft and this woman was talking about it, I'd

been hauling wood, you know that, I don't know if I mentioned it.

Q   Yes, you told me about that.

A   You see, I split that up, some stumps and everything, and I'd been working

at least 3 or 4 days there, you know, working at that wood and getting it ready, and

then I hauled it in and that would cover, you know, that time. I tried to find out

just when that happened, I guess you did, too.

Q   Herb did. I think Herb was checking into it.

A   I guess he didn't find out.

Q   No. Eddie, if you were to place your conscience on a scale or a balance -

you know what a set scale is - all of the reading that you've done, you've heard

about the scales of justice - if you were to place the question of Mary Hogan on

one edge of the scale or the balance and - - the other balance with a big doubt mark,

how would the scale tip, as far as your conscience is concerned, and what your

conscience tells you whether or not you could have taken Mary Hogan's life?

A   Well, the way my conscience and everything seems now, it doesn't seem

possible.

Q   How about Mrs. Worden?

A   Well, Mrs. Worden - the way I've been told (and I know that there's no lies

there) that there's some way - because I know the body was there - -

Q   What was your first recollection, Eddie, of seeing her body at your place

in the shed? Was she on the ground, or was she up on the chain hoist?

A   No, right now, I can't even - I thought that I mentioned that before that I

had seen her there -

Q   On Sunday you had a vague recollection. Remember Sunday you also told me

that you remembered putting her vagina in the box with the other vaginas - do you

remember telling me that? You told that to Herb - -

A   I believe -

Q   Yes, you did. Remember I asked you whether or not you remembered putting

the gambel between her legs, and you didn't remember that.

A   Right now I don't even remember of seeing her there. There's too many,

I think that's what - -

Q   Too many people talking.

A   Yes, talking. Talking, that's right.

Q   Are you tired now or do you feel partially rested?

A   You see, last night, whether, I don't know, there's something wrong there.

I couldn't sleep.

Q   Noise?

A   There was noise and my voices and everything going on there, gosh, it

was like I was drugged or something, you know.

Q   Eddie, do you remember my asking you when we had conversation together

along with Herb, whether you had ever heard voices or received signals. You told

me about the fireballs - that you had seen those once, a long time ago. Well this

noise last night, were those voices of somebody doing business at the sheriff's office, or —

A   That's right.

Q   I see.

A   The way it seemed — in the office — get louder, you know, and just like they'd step off farther or something, and I couldn't understand really. It sounded to me like the voice of that young fellow that was in jail there, too.

Q   Oh, he was upstairs. Well, I don't know, there were a couple boys upstairs I'd never seen —

A   That other one was gone already — there was just this youngest one —

Q   So maybe it was the fellow upstairs talking to himself?

A   There was other voices and it seemed something about a knife or something like that and cold — you know, disorganized.

Q   Is there any possibility that you could have been dreaming that?

A   It could be. This morning I was tired, you know, just like a drugged feeling, and I still don't feel just like I used to.

Q   But are you agreeable at this time, Eddie, to having conversation with me and are you willing to answer questions that I ask of you to the best of your ability?

A   That's right.

Q   I think we got along pretty well, didn't we, along with Herb also, we spent a lot of time together?

A   Yes.

Q   I'd like to hear now from you — do you feel that Herb and I treated you with gentleness?

A   Yes, as good as youse could, I guess.

Q   Well, I mean, was there anything that you feel that was unfair that we -

A   Well, first youse didn't know about it - the saw and stuff.

Q   That's right.

A   That seemed unfair because you know --

Q   But that's the only logical conclusion -

A   - - even if you insisted on it.

Q   Oh, no, since we knew and since we were satisfied that you were sincere in

your answers, although I must admit that sometimes you would get a little irritating

when you'd say "If you'll tell me where it was found,/I'll give you the answer -

or try to give -"

A   That would help, yes.

Q   You understand, Eddie, that it's so important - you've come along all of

this way - to tell whether or not you have any recollection of taking Mrs. Worden's

life. You understand(undistinguishable) and this testimony must be heard in a court

of law, and if the court of law feels that if you have committed a ???? - that a

person must be punished.

A   That's right. That's why I have admitted ?? I told 'em that. ??

(other side of Record 1)

Q   But there is enough physical evidence. I told you about the finger prints

and everyhing else.

A   That's right. That's why -

Q   That there was no other conclusion other than the fact that you were the

person that took Mrs. Worden's life.

Q   That's right. That's why I put my faith in your findings and everything --

Do you have any recollection as to why you struck her in the store?

A   That's what seems impossible, but I'd give anything if I could remember

that, if I'd have any cause to do anything --

Q   You remember my telling you that she did bleed in the store because your

bloody palm print was on the glass of the front door. You must have slammed the

door shut or something and locked it.

A   I see. I thought that was on the back door - where the garage was -- --

Q   Well, remember my saying I wasn't there, I drove by the place.

A   I was told that, too, so --

Q   Well, maybe, I'll check later on. We'll take a short break.

                         -- -- --

Q   Now, you remember you were the one that suggested taking the lie detector

test. Do you remember that?

A   Yes.

Q   And do you recall what you told me as to why you wanted the test?

A   Yes.

Q   I'd like for you to tell me again.

A   Well, when I was talking to the sheriff, I'm not sure --

Q   That's before I met you?

A   That's right. And if a lie detector test would help in showing that I

was unbalanced and things like that and kinda straighten things out, and they

said yes. So I said I'd like to have the test to see if that would show up.

Q   Tell me, Eddie, is there anything in your own mind to lead you to

believe that you are unbalanced on some occasions, because of spells or dazes that you get?

A   Yes, that, and these other things like in the cemetery. No sensible person, when I think of it now and I thought of it afterwards -

Q   That you hated yourself, didn't you tell me that?

A   Yes, so I know that there's something wrong - that no person in his right mind would do all that.

Q   But then again from one extreme to another - you say that you're unbalanced, the other portion of the time you are a very balanced rational individual because you recognized that you were doing wrong, and you tell me now and before that you know the difference between right and wrong, and I know that you do.

A   That's right.

Q   Now that is where we get back to Bernice again. Your conscience must have had a terrific shock when you recognized and realized what you did to Bernice. Were you verbally by words, either spoken or unspoken, told yourself what a terrible thing you had done? Do you have that recollection?

A   Well, I believe I talked to myself, almost like what you're saying and I guess it was mentioned that if I saw her that someone else had committed the crime and I saw blood on her that if I wouldn't ???????

Q   Well, remember my bring/that to your attention that, by your own explanation to me at the time after what you told me about what had occurred at the graves, in fact at your shack, that you would be shocked at the realization. Now I know that it has occurred and I also know that you are quite tired from answering these thousands and thousands of questions asked by all of us, but I know that it stands out very vividly in your mind the shock that you experienced when you discovered

88

what you did.

A That's right.

Q Do you have any recollection when and how that occurred – that shock of realization?

A Well, that is about when that was mentioned that gave me the most shock and realized the most when I was told, you know, about that body.

Q Yes, but, Eddie, I know that you were aware of that realization, that shock occurred when you were alone with her at your shack, at the shed, rather.

A Well, --

Q Maybe that's why you went to your friends and had supper with them.

A They came and got me – and then these others that I talked to --

Q All right, when you were at your friends having supper do you have any
not
recollection, I'm/quite sure that you had -- if it was sort of flashing back in your mind about her being at your shed.

  (Can't hear his reply)

Q Oh, well, how about before going to supper? It must have been gnawing at your heart.

A Well, you see, I couldn't say – because there was men like Milton Johnson, (indistinguishable) – that's got me confused ---- and how everything happened in sucha short space of time – –

Q Eddie, I don't know if you've been told or if you've been asked by many others – and even probably being directly accused of eating human flesh. I'm
n't
satisfied, Eddie, I can tell you this that you had, and I believe you. What was your intention – you told me and told Herb on Sunday what your intentions were

89

with theheart, but I would like for you again to tell me to see how good your

memory is at this time. Remember me telling you about Bernice's shoes and

stockings?

A   That's right.

Q   And I also told you about the heart?

A   That's right.

Q   What were your intentions with the heart? Now the inference that, the

talk, I mean all over the radio and the newspapers, has been that you had planned

on eating the heart.

A   And it was also told that it was on the table —

Q   No, I personally saw it on the floor within about 18 inches of your bed. —

You still don't remember about the stockings and the shoes? How about the heart?

You had told me what your intentions were with the heart.

                                with
A.   Was it in a bag? Or scraps of paper? — Well, that was what I always burned

for kindling.

Q   That's what you told me — and your answer checks out — your intentions

of burning it. You also told me what your intentions would have been if you

would have had an opportunity to continue your work with Bernice, as to what you

would have done with the flesh and other portions of her body that you didn't

want to keep. What did you tell me on Sunday? And to Herb? Other than the

portions of Bernice that you planned on keeping, what did you plan on doing

with the remainder of her remains?

A   The possibility would have been two things — that I would have buried

the body or (that's probably what would have happened) because of the way I

90

think now) I don't know what I would have thought then - because my stove there is so small - that probably would have been better.

Q   You told me that you probably would have burned it - do you remember telling me also, and Herb, - well, rather than put words in your mouth, do you recall telling us that you had done with the remainder of the bodies from the cemetery that you didn't --- how did you dispose of it?

A   The way I remember -- that was quite late in the fall -- (indistinguishable)

Q   Remember the other thing you told me about the burning - what the reaction was there on your part from the standpoint of the burning, not the fact that you were burning human remains but what was there about it that was displeasing or that you didn't like? Remember you told me that when you did that this certain condition did exist but it never got into the house ÷ will that give you an idea of what you told me?

A   You know what brought that to my mind? It was either the detectives or someone was telling me (no, it couldn't have been the detectives) it must have been some of these others - that must have been this year - that someone would like to buy my place and smelled something you know burning. You know that, of course, as I say, that makes it so bad when your memory is that way you know you can't pinpoint it down, but it seems to me in my conscience and everything that the only thing they said that was --

Q   Let me tell you, Eddie, who it was that -- it wasn't the detectives -- maybe someone had told - it was members of the road gang, probably the fellow that you worked with. You worked there on the road gang, didn't you - shoulders of the road and intersections and all?

91

Plainfield Dazed At Horror Story

PLAINFIELD, Wis. ⒨— This tiny central Wisconsin hamlet where neighboring farmers come to shop and swap small talk reacted with stunned disbelief — and anger — yesterday to the horrible story unfolding here.

They were caught up in the unaccustomed glare of publicity in the grisly wake of one of the most macabre crimes in the history of the state.

SHY, QUIET MAN

The crimes involved a suspect they knew as a shy quiet man and a victim they all respected, Mrs. Bernice Worden, a 58-year-old widow who operated a hardware store on North Street, the main thoroughfare.

Her eviscerated and decapitated body and 10 human skulls have been found on the farm of Ed Gein, a 51-year-old bachelor.

All this was as unbelievable as it was revolting for his neighbors who knew Gein as a retiring "Casper Milquetoast" type of man who liked to talk about women, but seemed too shy to talk to them.

Gein's farm is located six miles to the southwest of here in a quiet, scrub tree creek area where many a man and boy has dropped a fishing line.

Ed Marolla, editor of the Plainfield Sun, summed up some of the feelings when he said, "The town is stunned — I don't know any other word I can use."

But there were other, more emotional feelings.

"They don't have laws adequate to the times," said a man in a red hunting jacket as he stood inside Bernie and Jim's gasoline station across the street from the Worden store. "He'll plead insanity and then be paroled in two years to do it again . . ."

'A REAL PITCH'

"We're at a real pitch here," his companion said. "There's no use monkeying around. If the town got ahold of that guy, the town'd know what to do about him alright."

GRISLY SCENE
. . . 10 human heads.

What of Gein, who lived and kept mostly to himself for the last 25 years on his lonely, run-down farmstead?

Most of the townspeople know Gein by sight and to speak to, but, they say, he was the kind of a feller who had no real parents and a brother, who lived on the farm, died in the 1930s.

Those who did know him, like Bernie Muschinski Jr., said he always liked to talk about women.

Muschinski, who operates a filling station where Gein frequently brought his four or five-year-old car for gas and repairs, said Gein never said much.

"But, when he talked," Muschinski added, "it was usually about women. He mostly kept to himself."

A SLY GRIN

"He had a sort of sly grin when he would talk to you," another man recalled.

"You could call him an odd bachelor," said Franklin Otto, who operates a restaurant. "You could see the reason he never married. He was another Casper Milquetoast . . ."

"They came and told me," Lester Hill said, "But I can't believe it."

And so it went in Plainfield, a village of 700 stunned — and angry — folks.

92

Gein makes a soup bowl. (Lou Rusconi)

A   That's right.

Q   I don't know if they were riding by when you weren't working or what the circumstances were but it was some individual, I don't know him by name, it doesn't make any difference, either - it was somebody from your own community who had reason to be travelling up and down your road who gave the information to Mr. Murty. Do you know Mr. Murty?

A   Yes, that's right.

Q   That the odor was — it was a stench — - -. Did you have a garden patch or something or vegetable patch close to the house and the shed? Did you raise any vegetables at all? It was their first impression (Cigaret? - No.) that maybe it was a refuse or rubbish pile outside that was burning. Is there that possibility, I mean, that you could have had a rubbish pile and threw some bones or old flesh in the rubbish pile outside of the shed?

XA   Do you know how long ago that was?

Q   No, I don't. If I know, you know that I'd tell you.

A   That's right.

Q   We might ask Mr. Murty later on.

A   If it had been you know, happened - not that it would have been recent you know - why then I could remember.

Q   We'll ask Mr. Murty later on.

A   I know I've been burning mice that I've been catching.

Q   I imagine you have a lot of them at your place.

A   Quite a few, that's right.

Q   How did you catch them - in traps?

A   Traps, that's right.

Q   How many <del>did</del> ^{would} you catch in a day?

A   Well, sometimes there's be two and then again probably only one, sometimes two, and probably not for a long time --

Q   Eddie, one or two little mice, as you know, wouldn't give an odor that you could smell out to the road.

A   Well, if the wind would be right, it might, some. If it was quite a long time ago, I know I caught a rat but that wasn't big enough to make that much stench, still it made quite a bit, I suppose.

Q   Well, no, this apparently was a prolonged burning so that the air was heavy with the stench. Have you ever gone by a garbage dump, where the garbage has been rotting, you know, and the area more like a skunk the way the odor lingers like a cloud? It must have been a large quantity, a reasonable quantity.

A   This isn't what I was telling, about the disappearance, you know - they was asking about the disappearance of his big traps. I mentioned that strong smell that came from that -- that didn't get mixed up in this, did it?

Q   Well, I have been told by Mr. Murty, and this was told to me on Sunday, you know I was in an out from you so that I just got bits and snatches, this county or village truck driver, and I assumed that he was from the road gang, driving the big truck, was of the opinion that this odor came from the garden or something -- that's why I asked whether or not you had a vegetable patch.

A   That's what I was thinking - my exact words - my garden spot there and there's some pine trees and the wind was coming right straight from the south. I can show you just about here - you see my land is on this -- right here in

95

between the two farms is a field road where you go across, and right here - anyway

that was when ---- lived there - there is a place right here about, right here is

that field road, and right over here is this house, and right here is the garden

and right on the edge of that garden on the west is a row of pines, I guess there's

three rows, and that wind coming from the south brought that right over there.

The first that come in my mind was a chicken or something - the stench was so

strong --

Q   Were you - -- - (?)

A   That's right and also the folks that I told it to - they'd remember it.

Q   Who were the folks, do you remember, that you told -

A   Well, the state traffic cops wife, I told it to her.

Q   Did you see her in town or something?

A   No, I saw her right out in front of --- and I told her about it. She

said there had been a strong suspicion that there were bodies buried there and

that the authorities with probably the sheriff had been digging there. They

found one place she says kinda rounded up just like a grave, you know, but

they hadn't found anything yet.

Q   Did you know about the disappearance of Dick Travis?

A   Yes.

Q   From the people in town or from reading about it?

A   Well, I read that, I guess, in the paper and then others were telling

me about it.

Q   Did you know Dick Travis?

A   The only way Knew him was when I was about 13 - he was younger than me, just a couple of years, but he was small for his age. Anyway he was a lot shorter

than me. We was playing games at the school and he got mad at me and said he was

going to knock the dickens out of me, you know. Of course, my arms were longer so

I just reached out put my hand around him and caught him on the chest and he

staggered back and - - - -   And then they moved, I couldn't exactly say, but they
their farm is (?)
probably located up there on 13 somewhere. When he was in school is the only time

I remember seeing him.

Q   That would have been a long, long time ago, wouldn't it?

A   That's right.

Q   Would he ever have been known to come to visit in his old area?

A   To this Thompson place, yes. I guess they had a fire there, they was telling

me that in thesheriff's office.

Q   Well, Eddie, getting back to the burning

A   I think that must have been what that stench —

Q   Have you ever burned a chicken, we'll say, or the intestines of some live

stock, I mean have you ever -- well, you've smelled the odor of burning flesh,

haven't you?

A   Yes, and bones and where they burn stuff in Plainfield there on the edge of

the parking lot, sometimes I've smelled it like burning bones ——-

Q   These odors that you smelled in your, shall we call it the garden patch?

A   Yes.   That's where it came from.

Q   From the garden patch, would you think that it was garbage or do you think

the odor could have been from some human remains.

A   From flesh - flesh smells of chicken, you know. They bury chickens when

97

and ride along with them, and sometimes if it was kinda necessary that way, they'd want to do extra work or something then I'd take my own. That I'm pretty sure is where that got started.

Q   So you think that you know that you have spoken definitely at least to one person about it?

A   That's right.

Q   Do you remember her name?

A   Yes, she's the state traffic cop's wife. Ray Weis (?). She told me about that Herb had been digging around there for bodies and afterwards, I guess, that there had been FBI agents.

Q   It would have to be a pretty big amount of wood or something to kindle it or get it started to cause the flesh and bone to start burning, wouldn't it?

A   The way it seems to me just real decayed.

Q   Decaying rather than a burning odor?

A   That's right. A strong, real decaying odor - sickening.

Q   Allthis time I was under the impression that it was a result of being burned.

A   No, it was just a real strong decaying odor, the flesh had rotted. My idea kinda then I thought it was something buried --- some animal dug down - - - then afterwards, when I got to thinking about it - Travis had disappeared I guess they had been up to that place.

Q   What time of the year, do you recall, that you detected this odor?

A   Oh, that couldn't have been too awful long after he disappeared because Thompson didn't live there too long.

Q   Was it during the summer, what I'm getting at, Eddie, is - -

A   That must have been in the fall.

Q   Well, you know that a body, animal or otherwise, if exposed to the cold

decomposes very, very slowly and there would be very little odor.

A   No, I don't mean that it was cold like in the winter.

Q   More like the autumn when the sun is very hot during the day?

A   Because it was warm, there was no snow on the ground, and I think my idea

when I went in there was to look that ground over to see if it could be plowed for

rye. I'm pretty sure that was my idea.

Q   Eddie, other than what has been told - and a lot has been told to you so that

sometimes you can't separate from your own personal knowledge agains that what has been

told to you - I've asked you this before time and again, when was your first realization

that you had done something that you personally disapproved of regarding Bernice?

Was it before supper time?

A   No, I don't believe so because I - before supper there was no chance. I was out

side all the time.

Q   Outside your place? Do you recall what you were doing?

A   I was checking my car - - - - was right there.

Q   That was because of the noise in the rear end of it?

A   That's right. And before that Milton Johnson and the Tibbetts boy were there.

Then, of course, I went up there to Hills - I believe the first when I was told was

up here - - - about that body.

Q   Eddie, do you think when you went out to work on your truck to check it - you

knew the work was necessary, you had planned to check it to find out was wrong with

the truck. Do you think that that partially was an excuse or an alibi that you gave to yourself to get away from the shed because you knew then what had occurred?

A   No, to my knowledge, I couldn't swear to that, it might have been - - - (?)

Q   Tell me about your mother. I'd like to hear more about her. Was she a tall woman or a short woman?

A   Medium size - and a real good woman. When she was sick she was just as nice as could be. You know a lot of patients when they're sick they get crabby.

Q   Did you prepare her food for her?

A   That's right.

       - - - (indistinguishable)

QX A   - - - she tried to help some. Her eyesight was a little bad --(couldn't hear).

Q   Did she remind you of the factthat she always wanted you to be a good son?

A   That's right.

Q   What was your first name?

A   Edward.

- - -

J.C.W.: I was just wondering whetheror not in the past few nights when you went to bed

whether or not some of these things you were involved in with Bernice, whether or not

they could have re-appeared in the form of a bad dream. I know many times when I do

things, sometime I dream about them - things that actually occurred. Since you have

been a guest of the Sheriff at his place, do you recall whether or not having any dreams

regarding Bernice. Eddie, speak up, please.

Eddie: No, I haven't.

J.C.W.: Now you have indicated to me about these disturbances early this morning, about

hearing these noises and voices, could it have been

Eddie: No last night.

J.C.W.: All right, last night, could it have been the others, a dream, or a combination

of both?

Eddie: It could have been, but that was the first time I ever - Of course, being a strange

place, you know.

J.C.W.: You slept downstairs, did you, in the cells down below?

Eddie: Yes, and one voice that sounded like that voice, laughed once.

JCW: Well, did he know you were downstairs.

Eddie: No

JCS: Did he ever call down to you or try to talk to you?

Eddie: No.   These voices got quite loud and then it was just like

the cross-examination - it was just like "don't tell me this and don't tell me that" -

you know, it's hard to say.

JCS: How much time did the police from Chicago spend with you in conversation? Was it

short or relatively long?

Eddie: I think that was quite long. I told them all I could and in that way they kept on.

I told them to lower their voices.

JCW: Were they raising them?

Eddie: Naturally, when they were talking, you know, and I guess one couldn't hear too well

Schley: That's right. He couldn't hear too well. He'd get to talking pretty loud.

JCW: That's my bad habit. Since I can't hear too well, sometime I raise my voice and

beller like a bull. By the way, have you ever in your lifetime been to the City of

Chicago?

Eddie: No, never.

JCW: Remember I had asked you earlier how far you think you travelled away from home.

Have you ever been to Milwaukee?

Eddie: The only time I was to Milwaukee was for examination

JCW: And that was when - maybe back in 1940 or 41, or was it later than that?

Eddie: It was

JCW: Pearl Harbor was December of '41 so was it

Eddie: You see I'm 51 so it would have to be   for Army duty

JCS: You would have to have been 42 years or less

Eddie: Yes, that's right, so it does have to be figured out. That was - let's see -

time goes so fast - that was between Germany and this country, wasn't it, and the

Japanese at that time.

JCW: Your parents were still living when you went to Milwaukee - do you remember -

both your mother and father were living?

Eddie: That's right.

JCW: I bet that was a shock to you mother when you told her you had to go to Milwaukee

102

for a physical examination and that you probably were going into the Army and the Armed

Services.

EG: Well, at the time, but not too bad. The other boys had to go   and at the

time I thought the same thing that my duty was the same as the others.

JCB: Well, Eddie, remember my speaking to you about balances and the scale of justice.

Now, put Bernice on one of the balances of the scale and the word putting a weight on the

other end - if you felt as you have been directly accused of taking her life, would you

feel that there is any doubt in your mind at this time that you did not take her life.

EG: that is, when I think of all these things, you know - you know how it would

be with yourself - everything points to it.

JCB: Let's go on to the others. Could you speak out a definite answer when I ask you

about this little girl Mary Jean Weckler. Is there any doubt in your mind - could you

say yes I did it or I positively know that I am not involved.

EG: That's right, I could say that. That was in Wisconsin?

here

JCB: Yes that's only about 40 miles from you, southeast of here. I'll show you on the

map later on. Would your answer be

EG: Oh that, no I never

JCW: Definitely not

EG: That's right.

JCW: How about Evelyn Hartley?

EG: You see that happened in La Crosse, and I've never been there.

JCW: And Vic Travis?

EG: Vic Travis - I never saw him

JCW: And Mary Hogan? Is there a question, or could you give a definite answer on that,

103

or is there some reservation in your mind or conscience.

EG: I don't know just how many miles it is from there and   about that and I

have been there.

JCW: Yes, you told us that. And that you knew her.

EG: That's right. That I knew her and everything, but it seems impossible but there is

things that can be possible. The way I remember that I was - you seen it comes back to

me, you know what I mentioned to you, but I remember when I thought back - I guess I

thought back that time. I don't know. It's kinda mixed up, because I know when I was

hauling wood there - I don't remember just what day it was - I remember that my neighbor,

you know, he come from work - that's why I kinda was - I think that he worked until five

o'clock or sometimes he worked later, and he come around the corner and went home, and

he seen me out on the road and he should've but I don't know if he'd remember, but I

don't even remember the day. It must have been around three days that I split that up.

I piled it, you know, and then I hauled it so I could take it over the fence.

JCW: What was your first knowledge about her disappearing. Did someone tell you, or did

you hear it over - you have no radio at home, do you?

EG: That's right, I have.

JCW: You have.

EG: I have - a battery job.

JCW: Do you think you may first have heard about it over the radio or that you might have

read about it in the newspaper, or heard about it in town.

EG: I kinda think - you see that newspaper that we get - that comes once a week and that

way it seemed the way that woman talked like that was the real fresh, you know.

JCW: Maybe a day before, or maybe the same day.

EG: Well, I believe that was - must have been the day after or a few days after because that was in daylight - it was daylight when went over there. I don't remember if it was in the morning or right after dinner or something like that. It was real good daylight in Bancroft. We wanted to look at hay and we had to go, you see.

JCW: Eddie, did I tell you when I saw you last Sunday how the machine works that sits next to you - the lie detector?

EG: Yes, pretty good.

JCW: Well, I think - let me explain it to you once more. I don't think you'll dispute or disagree with me when I tell you that the best lie detector that there is is one's own mother. My mother could look at me and tell when I was stretching the truth, and you probably recall the same experiences. And, of course, this is just a secondayy device. Rather than burden you with a lot of technical explanations, let me cite myself as a true but poor example. I know that there have been many times, either as a young boy, a teen ager, or as a grown person that I have knowingly and deliberately told a lie.

EG: Oh, everybody has - especially children.

JCW: That's right. And I know when I told these lies, the person that I told them to believed me, but while I was telling these lies my conscience would say, "Joe, that is an out-and-out lie that you're telling. Have you ever experienced a feeling of your con- science telling you when you have exaggerated the truth or told a lie, whether or not it was to your mother or some acquaintance.

EG: Well mostly, probably when I was a kid stretching something. There's a , well a kind of a feeling now will I gg get away with it, will I get found out, will she know that I was telling a fib, and thoughts like that going through my mind.

JCW: Well you understand then what I mean by the feeling that we all experience and we

105

don't tell the truth whether or not it's a little lie or a whopper.

EG: That's right.

JCW: Now the questions that I will ask of you, Eddie, during the test will not come as a surprise. You will know what the questions are beforehand. They are based entirely upon our conversation that has taken place last Sunday with Herb, you and I plus my conversation with you today. I will read the questions to you beforehand so that No. 1 if you don't understand the question or if you feel that it is unfair for you to answer, you tell me so and I will rewrite them to your personal satisfaction. Now, based on my explanation to you and upon your explanation that you understand what I have told you, when you take the test regarding these issues at hand, the questions are so written so that in fairness to yourself you can give an answer by saying either yes, no or I don't know. As an example, if I were to ask you is it snowing or raining now, you couldn't give me a positive yes or no answer - you'd have to say I don't know because we haven't been near a window.

EG: That's right.

JCW: These questions which I will read to you, we'll go over them together. You will then answer by either yes, no or I don't know. Now in the event, and I don't think knowing you as well as I do now that you plan on lieing to me, let's say that should occur - in the event that your spoken answer whether or not it be yes, no or I don't know, bothers your conscience, besides yourself knowing it, Eddie, by means of the blood pressure cuff - have you ever had your blood pressure taken by the doctor where they wrap it around your arm and pump it up - by means of the blood pressure cuff and the tube that I will place about your chest which you won't even know you have on - it's like wearing a belt about your trousers - that feeling in the event you should not be telling the whole truth if you should experience a feeling that you have not told me all of the details or the

106

truth, besides yourself knowing it, I will be able to see it on the chart, and there is a

chart of paper that moves and a pen and ink that inscribes the pattern. There is no pain

to the test at all. Have you ever slept on your arm and have it go numb? Well that is the

feeling that you will experience from the cuff. The tests take no more than about 4 to 7

minutes a piece. Now, every person isn$t necessarily a suitable person to submit to a

test. Sometimes it's nervousness - it's natural for anyone coming down to submit to an

examination to be keyed up. Sometimes because of a physical condition - too heavy or

heart trouble would interfere so they're not suitable - so the way to determine whether or

not a person is fit for a test is by a little game. I will show you a card on which the

numbers and the words are written from 1 to 10, and you will see on this card that No. 1

and No. 2 and No. 10 are lined out. That leaves the numbers 3, 4, 5, 6, 7 and 8. I will

hand you a pencil and paper and I will turn my back, and I want you to pick unbeknown to

me any one number of your choice between three and eight. You write it on the sheet of

paper and put it on the desk so I can't see it.

EG: Oh, I see.

JCW: Then we'll begin just this test concerning the numbers. Now I'll ask you - did you

write No. 1 - you'll answer no. No. 2, no. No. 3, no. Did you write No. 4, no. Did you

write No. 5, no. Did you write No. 6, no. Did you write No. 7, no, and No. 8, no. Did

you write No. 9, no. Did you write no. 10, no. To one of those questions you will have

told a lie - do you follow me on that? Now, Eddie, the moment that chart is completed,

we will remove it from the machine and show you how it is possible by means of this exam-

ination to tell the number that you have picked and lied to me about. The test will also

then   Eddie, there is no pain to the test as I have explained, and further you will

recognize your conscience as it builds up to this lie and the relief that occurs after you .

107

have told the lie. Now based on that first test that will be the determining factor as to whether or not we will go on with the investigation at hand. And, as an example, I will ask you do you know or suspect who kidnaped the Hartley girl from La Crosse. Now, as a result of her disappearance, Eddie, what word do you have in your own vocabulary to describe what occurred to her. We don't know if she's dead, but there's good reason to believe she is dead because blood was found at the scene.

EG: That's right.

JCW: And a few other things. But what word would you have for what occurred to her? Was she kidnaped. Did she disappear?

EG: Well, a, I a, just what I'd really think in my mind?

JCW: Yes, what would your word be for it?

EG: The way I think, let's see what happened to her then would be like the question to this Evelyn Hartley.

JCW: Well, yes, Eddie, but what I would like would be your own word to convey

EG: To describe what I really think?

JCW: Yes, of course I told you nobody knows what actually happened to her. The only thing that has been definitely established is that she disappeared. Yes. Well, here, let me put. If I were to ask you the question during the examination, did you have anything to do with the disappearance of Evelyn Hartley from La Crosse, do you think you could answer that question? All right,

EG: No

JCW: All right, how would you answer the question Mary Jean Weckler, the little girl from Wisconsin. Did you have anything to do with her disappearance?

EG: No

JCW: Then, how would you answer - did you take the life of Bernice/or whatever your con-
                                                              Worden
science tells you.

EG: Well, I suppose that would be a - I don't know - I suppose that would be

JCW: Well, whatever your conscience tells you.

EG: That's right.

JCW: How would you answer the question do you believe that you did or could have taken

Bernice Worden's life? I don't know, yes or no.

EG: That, I suppose, would have to be the same. I don't know.

JCW: And is there any doubt in your mind now one way or the other?

EG: There is a doubt, that is, to tell you the truth. You know it goes both ways. Yes,
because there is so much evidence. When I think over, you know
and yet there could be a possibility, you know, that I didn't - that she might have been -

it couldn't be though. Oh that's where I'm so

JCW: Confused?

                                        There's so much evidence, and there could be a possibility -
EG: I'm confused, that's right./ And then yet it seems to me that I couldn't have - oh,

I don't know.

JCW: Well, Eddie, do you have a recollection of striking her with the jug of this anti-

freeze.

EG: No, I haven't even that. It could be possible and yet
                                            Bernice Worden's
JCW: Well, Eddie, do you have a recollection of placing her vagina in this cardboard box?
with the others?
Now remember Sunday you gave me and Herb an answer on that and I would like to you to re-

member what your answer was and, of course, did you put her vagina in the box with the

others?

EG: Now, let me see. I suppose, well if it was found there I - let's see

JCW: Well, let's go on

JCW: Let me ask in another way. Do you remember seeing Bernice Worden's vagina in the

box?

EG: That I believe I could answer/ no - I ~~don'txknowxjusixhow~~ suppose I don't know just how

JCW: Well you told Herb and myself

EG: That's right - that I did

JCW: That you did - that you didn't remehber putting it in but you remembered seeing and

knowing that it was hers.

EG: Well, ya, if I could get that straight - you know that kinda a little bit puzzly

JCW: Well, is there anything I can do, Eddie, to make it clearer?

EG: You're doing real good

JCW: Well, is there any doubt in your mind now with all the thousands of questions that

you have answered ~~anxyauxparx~~ is there any doubt or hesitancy on your part Eddie about

recalling of telling Herb and myself that you do remember seeing Bernice's vagina in this

box?with the other vaginas?

EG: I think that's what I said to you. Was a hazy recollection of seeing it.

JCW:Well, no you were positive about that and hazy about the other things.

EG: Well, that's the way it was. I know there was - There havebeen like you say -

so many questions. If there is anything that I'm sure about like that, that would be just

a straight no. That is , that is   now you see, it's just

as blank as can be. I don't know, but if it was there

JCW: You told Herb and myself about the heart

EG: That's right

JCW: And do you recall   Do you now still remember that? The heart

being *in the bag* with pieces of scrap paper?

110

EG: It's pretty   to me whether it's just like -   it's pretty clear that

I put it there.

JCW: Eddie, do you what word do you have where a person loses his life from the hands of

another person whether or not it be with an automobile, a rifle, a knife or otherwise.

EG: If it was deliberate like

JCW: Let's say that you were walking down your road and you weren't carrying a flashlight

like you should be and somebody is driving along with the car ripsnorting away and they

don't see you but they hit you. They recognize that they hit some hard object but they

don't bother to stop . They continue and don't report it. Did he take your life?
You lose your life

EG: Yes, that would be - he killed you

JCW: How would you answer the question, Eddie, for the examination - do you know whether
you
or not have ever taken the life of another person? The answer can be yes, no, or I don't
know.

EG: I don't know

JCW: Uh hugh. How would you answer the question do you remember taking the life of

Bernice Worden?

EG: Let's see, do you remember

JCW: Do you remember taking the life of Bernice Worden? And how would you answer the

question, did you take the life of Bernice Worden?
I guess
EG: That you see, would have to be yes, I don't know.

JCW: Uh huh. You told us Sunday   Your last recollection as I recall it

with Bernice, when do you remember being seeing her last at the store.

EG: As I remember is when she told about this checking deer

JCW: You were hazy at the time - do you recall how much time of an interval of time

there was while you stood in the store?

111

and she was, Eddie, up at the front of the store?

EG:

JCW: By the way, would you care for a snack, a sandwich and some coffee?

EG: Well, maybe a little coffee.

JCW: Uh huh. Would you care for a sandwich? What do you like? Ham?

EG: Just whatever you would think.

JCW: Well what would you like cold boiled ham?

EG: Would it digest good? You know this thinking and stuff, would it upset me. Would it be all right for me to eat something with your test?

JCW: I think it will. If you can eat the food. As a matter of fact, the coffee especially might freshen you up.

EG: Coffee would be

JoW: All right. Do you like sugar in your coffee?

EG: It will be all right.

JCW: How much sugar would you like?

EG: Not too much.

JCW: Would you care for a sandwich or would you care for a piece of pie?

EG: Would it be any bother

JCW? What kind of pie would you like? I imagine they have the old stock of pie, apple, or cherry pie.

EG: Well, apple pie.

JCW: I'll take care of that in a moment or so. And during the time if you will, Eddie, if you can still refresh your memory, because remember it's going to establish as far as your personal life is concerned , I hope the question that you want straightened up regarding the balance of your mind, plus these other things that we would like to know.

112

And ordinarily xxxxxxxxxxxxxyou heard me make some of these remarks   the possi-

bility of your envolvement of the taking of a life, the only other strongpossibility

that   the only one other than Bernice is Mary Hogan, and I would like to clear

that up. What do you suggest, Eddie that might be even . Eddie do you think if you had

an ßopportunity to be ina secluded spot we'll say a hotel room, or a some place where

you're guaranteed that nobody is going to disturb you, so that it's absolutely quiet

and everything -- many many hours of sleep might freshen your body and your mind?

EG: That's kind of hard to tell there'd be kind of a tension, you know, in a strange

place. That bothers most people, you know, so I couldn't say. It might help.

JCW: Yes. Are you tired now, I mean.

EG: Well, I am some - that's right. I don't know I didn't get the rest last night that I

should have.

JCW: While I,/Our little girl here at the office to send out to get us some coffee and a

piece of pie. Have you ever eaten cheese with apple pie? Would it you like a piece of

cheese with your pie? It might fefresh your memory a little bit more. We'll take a short

recess now because it's twenty minutes -

Disc -2- Side -2-

JCW: We'll have the coffee here in just a few minutes. Eddie, has there been any time,

now that you look back on it that you have this realization or recognition of your doing

something to Mrs. Worden that you knew was not correct other than when you told by the

authorities and prior to the time you were picked up.

EG: No, I don't believe so not   . I could say no to that because

JCW: Well, Eddie, in these instances where you removed the bodies from the cemetery

when did that realization occur to you? Would it be while you were working on the body

113

Bloody Fingerprint (Gein's) from Mary Hogan's Tavern.

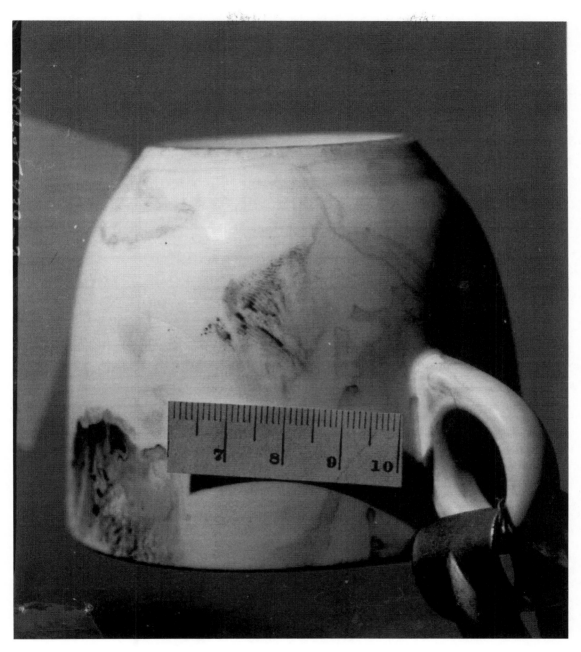

Coffee cup from Mary Hogan's Tavern with bloody fingerprints.

in your shed?

EG: Well, that's right. Sometimes it would be that way - sometimes when I'd just get to the cemetery and sometimes maybe when I had just taken a couple of shovels full of dirt or something. That would just snap me out of it like, you know, and gosh I'd be stark shaken and didn't realize.

JCW: What would your reaction be when you'd get the body up on the gambrel of the chain hoist?

EG: Well, gosh I can't really describe that. Well, I shouldn't - the only way I can say that would - the best I can describe it was kind of a numb feeling, like the body and mind

JCW: Sort of stricken dumb?

EG: Kind of a feeling something like that.

JCW: Come in. Close the door please. Let's see this is the one with cream and sugar and this one too is a little warm so watch it. Well how long would this numbness exist - would it be a matter of just a few short seconds, or minutes, or would it be prolonged?

EG: It would be prolonged a while

JCW: Well

EG: Well, I'd say about in different degrees until the body was either taken back and buried or something like that. And then there'd be a feeling of relief that it was back in the place where it should be.

JCW: Along, Eddie, along with the relief was there also remorse?

EG: That's right.

JCW: Uh huh. Did you recognize then I mean, did you recognize then that you shouldn't have done it?

EG: That's right.

116

EG: That would be the reason, you know, that I'd want to get it back.

JCW: As I recall it, you explained to Herb and myself that there weren't too many that you returned to the graves, were there?

EG: Yes

JCW: How many do you estimate that you returned?

EG: Let's see. Gosh, there must have been - let's see there was - see some of them were left right there and not taken away.

JCW: As I recall, you told me that you removed some?sections of the flesh.

EG: Yes

JCW: What section of the flesh did you remove? in those instances?

EG: The head.

JCW: The head. How about the vagina?

EG: . Well, that, not always.

JCW: In removing the head, did you first cut through and then snap the bone, or how would you separate it from the spinal column?

EG: I guess that would be snapping, or whatever you call it.

JCW: Snapping? Breaking the bone?

EG: I suppose.

JCW: By your recollection, you would cut until the motion of the knife was stopped by the bone, is that it? And then what would you do - work the head back and forth in the same fashion as you would when you attempt to break a piece of wire in two? I mean, I don't want to put words into your mouth - I mean, by your recollection

EG: That is a good description of it.

JCW: Do you recall any instance where at the cemetery you might have sawed the bone?

117

EG: No, I never took any saw.

JCW: Never any saw.

EG: No

JCW: Was it that knife that you made out of a file that you told us about?

EG: No, not all. You see

JCW: Why don't you go ahead and eat your pie? That cheese looks as though it's seen its

better days. You have to go out of the State of Wisconsin to get good cheese.

EG: Gosh, ain't that queer?

JCW: Well, that's like the oranges out of Florida and California. They leave all the culls

for the natives there and ship the best ones out.

EG: That's true. It is slightly curled, isn't it?

JCW: Slightly! If you don't want to eat it, don't. You won't hurt my feelings. Say did

you have much snow up your way?

EG: No, not a great deal. It was warm enough that it kind of kept melting and blow some.

JCW: How is the pie - any good?

EG: Real good.

JCW: It is, huh? Even when the cheese is dried out it adds a little different flavor to

the pie. What did you have for breakfast this morning? Eggs?

EG: No - just a piece of bacon, some oatmeal and a slice of bread.

JCW: What did you eat before you came to Madison? Didn't you say you stopped off at some

restaurant?

EG: That's right. I had a piece of pie, a hamburger and a cup of coffee, and a bowl of

chili.

JCW: Did you do any - did you ever have any warm meals when you were at home?

118

EG: Ya, most of them. I make tea and stuff like that, you know.

JCW: Well, how about solid food?

EG: Yes, I'd warm that.

JCW: Like a can oB beans or so, either spaghetti

EG: On my cereals I'd warm the milk and like that. Some like them real crisp and every-

thing, but I'd rather have it with - that's right.

JCW: What was your favorite cereal?

EG: Well, I'd change.

JCW: Would you buy these assorted boxes?

EG: That's right, that or else the real large. For laxative, for a change, I'd either get

this a either bran flakes. I'd make changes.

JCW: Did you eat much fresh meat? Or was it mostly sandwiches.

EG: Yes. I'd buy loaf meat and stuff.

JCW: You didn't have an ice house, did you?

EG: No

JCW: Yes. Hold it there. Do you recall how much money you had at home? Some money has

been found, but I just want to make sure that all of it has been found since the place

is going to be unattended, we want to make sure that in the event someone should have the

thought of breaking in - I don't think they'd want the junk you got there but they might

be on the lookout for money.

EG: No. Most of that - most valuable parts were taken or stolen anyway ahead of time

so there isn't too much. There might be some of them old dishes, antiques, or something

like that.

JCW: Were those your mother's dishes?

EG: That's right.

119

JCW: Well, Eddie, how much money do you figure should be at the home?

EG: Well, like I told the Sheriff and everything, what was in my cupboard - I don't know - they probably found it.

JCW: XXXXX Either in the cupboard or the dresser, I forget.

EG: There was a baking powder can where I put change in.

JCW: I don't know, but this was - I'll tell you that money has been found in excess of $20. It is more than $20. I was just wondering if you knew the exact amount, or close to it.

EG: Well, no I couldn't exactly say. You see I kept adding change to that and I should judge that it should be two-thirds full.

JCW: Well, the Sheriff has the money - it was turned over to him.

EG: There was some one dollar bills in a billfold. I don't xxxxxxxxxxx.know if they've been found or not.

JCW: I don't know. I'll check with. Where there many in it.

EG: Gosh, I couldn't say just exactly, and I'll tell you where it is so that if they have it - you know there's an old cabinet and I slipped that in there. There's stuff on top.

JCW: You be sure to tell the Sheriff so that he can have his men check to see whether or not it has been found.

EG: I told him about that, but I forgot to tell him this until just now when you mentioned it.

JCW: When you used to go shopping for food, and even though you felt that you couldn't afford it, what was usually the thing that you wanted the most that you ordinarily would splurge on it in the line of food?

EG: Most in fruits and fruit juices, and stuff like that. like celery and stuff like that.

120

JCW: Do you still have the bitter taste in your mouth that you were telling us about?

EG: That's right, I still have that. The doctor says that it's gall bladder trouble.

JCW: He was a very nice old gentleman, wasn't he?

EG: Uh huh.

JCW: He's a very famous doctor. He came all the way from Sheboygan.

EG: He wanted that xray.

JCW: Yes. Has it been done?

EG: Anda - that's right. They decided - they're not really too sure but thxxt their idea is a hardened gland.

JCW: Like a cartilage, you mean?

EG: Ya, kinda like that. But you press on that just right, you know, and it just pretty near doubles you right up.

JCW: Where abouts is it? Do you think it would be possible that that is a result of carrying logs or timbers and sort of a callous developed?

EG: No I believe that - here feel it here

JCW: I don't want to press on it because it might pain you.

EG: Well, if you don't press hard. It's right there almost below the collar bone. I'll show you. Right here.

JCW: Oh yes. Uh huh.

EG: It wiggles around.

JCW: Well, I'll wait until you get through with your pie. Don't hurry.

EG: If it gets kinda late, in here you wouldn't know it.

JCW: No. With no windows in here you can't tell what's going on on the outside. When you I understand now that they have what - found roughly is it 10 or 11?

EG: Ten

JCW: Now, of the ten, how many more plus do you think you have returned to the graveyard?

EG: That would be the full amount.

JCW: The full amount.

EG: Ya, that's right because there have been others thatI've opened but never done anything with them.

JCW: What prevented you from doing anything?

EG: That was the realization, I suppose, that it was wrong.

JCW: Well, how many bodies - yes

EG: So that would be the closest because most of them were left right there. Some wasn't. You see it has been in my mind now five years back and I couldn't exadtly say, but I think probably one or two, or something like that.

JCW: Well, did you finally come upon this realization - is that the thing that caused you to stop.

EG: Ya, that's right. It seems I'd get control, or something.

JCW: Did this urge re-develop then very recently? Even within the past week?

Eg: That's right. That's what I can't understand. Anything like that comes quick. I've told them about that. I've helped the person, and anything like that seems impossible.

JCW: Your napkin is right there. Here's another kleenex. Well, Eddie, when you removed Bernice's head, did you snap the bone also?

EG: That's right.

JCW: And it being a fresh body, you recall was there more difficulties since it was living bone to break it off?

EG: That I couldn't say. The whole thing is hazy. I don't even remember what kind of

122

knife I had. What I remember from before, you see, there was that other one that was one

that I found without a handle, and I put a handle on. And so, that, I guess, I threw away

when I kinda come to afterwards, and then it probably was quiteawhile til we was talking

about making knives out of files, and that was a nice kinda shaped file and only when I

made it it was longer than I had figured it.

JCW: Well, Eddie, Sheriff Schley tells me that you do - you correct me - you do have a

recollection and it's incorporated in your statement of withdrawing the blood from Bernice.

Do you probably think you put it in a bucket or something and disposed of it near your

toilet or outhouse.

EG: That's right.

JCW: Do you remember, I mean, was it the bucket?

EG: Well, that's what, I couldn't say, but it must have been some kind of a

JCW: Well do you recall was the draining accomplished from her neck? You placed

the bucket under her neck?

EG: Under the body.

JCW: Or rather under the body. Did you have to prop the bucket up on a box or something,

or because, as you recall, the distance from her shoulders as she was suspended was oh at

least five feet, as I recall when I saw her, from the ground. Was she - she no doubt had

to be hanging when you drew the blood.

EG: To my knowledge what I remember, I don't remember propping it up or anything. You say

that was

JCW: Her shoulders, I mean

EG: It can't be. How tall is that room there.

JCW: Well, when I stood in the pit, you know what I speak of, right beneath the chain hois

123

down on the ground. The hoist was right about where this ventilator is, and I stepped

down off the wooden floor down into this pit.

EG: That's right.

JCW: Her shoulders were about in line with my chest. So that's what I was wondering whether

or not you placed a container on a box or something, or whether or not you just placed the

container on the ground and let the blood drain from her from that distance into the bucket.

EG: Gosh, let's see. I can't say there.

JCW: Well do you remember - do you recall, I mean when you cut her neck - of course, it

hung back because it was only held by the bone in the spinal column, that is, of course,

probably the time that you drained the blood. So, of course, that would have brought her

head very much closer to the ground, and in wrenching her head off from the back bone as

I had told you, and you told me earlier that it required much motion on your part like

bending and snapping a wire in two, from those you had taken from the graves, did you let

the blood drain from her body when you cut her throat and just held the head back until

the blood drained out so then you could snap her head off.

EG: That must be

JCW: Well, I mean, that's why I'm asking you.

EG: I see - that and still I can't swear to that either just what position, you know.
That whole thing no I can't seem to

JCW: Cigarette?

EG: Maybe I could. Because it was such a short time, it was kinda fuzzy the whole thing.

JCW: Well, what do you mean, such a short time?

EG: It had to be, that's why that I can't even say what time it was because of course that

makes it so bad - if I could only - I can't even tell the time.

124

JCW: Well the element of time isn't too important, Eddie. It's probably if we can come upon the key, like picking out the right key to open up the door that's why I've been asking you these questions in an attempt that we could or did do to her body

EG: That height, and everything, that's what I was

JCW: Do you recall the nail on the/2x4 that held the chain?

EG: When you mention it, now it comes real plain to me.

JCW: Do you remember driving the nail into that studding into the upright? Or had it been there from a previous occasion?

EG: As I remember it, there must be more nails there, isn't there?

JCW: Well, this was, this was a new nail. It wasn't rusted at all. It was as though it was taken from a container, either from - is there a possibility that you purchased nails recently?

EG: Not that I

JCW: Well, it was a new nail - still a bright finish. The chain was held and pulled by the nail so that her body was suspended at the height that I have indicated and, as I say, the floor - here's your door. you walk into the shed, down into this pit, which was about oh 6x6 square, wasn't it?

EG: Probably something like that.

JCW: Yes, and in this pit off from the floor, as I say

EG: What would you judge the floor to be up about - 2½ feet?

JCW: No more than two feet - 30 inches, 24 to 30 inches.

EG: The way you remember seeing it, it was about that high, probably, huh?

JCW: Yes, because

EG: That would be higher, wouldn't it?

JCW: Well, I speak of the shoulders now. Her shoulders were right about in line with my

125

chest, and I am just slightly over 6' tall so this would make it roughly - her shoulders from the ground level were probably no more than 4 - 4½ feet off the ground

You wouldn't have to stoop to get to her neck.

EG: That would seem probably about right - the way you describe it

JCW: You have this recollection, Eddie, of the withdrawing of the blood from her body/ because you told that to the D. A.

EG: That's right. As I told them, you know that's blurry

JCW: Going back one step further, to get the blood in the bucket that means one thing that there had to be a large open wound in her body which presumably was the neck, so if you have a   from her body   the blood, do you have the recollection of running the knife through her neck to the bone?

EG: Now that you mention that, of course, and it seemed, well I really can't say, if you saw it you're right, you know, it has to be right.

JCW: Again reminding you of what I told you

EG: It don't seem right to me but you know

JCW: Do you disbelieve?

EG: No I don't disbelieve, but it just I don't know

JCW: Or is it you don't want to believe it because now you recognize what has happened

EG: No, it isn't that ½ it seems that way,

JCW: Eddie, getting back to these instances at the graves You say   removed portions right in the caskets   you would cut principally the head   cut through the neck and then what would you do to remove the head from the body?

EG:

JCW: Can you demonstrate to me   back and forth until it broke off.

EG: That's right.

JCW: What other portions of the bodies would you take other than the head. The breasts?

126

EG: No, that was only what ʲ ʲ found

JCW: Was that done at the cemeteries or at the shed? Eddie do you remember the wooden
stave barrel you had in the shed just as you walked in?

EG: That's right. I remember.

JCW: I looked at it with a flashlight - just a quick look but it looks pretty clean.

EG: Ya, I remember that. That was a water barrel.

JCW: A water barrel.

EG: That's right. I had that outside./ It was raining to catch watter, I'd use that and
sometimes, you know, for washing - soft water, and then I'd put that back where it was out
of the way. I covered it up so the dust - you probably noticed

JCW: The reason I asked you (remained indistinguishable)

JCW: Do you have any recollection Eddie/of these faces that you had plus this, how would you

describe this piece of flesh with the woman's breast, what would you call this section of

the body, the only big piece of

EG: Well, I couldn't just say how you would

JCW: Well, I mean do you   Do you recall any instances that you would place that

section of the upper part of the body over your body plus putting one of these faces

over your own, trying to inject yourself into believing that/you were a woman?

EG: Well, that I couldn't say, I don't remember it that way, I suppose I could say no, but

you know you can't

JCW: Um hum, that's why I was wondering/whether or not that is the reason why you have the upper portion of the body

and the/se various faces, because I am inclined to believe Eddie in conversation with you

Sunday and today, that because of the great love for your mother and recognizing it

in women generally that a part of the process of your own mind and conscience was that

you wanted to be like your mother, did you ever entertain the thought of wanting to be

as good as a woman as your mother?

EG:

JCW: Did you ever consider Eddie, prior to the passing of your mother that the love that your

mother expressed for you and the way that you mothered your own mother when she was ill,

that you felt that you should of been a woman, or that you would of preferred to have

been born a woman or girl?

EG: That I suppose I had to be answered properly, but it doesn't seem to come clear, you

know?

JCW: Yes, Well Eddie again------

EG: It's like you said at first there, that to be good like my mother that's a strong

128

EG: Well, I just know that

JCW: Um hum That is definitely and possitively a fact, fine. Now, I dislike/~~in~~ I mean having to

connect or associate your mother, your dear mother with this ~~instances~~ incident, but/i am trying the thing

to clear your mind in this respect.

EG: That's right.

JCW: ~~The/The~~ Because of the love that you had for your mother and she being that is

why I asked you the question, and I ask again whether or not you were trying to protect

yourself, understand what I mean that by putting yourself back in the days of trying to

remember your mother by making yourself her with the face and with this upper portion of

the body

EG: That could be, it's possible

JCW: I think Eddie, the other thing is the same question again, did you ever consider the

thought where you would of preferred to have been born a girl or woman?

EG: That, I don't know how you would say that, it doesn't---

Well, what is ~~the/~~
HCW:/ The best way that you would ~~did~~ answer it. Let me ask you this question Eddie, we know

each other well enough seemingly personal and embarrassing questions that I

ask you. Did you ever have the thought that you would of liked to remove or cut off

your penis and preferred to have it like the/sexual organs of a woman, I mean without shape of the

anything between your legs.

EG: Well, part of that is true.

JCW: What part of that is true?

EG: That, like removing part of myself, that does--

JCW: Well, specifically does that part mean your penis?

EG: Well, it does seem like it

JCW: Had it occured to you when your were a young boy or after the passing of your mother?

EG: Well, that seems to me like that was before when I was young.

JCW: Um hum. Do you recall any instances when you even considered the thought at the time

        of cutting your penis and testicles off, other than recognizing---

EG: As far as I know, no.

        Because
JCW:/   You probably realized the fact that you could of died I mean, have you ever assisted

        in the castration of animals, have you ever seen it done.

                                                             once or
EG: I've seen it done, well I'd say about/twice, well I'd say about twice.

JCW: Hog or steer?

EG: Hog, I helped hold the hog.

JCW: Um hum. Getting back to the question again, do you ever have any recollection where

        you feld that you didn't want to have a penis, that you'd prefer to have the sexual

        parts of a woman, that you wished you could of been born a woman?

EG: That doesn't   that could of been in my mind

JCW: Did you ever   Your membry now I think we'll be able to patch this maze or

        puddle together. Do you agree? That we're coming upon it?

EG: That is, as far as I know is that feeling too.

JCW: Um hum. Do you ever have any recollection Eddie of taking any of these female parts, the

        vagina specifically and holding it over your penis to cover the penis/ so you couldn't

        see the penis, and just see the vagina of a woman?

EG: I believe thats true.

JCW: Um hum. So you see that I know about these things, that I understand.

EG: Now it's coming.

JCW: Sure. Do you recall any instances after you removed Bernoice 's vagina, of putting it over

                                    130

JCW: over your own penis?

EG: No, I don't remember that.

JCW: But, do you recall doing that with the vaginas of the bodies of the other women?

EG: That I believe I do remember, that's right.

JCW: Now, these faces and I know that you selected these heads and faces because of some

particular association. Was there a resemblance in some of these faces that you had

to your mother?

EG: I believe there was some

JCW: Was the particular one that was in the plastic bag that I first told you about on
first
Sunday when the/face was found?

EG: Well, I don't reme mber even that very well, but It probably did.

JCW: Well Eddie, do you recall if I have told you and again I remind you as often as I have,

just because I tell you about these things I don't want ƒƒ you to say yes in the hopes

that you think that you're trying to satisfy me, I'm interest@d only in the truth.

Now, do you have any recollection of ever wearing this upper portion of the body and the

vagina and a face?

EG: That part of the body, I don't, that doesn't

JCW: Well, how about the face, have you ever placed the faces over your own face?

EG: That I did, I'm pretty sure of that.

JCW: Because in this   well, I'll tell you truthfully, I have only seen one of

these faces.

EG: That's right.

JCW: But, the odd things, if you want to call them odd, is that the eyes were open and the

131

JCW: mouth was open, have you ever seen a Halloween mask is a good example.

EG: That's right. Um hum.

JCW: Well, they are always made with the mouth open and the eyes, so that you could look thru

the mask.

EG: That's right.

JOW: And, that's the thought that occured to me immediately, when I saw that as to ////

whether or not that was the purpose for which the mask was meant, because of the open

mouth and the   eyelids. Now do you have any recollection as to how recently

would you hold the mask with your hand or would you put a rubber band on, or

how would you hold it on?

EG: The way that I remember now in the back of my mind is   isN't there just parts,

JCW: There are eyes, nose and mouth

EG: All of them?

JCW: interested in the ten faces, I speak of them as faces or heads or whatever

you'd like, there was also a bag that was found that was containing some eyes, some

nose and I think one mouth and that's all I know, I don't know how many there are I

just say some I didn't know definetely ////////   one mouth. Um hum.
                                    that
EG: I think when you meantion that,/it brings it to me, you know that the parts, sort of
                                    a
like eyes, those parts of /// heads there should be some parts of just a head and I

suppose there would be about two or three?

CW: I don't know, I do know there is some. I don't know by numbers.

EG: Have you mentioned the fact that   what was the lower parts of the faces

that's right.

JCW: Do you have any recollection Eddie, how you held the faces ¢/¢ on? What do you do, firs'

put the hair on the head, on your hair?

EG: That's right.

JCW: Um hum. Then how, would it stay on, I mean just like a piece of paper, how would you

put the face on, so that it wouldn't fall off.

EG: I don't believe that I put that on, that's just a part of that was

JCW: Well, I don't understand that point.

EG: You see, like if there would be a head there you'd just cut the lower part off here and'

just leave the   part.

JCW: But, the lower part I speak of was just the hair, back of the ears and down to this

portion of the neck and look just like a Halloween mask. Now as I ------ .

EG: Oh I see what you mean   you're right there, yes I remember that now,

you bring that back to me.

JCW: Well do you remember how you held the faces over your own face?

EG: I believe that there was a cord here.

JCW: A cord?

EG: Um hum, that's right. And, I never thought of that until you brought that up now.

Yes
JCW: /I think your memory is gradually becoming refreshed more and more. Now, this other

thing and it is very embarassingtoo, and remember I think I sort of took you off your

feet, wait ¢/¢/¢/¢/¢/ I want to check again with our operator-----Mr. Wilson just told

me ¢/¢¢/, and you know him, he's the Superintendent or the boss, you met him when we

were up there that the Firearms gentleman you've met him, you're acquanted with him,

Allan, he's the young man, that he has just identified the bullet from Berneice, from

133

JCW: this particular rifle at Worden's, which means, that she was shot in her store. Now,

when I say ~~where~~ in her store, ~~it~~ it could of been in the back of the store, it could of been

outside, but neverthless the rifle was from the premises, and she was shot and the rifle

was put back. Does that bring back any recollection to you?----------- that's the

test shot that he fired from your   we have a range downstairs and he is

going to check that against Mary Hogan. Now, you think about that for a moment, but

getting back to the question that I was drawing up when I left the room, I think I

sor t of took you off your feet/on Sunday when I asked you a very direct question you

sort of hedged on it, but/then you told me the truth, when I asked you whether or not you'd

ever masturbated, remember when I asked you that question, ~~that~~ and what was your answer to

the question.

G: That would be yes.

CW: Do you have any recollection Eddie if you would wear the face and the vagina, would

you become sexually excited and masturbate.

G: No, /I don't believe so.

CW: You don't believe so. Um hum. Do you think you would wear the face over a prolonged

period, or just for or ~~o~~ for what length of time?

G: That's kind of hard to tell, but it would seem to me not toolong, I had other things to

do.

CW: Yes, but I mean------

G: Maybe about an hour or so.

CW: Would you at any time ~~er/es~~ ever put a pair of women's panties over your body and/then put

some of these vaginas over your penis?

134

G: That could be.

W: Um hum. Do you recall,--------yes

G: Well, I couldn't   that I know------I think's thats the best decision, could
be.

W: Yes, do you have any recollection Eddie of wearing this upper portion of the body, be-

cause of it having women's breasts?

G: That doesn't come clear at all.

W: But, the face does?

G: That's right.

W: Um hum. When do you recall was the most recent incident in which you have had this face

over your own face?

G: Oh------   I should judge that it's about five years ago at least since I

        so that's
ever, //// kind of hard to tell just---

                  I mean
W: Course, her'es the other thing/to raise a question,   since this face was in

a plastic bag, do you have the recollection   that you had placed

                                originally
this face in the plastic bag, the one that I ///spoke to you ////   cause I think you
as /// I ---you was scared
/recallwas so that the moths wouldn't get at it, remember telling me that?

G: Yes, that's right.

                        ///////////
W: I was wondering when you did that,/whether or not as recently as it was, whether or not·

you did have the mask on again?

G: No, I can say no I guess to that.

W: Yes, I understand. Did you entertain any thought ---if Berneice in any way reminds you

of your mother?

G: No, I don't believe so.

Gein 'Didn't Know What Happened, Was in Daze'

New Sheriff Gets 'Rough Initiation'

By Sentinel Staff Writer

WAUTOMA, Wis., Nov. 18 —"Believe me, it was a rough initiation."

Art Schley, appointed sheriff of Waushara County only six weeks ago, made this comment Monday night after being handed Wisconsin's most macabre murder case in years.

Schley has snatched only five hours sleep in the past three nights in his investigation of the murder and grave robbings confessed here by Edward Gein, 51 year old bachelor handyman who lives on a farm 16 miles north of this county seat community.

But Schley is a big man, 6 feet, 246 pounds, and was un-

Describes Events in Store

By Sentinel Staff Writer

WAUTOMA, Wis., Nov. 18 —"My memory is vague . . ."

These and other phrases of a similar nature recur in the confession of Edward Gein, 51, to authorities who identified Monday the butchery of a Plainfield, Wis., widow and ownership of a macabre collection of female skulls.

RELEASED DETAILS

The statement was released Monday afternoon by Dist. Atty. Earl Kileen.

In his statement, Gein admitted going to Mrs. Bernice Worden's hardware store at Plainfield Saturday morning.

"I went into the store with a glass jug in order to some anti-freeze. Gein was guessed by Kileen. "Mrs. Worden said,

Ed Gein (Nicolas Castelaux - facebook.com/nicolas.castelaux)

JCW: Did she in any way resemble her in size or in shape?

EG: In size, I believe she did, yes she did.

JCS: How about facially, was there anything about her face ~~that~~ or/head that ~~that~~ wer're/close

to the appearance of your mother?

EG: May be a little.

JCW: What? Nose, eyes, hair, neck?

EG: Her hair / would be a different color, but there's some parts of the face which might resemble

her.

JCW: Um hum. Did you often see in Mrs. Worden, did you often see your mother in her?

EG: Well, well not that I, it doesn't come to me now.

JCW: What was your reason for taking the cash register from the store?

EG: That I can tell you right now is I go back, there is no reason that I can think of at all.

JCW: Was it because it/was a mechanical device ?
        you'd liked and it

EG: I believe you about struck it there. That's the only reason I can think of.

JCW: Was it and adding machine type, I haven't seen the machine I know it was there.

EG:

JCW: Do you recall after you got it home of trying it out?

EG: That's right.

JCW: Um hum. Did you try to add up any figures or did you go thru the motions of making change as though you were
        for
        /people?

EG: That's right, I was adding, say that comes clear now.

JCW: That's so, tell me about it.

EG: paper coming out on top now.

JCW: Where did you do that, in the shed?

138

In the shed.
EG: /Yes, that's right.

JCW: Had you brought Berniece in then? Or did you bring the cash register in after you

brought Berniece in?

EG: I couldn't say.

JCW: Did you spend much time playing with the cash register?

EG: It seems quite a while to me,/cause time goes faster

JCW: Yes, with Berniece, did you have any thought in mind of removing her face because of

slight resemblance to your mother?

EG: That I couldn't   seem possible, but I couldn't say. That I couldn't say.

JCW: Yes. Why don't you read this over, I imagine , read this over, maybe sort of refresh

your memory until I get back.

CI #4781 - Disc 3 - Side 2

JCW: Of any portion which you have read Eddie, come through or in   -----

EG: Well, /the only thing, it had to be

JCW: Will you /speak a little louder Eddie, so I can hear you.

EG: The only thing, taking the body out of the car and hanging it up by its heels

cause I can't remember it clear   right now, then I drove out to my farm I know that

cause I realize that I was driving out the farm, so that's true. Could be right too.

JCW: What is that?

EG: Cause, after that   exactly that must be it, now

it doesn't come to me exactly what I did think, but when they mentioned

JCW: Look,/you & I should straighten up at this particular point, you explained to me that the

as far as you're personally concerned, that there was some thought regarding the re-

139

JCW: semblance of Berniece and your mother, is that correct?

EG: Yes, there was some.

JCW: Eddie, I don't believe that your thoughts were directed to her as being a deer, animal

I think your thoughts were more directed to the fact, that she bore some resemblance

or relationship to your mother, now which are you more inclined to believe?

EG: Well,

JCW: Understanding this, that you removed her head for the same purpose which you had done TO
the others.

EG: That could be, that's right.

JCW: You removed her vagina as you did in the case of the others. Now, in dressing out a

deer, or anything else you know that the purpose of dressing out a deer is to get it's

the
flesh   that its necessary to remove the head or/skin of the body entirely, but

the sexual organs of a deer are not removed separately.

EG: Hey, that's right too.

JCW: So, with what I have explained to you Eddie, I think we can get closer to the reason

as to why you did take Berniece's life? Based on what you have told me Eddie, that

you used to joke with her about roller-skating and that you can't roller skate and

everything, things marked out in my mind that you applied every excuse or reason to

it was
go to see Berniece to buy, whether or not/a half pound of shingle nails   ball of

twine or something, just so that you could have conversation. Is that right or wrong?

EG: Well, I believe you're right there. I liked her that way, she was nice.

JCW: Was she   your mother?

EG: I think so.

JCW: Did she ever talk to you about your mother?

140

EG: She must of   all of that to me.

ICW: Well Eddie, now that we are trying to clear these things up, can you explain the meaning

your reason now for taking Berniece? You took Berniece because you wanted her.

EG:

ICW: Right. Now, why did you want her?

EG: So, that must be the reason.

CW: I don't want to put words or ideas

EG: I know, but that must be

CW: I know it's a slow process, but I think if you're agreeable to talk this thing out here

we might come up with a complete story. Do you agree?

     That's right.
EG: /As far as you said, you come out   story   ~~true~~ true   that I'd remember

CW: Now, Eddie, what is the answer or why did you take Berniece?

EG: Cause, I -----

CW: Did you have sort of a faint notion?

EG: Yes, that's right.It was a notion. That I did take her for the resemblance, of my

mother, her height and everything was the same and she had   resemblance
                                                                     ~~resemblance~~ ~~of~~ to

the cheek bones here, but   well, we'll talk some more.

CW: Fine. Would you rule out definetely the remark that you made in the statement about /

associating her likeness to a deer?

EG: I believe I would.

                                                            a boy or a young man or as a grown
CW: Tell me, Eddie, as far back as you can remember, either as/   had you ever wished that
                                                                .man
               give birth·or
you could be a woman, ~~pith~~ carry a child?

CW: You know Mr. Wilson, don't you Eddie?

141

not distinguishable - -

Q   That was just about the time you

It was fired   32765 mill. automatic pistol which was

found

Q   Do you know what time - well

A   I can't tell the time.

Q   No, I mean that that shell was fired from that gun.

A   Well, that wouldn't do much good to think of that because I

couldn't say just when.

           The
Q   ~~That~~ important thing in that is what became of Mary Hogan's

body. It was never recovered.

           right
A   That's ~~funny~~.

Q   We may have parts of it   coming down here in the field, I

don't know, but that's a matter for you to work

but we want your permission

A   That's right.

Q   let the Crime Lab. find out.

A   That's right.

                               You work that out with

Thanks for the information.

Q   Well, let's drop that matter, so that we can think about it

later.

Q   You don't know the time or about when she was

      The time of the day?

A   That's right.

Q   Yes I can find that out from her. XXXXXgaXXX That's what I

said to the sheriff - I'll get a hold of her because I saw them out

in the hall way before and I'll ask him

would that refresh your memory?

A   Yes sir that would help.

Q   I talked to Mr.   and Miss Hogan disappeared some time

between 4:40 and 5:30 P. M. That was in the late afternoon

A   December 8th and the time was - of course that can't be absolutely

accurate - 10 minutes to 5 to 5:30. See,   a neighbor came

to the tavern about 5:30 P. M. and found the door unlocked. The lights were turned on and a trail of blood leading from the overturned chair

and so on. I used or rather I found a 32 automatic pistol cartridge

case was also found on the floor

but now in view of the information that you have at hand, has your

memory been refreshed any on that?

A.   which I can't seem to

recall but apparently it did happen. You would think a large amount

of money had disappeared. Look what the paper says here, Gee - of

course they found that much money there   there werecoins

found in plastic bags and everything else. She apparently was quite

a wealthy woman because they say that she had deposited $1500.00 at

the bank about two weeks ago before she disappeared. They believe

that money was taken along with Mary. XX Do you have any recollection

of taking money when you took her?

A.   Gosh, if I took - I don't believe there was any money taken - it

must be-but still-well I   .   If I could remember you know

as time goes on   but that day

Q   Tell me, did you use this gun?

         Yes, let's see that was 3   well, we'll say

Q   Do you recall removing her face?

A.   I don't, yes, maybe the pictures show it differently. You know

I said

Q.   Do you remember seeing the picture Mr. Haack showed you Sunday

night?

A.   That's right, but

Q.   And the dog there?

A.   But she doesn't look like - of course it's been, you know a long

time.

Q.   Yes, tell them about not looking like her from the last time you

saw her. Was there any resemblence between Mary Hogan and your Mother?

A.   I believe she was closer than

Q.   What is there that you remember about the place, there's a

picture of the place. Did you ~~Juke box~~ and   table and see the over turned

chairs and/the ~~see~~ blood. Blood on the oil cloth. Do you remember my

telling you on Sunday that there was a bloody portion of a palm print

on this oil cloth? That is now being checked also. What is your

recollection, ~~Eddie~~? Yes,   you can see also that I just got

the report that there is blood, positive identification of human

blood in the trunk of your car. That's just evidence, but

of course we know this already but that is a good thing to know.

What's your recollection, no matter how much or how little, regarding

145

Mary Hogan% now?

A.   I remember her.

Q.   See, we had a report, a young little school/girl passing by,

I don't know whether she's a neighbor or was a neighbor of Mary

Hogan's, that recalled a pick-up truck, recalled a canvas - % or

                                    covering something
tarpaulin in the back of the truck/oxxxzzzzzzzzzg. Do you remember

putting
haXing her in the body of the truck and covering her?

A.   No, I don't and this tarpaulin or canvas, I haven't got any of

that.

%.   Well, could it have been some - some

Q.   Any other covering, ha.

Q.   Some farm equipment or something? Do you remember just roughly

how many feet you stood off when you fired the gun? at her?

A.   I don't X remember that, you know this was so sudden I did not

realize anything of that.

Q.   Is there any- . What was your feeling about Mary Hogan? Were

your feelings about Mary Hogan the same as you had toward Bernice?

A.   That's right.
XXXXXXXXXXXXXXXXXXXXXXX

Q.   And what was that feeling?

A.   Every time I went there, she was friendly and nice.

146

Q.   Mary Hogan ~~was~~ also?

A.   That's right.

Q.   Other than being friendly and nice, did you in any way associate Mary Hogan with your Mother?

A.   That's true too.

Q.   That's true too, ha.

What in / particular about Mary, did you find was the same as your Mother's?

A.   That friendliness and thinking it over now I believe she/that must have been just about the same, same height,/and everything must be about the same.

Q.   Do you remember what - Yes?

A.   You know it doesn't just - now that - doesn't seem possible you know that   my mind. That's what upsets me.

Q.   Eddie,
/ What recollection do you have, do you have a recollection of, conclusive recollection as to whether or not your putting Mary up on the gambel and on the chain hoist?

IXᴀᴍᴋᴋXᴇᴀᴍᴍᴇᴀᴋXᴇᴍᴀᴋX

A.   I can say no, that I don't remember that.

Q.   Do you remember removing her head?

A.   Gosh
~~Yes~~/ I am trying to think

Q.   Well, what recollection do you have as relating to Mary Hogan, other than the fact, that she bore a/ɪʀɴʐʐ ~~the closest~~ resemblence to your Mother,

being friendly, ~~her~~ ~~the~~ age / ~~being closer to your mother~~ than Bernice?

A.   Well, there wasn't much difference.

Q.   Do you recall how you disposed of her body? I think if you remember,
she/ɴʜʐɴɪʐʐembalmed./ɪsɪ̱ʐ was not Eddie, there any possibility that you could have put

her in a casket/ in the cemetery?

A.   Yes, I guess anything is possible the way things are going.

Q.   Could you have taken a body from the grave and you knew that the

casket was empty and then in a matter of let's say a day or two days

or a week, you could have taken Mary and put her in the casket that

had formerly been occupied by some other womanX or - yes?

A.   Could be.

Q.   Do you think it's

A.   I can't - it doesn't really come to me now

            not distinquishable

Q.   How did you use the formald e hyde, the preservative that you had

at home?

A.   I believe that's been there a long time. I believe that's for

the squirrel tails that I was   . I had a whole box of them. I gave
some of them to the kids. I seen them putting them on their cars.
Q.   Did you ever try tanning the entire squirrel?

X A.   No, I don't think I did.

Q.   Well, do you have recollection of ever using any/formaldyhyde
of this   e

solution on any of the flesh that you had?

A.   No, I don't believe so.

Q.   This mask that you wore over your face, could that be Mary Hogan?
but
Because there is a little resemblence/ that I don't know when I tell

I'll be very truthful with you.
you whether or not this mask has been embalmed or not./ ~~How are you~~

~~going to~~

Q.   What color was the head?

A.   Dark, remember I told you I looked at it   - brown or black.

     hm-m

Q.   Did you ever try your hand at preserving any flesh with for-
e
~~maldyhyde~~ maldyhyde?

A.   Not - you know I can't say for sure anything the way it seems.

Q.   Well, do you remember bringing Mary home with you?

A.   The whole thing seems impossible, but it could - can be - must be

     (not distinguishable)
     You know that we haven't lied to you.
A.   That's right.

Q.   Do you remember removing her intestines?

A.   See I don't - that is all a blank.

Q.   How about her vagina, do you remember removing her vagina?

149

A. I don't - you see I don't remember that whole thing.

Q. Eddie,

A. I remember that and when I was telling that. I guess I do need

treatment and

Q. No, I know that the doctors can help you, especially if you yourself

want help.

A. That's right, I sure do.

Q. Do you remember her drinking coffee when you walked in? Do you

remember whether or not she was at the bar or whether or not she was at this

table when you first saw her?

A. The only thing that registers now is, when you said that coffee,

was that I seen that   or something. I seen that in the papers

what it said about

but - it doesn't seem possible but it is. Must be.

Q. Just get a hold of yourself. Just sit there for a moment and sort of

think it over and try to refresh your memory.

A. Or lose it altogether.

Q. No, I don't think you will, Eddie, because your memory is remarkable

do to the fact that you have been able to refresh it. You just sit and relax

and I'll be back in a moment.

JCW   able to refresh your memory any atall?

E.G.   No I haven't but

JCW   But what?

E,G,   Is it, that is, would it be possible just -- that is -- could I, how would

           you say that - a

JCW   Just use your own words.

E.G.   say that I doubt it?

JCW   I wouldn't say anything that I know not to be the truth, only speak out the

           truth, let your conscience be your guide. If you know that you did it

E.G.   That's right, if I was just sure, why

JCW   Do you have a strong feeling or suspicion that you did do it?

E.G.   That's it -- just that chance -- that's what, that's why I kinda wanted them

           to test

JCW   Yes. Do you think that if, sure that's why you, remember at that time I was

           not aware of the fact that you were taking bodies from graves. You were

           constantly telling Herb and myself, "If you have them checked by the

           Laboratory, the Crime Lab, they'll find that they've been embalmed."

E.G.   That's right.

JCW   And that's the way it worked out. Then later on, I mean you'd indicated

           that these bodies came from the graves.

E.G.   Do you think that you might be able to better refresh your memory if you were

           to take the test now? Of course the thing I'd like to bring to your attention

           Eddie, is that you must speak out the answer as your conscience wants you to,

           to give it. You let your conscience be your guide.

E.G.   That's right. It's That I should say it out, you know, that I know, I will.

JCW   That's right. How are you going to answer regarding Bernice, when I'll

         ask you whether or not, did you take Bernice's life?

E.G.   Can't be sure.

JCW   What does your conscience tell you, Eddie?

E.G.   Well, it could be -- I don't know just how you would   to say that, but

         you see I don't, it doesn't come correct to me, but you know like my mind tells

         me that that it's so.

JCW   Oh, your mind, you mean by your mind your conscience?

E.G.   Well just, you know everything points to

         my sense of reason I guess you would say, or something like that, it points

         right to it.

JCW   How does your sense of reason figure out the disappearance of Mary Hogan?

E.G.   That is a - gees I can't really figure that out at all yet, but if that shell,

         and Beck said it is, why that had to be because I don't, it wasn't

         out that I or anything like that, and I wouldn't want to accuse anybody anyway,

         even if it was

JCW   It being your own gun right under your own pillow. I understand there were

         very few if any people that were ever into your home.

E.G.   There were some, quite a few.

JCW   Weren't you ever fearful of their finding portions of the bodies.

E.G.   Well, as I mentioned to you, after that why it was no, well the bodies wasn't

         hidden in view, no, it was just like it was, oh   it was just like it was

         forgotten, but I am glad that that was brought out that way about

JCW   Unhun. Well, I'm going to start writing up these questions.

E.G.   Right away?

JCW   Yes.

E.G.   You know what a

JCW   What were you going to tell me?

JCW   Eddie, what's your middle name?

E.G.   Theadore.

JCW   Theadore, that's right you told me. You were born when and where? At La Crosse, but the month, the day and the year?

E.G.   August 28th, that was 1906, that would come out 51, I guess.

JCW   Yes. Do you remember having Mary Hogan at home, or in the shed? Or _____

E.G.   That I can't do, it don't seem possible you know, but there is a positive indentification of that shell, you know?

JCW   Yes there is. Well, I'm drawing up these questions now, Eddie. How will you answer the question "Did you take the life of Mrs. Worden?", of Bernice Warden? I don't like to use the word "kill", it is not necessary. You heard me tell you also that the bullet has been identified from the rifle from her store, was fired in the back of her head, and I understand you told the Sheriff in your statement that you have a recollection, a vague recollection of striking her with the anti-freeze. Is that correct?

E.G.   No, that isn't correct.

JCW   Have some forms here, let's see what it is. I stand corrected. You might have told them that maybe it might have happened.

E.G.   That's rightee.

JCW   Well do you remember taking Bernice's life?

E.G.   You can fill all the rest out and I'll   whatever you feel is necessary,

      I'll try to think that over while you fill it out.

JCW   Okay

E.G.   you - - - -

JCW   You just sit back and think it over. How would you answer the question, "Bernice's

      is the only human life you've ever taken?"

E.G.   Well I could say

JCW   Are you getting tired?

E.G.   Well, it isn't that so much, it's

JCW   You see, Eddie, the reason I have been delaying the test is that it is most

      desirable under the circumstances that a person be sure in his own conscience

      that he can give a yes or no answer to a question, because, sure all along

      you've been saying, it is possible that I've done these things

E.G.   That's right, the truth

JCW   but, plus all these things you've been told that you were said to have done.

      I know that your memory is becoming fresher and fresher as each moment goes

      by, therefore, and I know that you are extremely remorseful, aren't you at

      this particular moment?

E.G.   That's true

JCW: If that is what it is, is that preventing you from mustering up the necessary courage

to speak out what is true?

EG: No, it isn't that. What is in my mind is just like I said to you if it would be that

if it would be for that it wouldn't have to be put in black and white, like the thing goes just what I do if I do not remember any things like that   (all indistinguishable)

JCW: ?

EG: It isn't that at all ? ?

JCW: your memory regarding Bernice and Mary Hogan

is extremely hazy. Now is it that you just can't get yourself together to actually believe

that you are the person that do these things - taking the life of Bernice Worden and taking

the life of Mary Hogan?

EG: Well, it's that and it isn't clear in my mind how and

JCW: Well, Eddie, / ?   All right, now what do you think the

reason is, especially as far as Bernice is concerned?

EG: That's the only thing, the wild(?) reason would be because of resemblance or something

to my mother, xm or someone I liked   but I can't the only thing there is   why

I would harm them, that's what I can't

JCW: Well, probably as far as you considered at that time/that you had no intentions of

harming them but that you wanted to possess them, to have them for your own because your

mother was buried and you know ~~thatxthexexthxxxintxxextxx~~ thought of removing her body, or

did that thought ever occur to you?

EG: I couldn't say.

JCW: All right. But at least you did possess a portion of bodies of others who probably bore

some resemblance to your mother. You say that (~~all indistinguishable~~) you were attracted
because of the relationship Bernice had to your mother. Did that same
    resemblance or relationship between your mother also reproduced in Mary
EG: Hogan?
       That's right.
JCW: Do you remember taking Bernice from the store now that your memory is becoming refreshed?

EG: Yes it seems pretty clear that way

JCW: Yes, but regardless of how clear or ~~flxxty~~ false, what do you remember about now of tak-

155

ing Bernice? You remember picking her up? Io you remember that? You

remember where she went when you picked her up? You remember where she

walked? You remember where she was on the floor when you picked her up?

A.   No, I couldn't say and be exact.

Q.   Could you say within a matter of 3 or 4 feet? Now that your memory

is coming back, Eddie, do you.....

A.   Wait a minute

Q.   I have never been in the store so that I am not familiar with the

location but here let's just generalize. Now, you remember, or do you

remember picking up Bernice?

A.   I'd rather tell the truth....

Q.   If you can remember, that's all we want. Can you remember picking her

up? Have you any recollection of what happened just before that?

A.   I took her up careful. I don't remember.

Q.   Just before you picked her up do you remember holding the rifle in your

hand; do you remember having the rifle in your hand?

A.   That.......there were fingerprints on the stock.

Q.   Yes, on the stock but there are fingerprints on the stock in blood

but I'm not going to tell you they are yours because I don't know. The

rifle was returned to the place where it originally came from. Do you

remember whether or not you took the cash register out first or whether or

not you took Bernice out first? Eddie, just a split second before you

recall picking her up, do you have any recollection of what had happened

just before that? Had you just come back from putting the rifle away?

156

A.   I don't remember that.

X.Q.   I don't doubt that at all. Do you remember getting the rifle? Do you
remember loading it?

A.   That's it....I can't remember it.

Q.   Do you remember firing it?

A.   I remember before that I took the rifle.

Q.   Was that the same day or previous to that?

A.   No, that was about 2 days ago or something like that.

Q.   Do you remember did you have a shell, a cartridge in your pocket, in
your coat, in your trousers?

A.   I can't get it through my head...It is possible.

Q.   What is possible?

A.   That I had a shell in there.

Q.   Do you remember putting it in the rifle?

A.   That's what.....I can't.....

Q.   Well, Eddie, do you remember pointing the rifle at her?

A.   No.

Q.   Do you remember hearing the report of the shot when it went off? That
is something that should have been registered on your mind because of the
noise that it makes. It wasn't a loud noise but you have heard a couple
shots fired on the range downstairs while you were here. You remember her
reaction the moment she began to fall? What did she say or what did she do?
Did she fall on her face or did she fall on her back or did you try to ease
her before she fell to the floor? Because she didn't die instantly; it could

157

SNOW, RAIN
Heavy snow warning for west, north. Freezing rain south of Green Bay. Details on Page 2.

Oshkosh Daily Northwestern

Associated Press and United Press   Ninetieth Year   Oshkosh, Wis., Monday Evening, November 18, 1957   22 Pages   Price Six Cents

10 Skulls Found in House of Horror

Wintry Storm Rips Midwest

Traffic Snarled, Schools Closed As Heavy Snow Hits; Wisconsin in Path

By THE ASSOCIATED PRESS

A wintry storm bolted parts of the Midwest Monday, snarling highway traffic and closing some schools.

The storm spread a heavy snow cover from northern Oklahoma into Wisconsin and accumulations up to a foot deep were forecast.

The Midwest storm came on the heels of a rash of out-of-season tornadoes which killed at least five persons in Alabama and Mississippi.

Russell in north central Kansas had eight inches of snow on the ground; Hill City, Kan., seven; La Crosse, Wis., five; Council Bluffs, Iowa, nine, and Dumont, Wis., nine. Parts of Nebraska reported 10 inches.

Many Schools Closed

Scores of schools were closed in Iowa because school buses couldn't move over the snow covered roads. Highway travel was slowed in northwest Iowa. A heavy glaze warning was issued for motorists in parts of Iowa.

The U. S. Weather Bureau in Kansas City said snow was falling through eastern Nebraska and western and northern Iowa, Kansas and into northern Oklahoma and that strong northerly winds would cause considerable blowing and drifting.

The mercury nosedived in 32 degrees below zero in parts of Wyoming.

nado damaged homes and buildings at White Settlement, near Fort Worth. Three persons were killed and nine injured in Alabama and two killed and several injured in Mississippi. Several homes and buildings were destroyed or damaged.

Rain, Thunderstorms

The thunderstorms and showers extended from Virginia southward to the Gulf and westward through Missouri and southeast Kansas and all of Texas except the Panhandle.

Northwest of the rain and storm belt, snow fell from Iowa to the Texas Panhandle and westward into eastern Wyoming and Colorado.

The snowfall was described as heavy in a band from Green Bay to La Crosse, with the latter city reporting a total of five inches on the ground at 6 a.m. By mid-morning the snow there had changed to a freezing drizzle.

Elsewhere in the state this ...

BULLETIN

Gein Admits Killing Woman, Kileen Reveals

WAUTOMA — In a statement released to the press at 1:45 p.m. today, Dist. Atty. Earl F. Kileen said that Edward Gein had admitted the murder of Mrs. Bernice Worden.

In a somewhat incoherent statement, Kileen said, Gein confessed that he recalls dragging Mrs. Worden across the floor of her store, loading the body into her truck, driving it to the edge of the village, walking back to the village to get his own car, and then transferring the body to his vehicle.

Gein insisted, however, that he "was not sure of, is that killed her, because I didn't have a weapon with me or on my property." Dist. Atty. Kileen said, however, that he had been informed Mrs. Worden was shot to death.

According to the district attorney, Gein then told how he took a knife to look for the body of the Plainfield merchant to his own home, hung it by the heels, and dismembered it.

To Be Arraigned

He is to be arraigned in County Court this afternoon on a robbery charge, the district attorney indicating he wanted to check with ...

RETURNS TO MURDER SCENE

Ed. Gein, farmer, who is being held for questioning in connection with the death of 10 persons, leaves county jail handcuffed and escorted by Sheriff Art Schley. He is taking the sheriff to his farm at Plainfield near Wautoma where he said "he had something to show him" at the house where he lives. The portions of 10 bodies were found in his house. (AP Wirephoto)

Dulles Gives

Gunshot Wounds

Handy Man Is Grilled by DA

Body of Missing Plainfield Woman Discovered at Farm Home of Ed Gein

PLAINFIELD (AP) — The Waushara County District attorney said today that five more human heads have been found on an isolated farm near Plainfield, raising to 10 the number of cadavers discovered so far in the house where a mild-mannered handy man lived alone.

Prosecutor Earl Kileen said that Edward Gein had broken a stubborn 30-hour silence and admitted that he "knew something" about the macabre collection.

Kileen said that Gein told him he "might of" killed the victims, and admitted the ghastly butchering of a 58-year-old Plainfield businesswoman Saturday.

Gein was asked whether, in connection with the disemboweling of Mrs. Bernice Worden, he had intended to eat his victims.

"On that point he still has a lapse of memory," the district attorney said.

The five latest heads to be found were wrapped neatly in plastic bags.

Shortly after 11 a.m. (CST), the 51-year-old Gein—a frail looking 160-pound bachelor—wearing rubber boots, and with his red cloth gloves handcuffed before him, was taken from the Waushara County Jail at Wautoma by Kileen, Sheriff Art Schley and County Judge Boyd Clark.

"He has something he wants to ...

10 Perish In Weekend Road Mishaps

By THE ASSOCIATED PRESS

Dr. John Schindler, Monroe's famed physician-author, headed a list of 10 weekend highway fatalities that raised Wisconsin's 1957 traffic death toll to 704 compared with 644 on this date last year.

The State Motor Vehicle Department revised the total on the basis of reports of deaths attributable to accidents previously unreported.

A sailor died at Manitowoc Saturday night when he was hit by a car while standing near a stalled automobile. Authorities identified him as James E. Redl, 22, of Elroy, Wis., who was stationed aboard the Destroyer Escort U.S.S. Daniel A. Joy. The craft is berthed at the Manitowoc shipyards for repairs. The accident occurred on Memorial Drive between Manitowoc and Two Rivers.

Hits Bridge Abutment

A man identified as ...

The Cold World of Ed Gein. (Sam Hane. - artgrinder.com)

have been a matter of seconds or minutes or even an hour; I don't know, but

I know one thing positively, that she wasn't, that she didn't die

instantaneously. That is, because of the fact she didn't die instantaneously

is something that is etched upon your memory as to what...

......

Q.   She was hit in the back of the head with the bullet. Now in picking

her up, do you remember, just generally, let's use a point on the compass so

as to speak, the barrel of anti-freeze, was she near there? or was she

near the front or the back door, or did she see you standing near the rifle

when she began to walk toward you? She couldn't have been walking toward

you because she was shot in the back of the head.

......

Q.   Did you have to get on your knees to pick her up, do you remember that?

Did you get down on one.....

A.   That will be right.

Q.   You remember whether or not it was one knee or both the knees...because

I know you were very gentle with her in picking her up. You were, weren't

you?

A.   That's right.

Q.   So if you remember

....

Q.   It doesn't have to be step-by-step....you new remember that you very

gently picked her up but did you get down this way, which would be most

natural, with of course, one leg up.

A.   I believe that is it.

Q.   Now, in relation to where you picked her up, do you remember where she

was laying when you picked her up? Was it near the anti-freeze drums or

was it near the front door?

A.   Well.....

Q.   Between the front door and the back door?

      ....

Q.   Yes, uhhuh. Do you remember her saying anything.........the moment the
shot was fired

A.   That's what I think .....

Q.   Huhuh. Do you remember holding ....in your hands on Saturday

morning when you went in to buy the anti-freeze?

A.   I don't remember. I remember........the day before,...not the day

before, two days before.

Q.   Let's try....for what reason did you look at the guns then?

A.   That was because we were talking about deer hunting.......I think......

Frank......Frank was there.

Q   When did the thought first occur to you that you wanted Bernice for

your own? Was it before Saturday? Had you thought about this for a long

time?

A   No, I didn't....

Q   .....it came on all of a sudden?

A   That's right.......

Q   Do you think that it happened on the day that you took her?

A   ....anti-freeze, yes.

161

because I was short of kerosene. That's just as clear in my mind.

Q   ......I believe you.....the thought developed on the moment.

A   That's right. Otherwise I probably would have taken something along.

Q   Hhuh. .....possibility that you could have had some ammunition in your

pocket or there is a possibility that you could have taken it off the shelf

or.......in the store. Had you been hunting squirrels at all or rabbits

last week? Remember I told you about the tin cans which.........

target practice.

A   Well, I believe he had some too.

Q   Do you remember, did you some some ammunition in your pocket at the

time when you were target practicing?

A   I believe it........

Q   Do you know what kind of ammunition you were using?

....

Yes.

I believe the last time ......but I believe ....target practicing

ourselves after that which .....

Huhuh......Do you remember the mink? Winchester or,......or.......

Remington.....

Let's see...I believe....I believe the shells were bought from

.....What brand of ammunition do you believe these 22 shorts were?

......Federal Cartridge Company, ...Minnesota, and that they had I

think........Winchester.......

.....Yes

162

Do you remember the color of the box?

.... red

Well, that's all right. That's not too important. Do you think that you might have had some 22 shorts.

.....something like that. Red and white or something like that. Red or black.

And yellow in it?

DISC 4 - SIDE 2

Do you remember whether or not you had any cartridges in your pocket? ....

.......but I..

I think it.....It's much better to add some straight....answers ......

Better than an "I don't know." That's right.......and I have enough respect for you, Eddie, so that I feel that I - when your memory becomes sufficiently refreshed, if you don't have to have.....to back up your story .....

That's right.

....test anyway.....if you want to.......Eddie, getting back to..... ...midway in the store , do you recall whether or not you slipped your hand under her, put your hands under her back or on her front part of the body? ....

....

You remember.........underneath her arms? When you picked her up do

163

you remember you say you remember picking her up.

That's right.

What is the next thing - you say you remember picking her up.

That's right.

What is the next thing that you remember? Do you remember walking out the door with her?

. . . .

Here's the thing, if you do remember dragging her. Is that correct?

That's right.

And her legs dragged?

That's right.

See here's....remember her dragging her across the floor like dragging a carpet; did you drag her like a carpet? or did you have her feet dragging?

.....I remember......her into the.......

Do you remember covering her?

To what I was.....outside

Eddie, do you remember realizing when you picked her up what had happened? When you picked her up did you know then what had happened?

....I don't believe I did......lifted her up and

Did you know that she was...did you know that she was hurt bad?

. . . . . .

You,...there for a moment and think it over......You remember picking her up, but do you recall or did you recognize or know then that she was hurt?

164

I believe I did.

What did you think? I mean, when you picked her up .....her to be on

the floor?.....

That's right.

....thought was transmitted to ....on the floor.

....

.....on the floor.....personal control....part of her.....

......

Yes

....

Yes

....

At the time you picked her up, Eddie, ...we'll try all angles. When

you picked her up...tried to pick her up did you then know something had

happened to her? that you, yourself, were responsible?

......

When you put her in the truck

Yes,......but I'm not sure

To take her somewhere? perhaps?

That's the way.....

Were you at that moment......

Yes, in a way it seems so........

Why do you think you were......

........that's the way it seems to me when I took her.......but ....

I know I'm not lying...that's the honest ......right out.......to take her

out and

Is it possible that you wanted to take her for yourself? ....

That could be it.

Well, Eddie, when you were driving home did you know then that she was

injured? as the result of something you had done to her?

....

.....that she was dead

.......my mind

.....I realize....and then prior to that you must have had some inkling

of her being dead. Did that occur when she was in the shed? ......you were

extremely careful .....and kindly....truck......her down...so she was.....

.......Did you know then, did you think you were trying to help her at that

time when she was in the shed?

....

Outside......

I can't...it seems to me....I'm not sure of it. ......

.....blood,....wash cloth and some rags, sponge, or what?

....

Where did you get the water from?

In the house.

In the house? Did you use your own washcloth?

That's right.

Remember what portion of her body you washed?

166

Her shoulders.

Her shoulders? Was she on the floor then, or was she.......?
washing her would be
...quite difficult especially with all the clutter of stuff that you had

there. Do you think that you washed her in the shed?

Yes, that's right.

Now, you and I .... shed.... a lot of clutter in the shed.

That's right.

Which would make it a little difficult under the circumstances to wash

her unless you had her down on the dirt floor. ....Now if you wanted to

wash her she had to be washed while she was suspended on the.......See if

you can refresh your memory on that. Do you remember.......Did you heat

the water? or was it cold water?

......

You remember when you picked up the washrag....

....

Do you think that you put her up on the....so it would be easier to

wash her down?

....

Then maybe later on you put her up on the......

....

Well, that's not too important. ......your memory.....refreshed. Do

you remember bringing her from the truck into the shed?

....

Do you remember undressing her?

167

Getting back to Bernice's store. Just the moment before you picked her up you........just before you picked her up, do you remember was she.....

......

.....after that......

....

....the bathroom ......positive either yes or no; then we can get the test over with. Why don't you sit down? Unless you can rest by standing. Now.......

....

Are you familiar with........

....

<u>You know how to load them, don't you?</u>

Yes........

.......different model. Do you have any recollection of loading the shells either into the chamber or into the magazine of that......?

......

Do you remember loading it into the magazine? The tube?

I can't be positive.

I see.

Because.....

No, I don't want you to....unless you're sure.

That's right.

Eddie, do you......sure?

Yes.

168

Eddie do you remember any time ......

That's right.

OK. Mind telling me about the number.....

That's right......

.....all right. We'll go on a little while after dinner.....down for
tonight. ....run that test? Couldn't the rest be......? ...satisfaction
We have to get these tests over. Can't run a test unless you are getting
the proper rest....I'm thinking of terms.......concerning tonight.....
after dinner we have in mind, not too late, we have some additional tests
to run tonight. Now, we may want to go on tomorrow but in that event we've
got to think in terms of some place for you to sleep tonight and instead of
putting you in a jail cell they have a couple of rooms at the Madison Police
Department...security area....hospital.../ connecting rooms and we can....Mr ....or whoever
you feel at ease with ....put him in 1 room and 1 bed and/you'll you in the other and get a good
night's sleep. Now, if that's acceptable to you in lieu of a hotel room
it would simplify things for us. Otherwise we've got to get a hotel room
and then change off with the bed. Because you are actually, technically,
in the custody of the sheriff in of that county. If that will be all right
with you, I'll make those arrangements, which will probably be around 10
o'clock or so; then we can bed you down there and then at that time when I
talk with Mr.......later than that.......Is that OK, Eddie?

Yes.

You'll get a good night's sleep. If it's going to cause any. /difficulty ...in
your mind......

What is it you would like to consult with him about?

Well, just to see what he thinks of this.

.....

I don't know anything about law, like that, and then everything that he

....

Yes. Well, Eddie, what specific reason, if you would care to tell me,
the question or advise that you would like to ask of your attorney.

Well, his advice, first,.....,he can talk to me.....saying too much.
He said I shouldn't sign anything

I'm not going to ask you to sign anything.

....   good as I can.

Well, Eddie, tell me this, have you had conversation with me voluntarily?

That's right.

          used any
Have I./...pressure or threats or anything to force you to talk?

No. Youv'e been very nice.

Is there anything you have told me, Eddie, today that I forced you to
tell me?

No.......as far as I know........

You're doing the right thing. As a matter of fact ....Who was the
first person who suggested that you must get a lawyer?

You were.

Exactly. When did I tell you that? Before you left me on Sunday.

That's right.

So I wanted to make sure that you were aware of your rights as an

170

American citizen. We all are interested in your personal record rights and want to

help you. and I think you believe that, understand it.

That's right. ...fair without any stories, such things......

....our investigation too.

That's right.

That's what we're trying to do without any suggestions, anything

improper. We've treated you well.

Nobody treated me any better.

.....Nobody's promised you anything.?

No.

I'm sure nobody here would do anything of that kind. I'll make these

arrangements ....

.....

How about going on tonight as we suggest? do you agree? would you like

to try this out? with the numbers?

That would be the test tonight. ....

......which one of these numbers pick /...out and write and it must be any one

number between 3 and 8. See it can't be any one number with the.....

.....let me know and write it on this piece of paper so I can't see. You sure

that you put only one?

There.

...You have picked one of the numbers.......When is the last time that

you had your/......In Milwaukee for the.......test?
blood pressure taken?

171

Q   That isn't too tight, is it? If it is, tell me so.

A   Well, I don't think so, that won't bother too much.

Q   Let me loosen -- let me put a little - - how's that, better?

A   That's just about right.

Q   You probably recognize, Eddie, that this is a very sensitive and delicate instrument, so whenever this is pumped up, puffed, it's very important that you try to remain as quiet and relaxed as possible. If you should have to sniff or clear your nose or clear your throat, please do it. Otherwise, try to remain as comfortable as possible.

A   That's right.

Q   Just rest your hands comfortably with your fingers extended. Just natural.

A   That's right.

Q   I'm going to measure your blood pressure and pulse for a few seconds. As a matter of fact, that will demonstrate to you exactly what the entire test will feel like. Just sit quietly and relax. Now, I'm going to pump up the cup. You notice the air flowing into it? Now, that's the feeling that you're going to experience. It's not too uncomfortable, is there any discomfort at all?

A   Oh, just a tiny bit, you know, that being a little tight on the arm. Otherwise -

Q   That's only when it's pumped up.

A   That's right.

Q   Now, I don't want you to tell me this number, but do you remember the number that you've written down?

A   That's right.

172

Q   And you heard me tell you earlier that I would ask you on 10 different

questions, did you write No. 1 through to 10, and to each one you will answer "No"

so that you automatically lie to the number that you've written down here. Do you

understand that?

A   That's right.

Q   And the minute that test is completed, I'll show --

You'll find this very interesting. Did you write No. 1?

A   No.

Q   Did you write No. 2?

A   No.

Q   Did you write No. 3?

A   No.

Q   Did you write No. 4?

A   No.

Q   Did you write No. 5?

A   No.

Q   Did you write No. 6?

A   No.

Q   Did you write No. 7?

A   No.

Q   Did you write No. 8?

A   No.

Q   Did you write No. 9?

A   No.

you to understand, Eddie, that I know that when you tell me that you do not remember some of these details, the lesser details, I know that you don't know. But I want you to tell me now before we go on to conclude this your recollection of what you told me in this private room which is a hospital room in the Madison Jail when I asked you about Mary Hogan. Tell me as best you remember. Did I ask you whether or not you took Mary Hogan's life? Do you remember my asking you that?

A   I remember that, but I don't know if that was when you asked here, or - - -

Q   I asked you here but I again asked you while we were waiting for the bed to be made up. When you were here last with me you told me I don't know or I don't remember. Now when I got to the jail with you I told you directly - I said, Eddie, just between you and I, I must tell you that I know that you have more specific knowledge regarding both Bernice Worden and Mary Hogan, and I prevailed upon you as a man, and you had told me earlier and I asked you again, do you know the difference between right and wrong? Do you?

A   That's right.

Q   I am convinced of that fact - - -

A   Now when you mention that fact, now it comes to me, I couldn't have thought of that.

Q   About what?

A   When you were asking me about Mary Hogan. I couldn't have -- it was just a complete blank. This tension - - -

Q   Sure, that's understandable - -

A   Gee, I didn't sleep too good, it was too hot, and they was working, I guess, in there, or something - -

Q   It's a new building, you know.

A   I know. Opening them cell blocks, I guess, prying, bang, wham. People marching

174

back and forth to - -

Q   But it was clean, wasn't it?

A   Oh, gee, that was swell there.

Q   I'll bet that Sheriff, Schley, would like to have quarters like that for his

police -- beautiful.   Well, Eddie, why don't you drink your coffee? Tell me again

now that your memory is becoming refreshed, when I asked you about Mary Hogan at the

jail, do you now recall what you told me? Let's talk about Mary Hogan now, whether you

remember telling me when I revealed to you, when I told you directly, Eddie, I tell you

this privately, we're in this room, I speak now of this special hospital detention room

in the jail, I says, Eddie, I know that you have a better knowledge, a more specific

knowledge about the Mary Hogan case.

         That's right.

         And then did you answer yes or no? In reply to my question?

         I think yes.

         Well, is there any doubt in your mind?

         Well, --

         As a result of what you told me further on --

         I'm pretty sure that it was yes.

         O.K. now, what did you tell me, as best as you can remember, about Mary Hogan?

Did you, Eddie, did you - -

         I don't know if that bump I got on the head is bothering my memory or not.

         What bump?

                        aches like the dickens right now
         Well, it ~~aches~~ - - - right now, I guess. Well, when I first came there - -

         What did the doctor that examined you at the sheriff's office at Waushara tell

you? Did he examine it at all? Did he say it was -- you had an x-ray, I understand,

175

the day following, which was on a Monday.

A   That wasn't just real clear -- they couldn't agree, the two doctors there.

Q   Well, I think what we'll do very shortly, we'll tell Mr. Schley and Mr. Murty, either here or the moment they get back home - I know they'll have it taken care of. Now getting back to Mary, you say that now your memory is refreshed as to what you told me last night in the hospital detention ward at the Madison Police Department, and I explained to you that I was aware of the fact that you had more concrete or definite knowledge about the disappearance of Mary Hogan, and you gave me an answer. Which was it, yes or no? Eddie, do you recall whether or not you - -

A   The only thing I remember is, you know, when we took the test here, I told you that I knew that I was guilty of it, but I would say - -

Q   I don't know and I don't remember.

A   I remember that when I said that here, but this other, it won't come to my mind. I think I said yes, but I - -

Q   Well, here, let me try to refresh your memory without putting words in your mouth. Did you tell me anything last night when you and I were alone at the Madison Police Department waiting for the beds to be made up, did you tell me something more about your knowledge of the Mary Hogan case? While you and I were together. Allright, Eddie, here, you had mentioned something about Mary Hogan standing up at the table. Does that give you a clue?

That's right. Isn't it queer that I can't think of that?

Well, I hope it does, you're no different than anyone else. I need just one word or key to open the door and then, yes, I can follow through. Now as a result of my remark you said something about Mary standing at the table. Now as there a result of my

176

A   My answer would be now, and probably was then, that I, as you say, I just

- - -??? possessive, or I just wanted them, that's - - -

Q   Because they - -

A   There was no robbery motive.

Q   And I believe you, Eddie. You wanted to posses them - why? Now, see, there's

one person, Eddie, that is the answer as to why you wanted to possess either Bernice

or Mary, and who was or who is that person even though that person is not alive today?

A   The only thing that I can say is, as you explained to me, she resembled even

more than Bernice, she resembled my mother, a lot more than Bernice. She was about

                                fuller   plumper
the same size and she was oh plumper, you know,/and my mother was plump - and just

exactly;otherwise but my mother was quite a bit German in her and there was German

                        and stuff
in Bernice so her face/had the same shape.

Q   You explained also to me what happened to Mary Hogan after you shot her.

Will you tell me again? What happened to her, did you leave her in her place or did

you do something with her?

A   Well, I was talking with Specks, I don't know if it was - if I mentioned

that to you or not - it came clearer to me that I went out after this, went outside,

whether I wanted to go home, I'm not quite sure about that. Anyway I remember going

out and I believe I left the door open, and I now went back in again, and took her,

she was laying on her side, it must have been, because I didn't have to raise her up.

I just took her - - -

Q   Eddie, as a result of what you told me in the beginning and ultimately

repeated in detail to Mr. Murty and the Sheriff, do you feel better or worse for the

fact that you have now told the truth?

remark, you said something about Mary standing at the table. Now as a result of my

remark at this moment, just generally, can you remember now what else you told me? Who

was standing next to Mary Hogan?

That would be me.

That was you. Is there any doubt in your mind that it wasn't you?

No.

All right. Then, what is the next thing that you recall telling me generally?
Did you do anything to Mary Hogan?

Yes. See I was standing next to her and a little bit, you know, farther back.
The way I remember, Speck asked me about that, you see I got this, oh, I hadn't had it
too long. You know things that are more valuable I generally take along from home
so things don't get stolen, I know I took this gun. . .

Do you remember what kind of gun? What kind of gun was it?

It was automatic.

Was it an American or was it a foreign?

A foreign gun.

Can you further identify it, I mean - -

A Mauser. I'm sure this is right as it comes to me, that I had no intention
even then, but I just took it out that way, and I still can't understand it - why I
shot her, just I took it out like, whether I was going to show it to her or - -

Do you recall the discussion that you and I had yesterday regarding whether or

not, and based on information that you had given me, whether or not your motive in

either of these cases I speak of - Bernice and Mary - whether or not it had anything

to do, No. 1, with robbery, or whether or not it had something to do with your mother.

178

A   Well, I feel better that it's come clear in my mind.

Q   We appreciate the fact that you've always been cooperative, because nobody can deny you that, but gradually your memory has become refreshed. Remember my asking you last night at the jail whether or not the bullet that you had on that beaded chain and that tuft of hair, whether or not that bullet came from Mary Hogan?

A.   I was just talking about -- he asked me -- too, like you, no, it isn't because you know she was shot in the head and the bullet remained inside, see. If it woulda went through it woulda been in the building.

Q   When you dressed her out, didn't you - removed her skin from her head, did you do that?

A   I took that, that's right.

Q   Didn't the bullet drop out then?

A   No, it didn't. It was inside, it must have been inside.

Q   You just peeled the skin off of the skull and disposed of the bone and the other material that was in the head, is that it?

A   That's right.

Q   I want to ask you this also, remember I spoke to you on Sunday. Do you recall having a piece of Scotch tape on the port, or where the shell comes out?

Q   That's right.

A   And you had told me earlier that you were having trouble with the gun.

Q   With the ejection.

A   I ask you this question directly, Eddie, I mean you've told me what you had done - as a result of your extensive reading on all subject matters, your acquaintance with bullets and cartridge cases can be identified, was there anything based on your personal knowledge which you felt that if there ever was an thing found from any of

179

Gein Prepares a victim's head. (Lou Rusconi.)

Gein Creates an outfit from human skin. (Lou Rusconi)

your guns at a scene that it could be linked up to your gun? Is that why you would

have put the Scotch tape over it?

A   No, my idea was, you see when that would catch — I don't know if it bothered

you when you tried the gun out —

Q   I don't know, we'd have to talk to Allen about it. Allen is the one that made

that examination.

A   You see, when it would eject the shell it either closed too quick or didn't

come back far enough so it would eject the shell, and when she closed she catched the

shell right in between the port and the back part.

Q   I'll give you an explanation as to why that did happen. A person that is

not familiar with weapons that use magazines or clips, if they are not careful in

putting cartridges into the magazine, they can very easily spread the lips at the

top of the magazine so that instead of these cartridges, when they're in the gun,

to slide on an angle into the chamber. If those lips are spread, when the cartridge

begins to move out of the magazine or clip, since it isn't held by the lips, it

jumps up partially, and that's the reason that it jams.

A   Oh, I see. I was afraid it would damage something inside.

Q   Last night you also told me about removing Mary's face from her skull.

Is that correct or is it not?

A   That's correct.

Q   And what other portion of her body did you retain? Remember I asked you Did

you remove her flesh from the upper part of the body and you answered No.

A   That's right.

Q   Then I asked you Did you keep her vagina and what was your answer to this?

A   My answer should have been No.

182

Q   You had told me Yes. Now that you've been able to refresh your memory, are
you quite sure that the face was the only thing?

A   That's right.

Q   Was there any thought, consideration or association as far as Mary Hogan was
concerned, being a woman, other than her face which you say reminded you of your
mother? Was there any association, as far as you were/concerned, with her sexual parts?
_{personally}

A   No, I don't believe so.

Q   When I asked you last night, you were definitely saying No, I did not remove
the flesh from the upper part of her body, meaning her breasts and stomach, but I did
keep her face and her vagina. You were positive about the face, and you were a little
hazy about the vagina. You were definite about not taking the chest - - -. Now, are
you in any better position to determine now whether or not you did keep her vagina?

A   Well, it seems quite clear, you know, as clear as it possibly can in my mind
that I didn't, like I told xxxxx the sheriff.

Q   Did you at that time have any recollection of utilizing the gambel and the
chain hoist for her?

A   No, the way I - I can almost see it - the way it probably is right, that
I didn't.

Q   Did you conduct your work in that same pit or shed?

A   That's right.

Q   Since you had told me that your dad had used that particular area in your
shed for dressing out cattle, do we agree, I mean, on the particular area? Is that
the same area where you had done this work on these women?

A   Yes.

183

Q   I believe you, without putting words in your mouth, I'll tell you very

directly
frankly that I am, I feel quite sure that in the case of Mary Hogan that if what

the newspapers say that it is believed that a large sum of money was taken that you

did not take it. Do you have any recollection of picking up any change or anything

else?

A   No.

Q   You see, that was a suggestion that someone could have arrived after you

left the premises and rifled the place.

A   That was what I was telling them.

           had suggested
Q   You would suggest, and brought up the question, as I recall yesterday when

you told me something about the Hill boy, is that it?

A   No, it's this Seymour Lester.

Q   Lester?

A   He's the one that found the body.

Q   Oh. I see.

A   And, like I described to you the sheriff, well I can describe it here -

(indistinguishable about the highway,etc.) There's the tavern and right here on

this corner is a road goes this way. Right here on this corner is a house and farm

right across the road. Instead of going to here and reporting it like anybody would,

he goes back down this road where he lives - he lived down on that other corner -

        (Excuse me for a moment)

Q   You were talking about the man that found Mary Hogan. Are you acquainted

with Seymour?

A   No, except that after he moved up in our country I have seen him.

Q   You've seen him.

A   I've seen him , that's all.

Q   Do you have any reason to believe that any given individual could have

taken any money from her?

A   That I have, of course, I couldn't say just exactly who it is, but he acted

and probably went home.

so suspicious instead of going over there he went down this way toward his home/ If

he went home, when he come back this George Cummings is where he stopped, it's

either the first place or the second place - I think it's the first place from his

home. He reported it there, going 3/4 mile - it must be at least 3/4 mile - before

reporting it when there's a house here and there's a house over here, there's

another house over here, and I believe there's another house over here. He goes

past all them places and goes there, is that natural?

- - -

185

A -- from the stove, you know, in that other room, and sometimes, if I start a

fire in the[illegible] you know, put kerosene in, or something, that flame goes up and sometimes

starts a-burning.

Q Is that so?

A So I had that syringe, I'd just take water in it, you know where these joints

are in the pipe?

Q Yes.

A Squirt some in there and save a chimney fire. That's what that - - - I used - -

Q Oh, I see. Well, I can tell you, the suspicion up your way was that you used

that on the bodies. Did you use any preparation, neats foot oil, saddle soap, or any

other item, formaldehyde, or any other substance or solution? You have probably your

own name or description for the preparation of the flesh?

A The only thing probably on one and probably on some of that skin probably,
   from
you know, that one woman, I probably put some oil on, possibly, that's all, to keep

it soft, you know.

Q Which woman do you mean?

A That is closest I can remember, you know, it's where this upper part her is

taken from, the Adams woman.

Q From the Plainfield cemetery.

A That's right.

Q What kind of oil, ordinary --

A Penetrating oil. It might have been I run on to that other oil - just to keep

it soft. That's the only thing. I didn't know how to make any other preparation.

Q Are we mistaken when, based on the personal information that I have, that there is a strong possibility that you did have formaldehyde in the house?

A   At that, I believe there was a bottle or part of a bottle.

Q   Did you use that in taxidermy? You mentioned something about squirrel tails.

A   That's right.

Q   Did you ever use any of that formaldehyde on any of the flesh?

A   I don't believe so - pretty sure of that.

Q   I found - not I found - we all, this is a we operation, so when I speak of I disregard it - a pair of red rubber gloves in the shack. Did you wear those?

A   Yes, I wore that quite often, lots of times I'd wear them in taking down the pipes.

Q   I see.

A   To keep my hands clean and I didn't like to use my other like cotton gloves or anything because it's quite a job to get that soot and stuff off.

Q   Did you wear the rubber gloves as far as Mary Hogan or Bernice Worden were concerned?

A   No, not with Bernice. No, I could be sure of that. But with Mary Hogan, I wouldn't say for sure. I believe - it seems that I did - pretty close - I'll say right out that I did, otherwise it wouldn't be in my mind.

Q   How about the bodies from the cemetery - did you use the rubber gloves in those instances?

A   That I couldn't be too sure.

Q   Based on information given to me, and as you know people have very vivid imaginations and like to say things that are untrue, but were you ever referred to or kidded by your neighbors or friends or people in the community about being an undertaker or an embalmer?

A   No. Not that I know of.

Q   Is it possible?

A   No.

Q   Do you recall having a conversation late last week, ~~possibly~~ maybe Thursday or

Friday, well, here, let me ask this question: Were you ever known as lover boy? Or

a ladies' man? Probably you were the butt of jokes that --

A   Oh, it might have been one - something like that - sombody might have -

Q   Lover boy and lady killer, I understand that that is the names that some

people had used in referring or identifying, that it was based on the fact that you,

on numerous occasions, would like to talk about women and your ability with women.

A   No, that's wrong.

Q   Well, see, like I prefaced my remarks, people are ever ready to embellish or

put extra heavy topping of icing on a cake, when you give 'em an opportunity. I don't

think, I know, let's say that, that if the people that have been most closely associated

with you in this investigation, Herb (you know Herb), Mr.Murty, your Sheriff, and if I

may include myself, I think that we have all gotten along very well with you, that,

yes, we have had lengthy conversations -

A   Sure,but that was necessary.

Q   And, do you agree or disagree that during all this time every effort was made,

whether or not it was by myself, Herb, Murty, George Schley, to see that you had food,

here and up in Waushara, that everything was within the limitations that were imposed

upon us, that you were looked after, like we were looked after, like we'd like to look

after ourselves.

188

A   That's right.

Q   You will, at this particular point, also recognize that you have made

statments, some to me directly and then you repeated them later on to others, and

with the others you probably went into detail further.

A   That's right.

Q   In the admissions, if you want to call it that, or remarks, or basically to

further identify it so that you understand it, so that I understand that you know

what I'm talking about, that you eventually refresh your memory and told all that

you have remembered to the best of your knowledge and belief.

A   That's right.

Q   Now, did you tell that to me and the others on a strictly voluntary basis?

A   Yes.

Q   Has there been anything that I have ever said or done or demonstrated to

you so that you -- and even at this point - would be fearful of me? Have I ever

frightened you, have I ever threatened you?

A   No.

Q   And you feel that under the circumstances the treatment that I personally

have given you, that it was fair?

A   Yes, that's right.

Q   So you say, Eddie, that as far as you are concerned, and I'm at a point

now where I know you are levelling with me and telling the truth, that the syringe

never was utilized by yourself in regards to anything you did to the bodies.

A   That's right.

Q   I believe you. And that the only preservatives that you could have used

was some oils, oils that you had at the house for another purpose, either for your

189

machine or your - some car or other devices, and I believe you on that.

A   Yes, that's right.

Q   Now, in the case of Bernice. You told me at the Madison jail yesterday that your memory became refreshed and that you did have a recollection of taking her life. Is that correct?

A   That's right.

Q   You either, you also indicated to me - and all this has been repeated in detail after I left, I've been told - you told me before I left the approximate distance, it was a distance of 10 feet plus, do you recall? Well, that's not too important. Nevertheless, I mean you were many feet from her, is that correct?

A   That's right, many feet, that's right.

Q   She was standing with her back to you -

A   Not fully, you know.

Q   Well, sorta just sideways --

A   That's right.

Q   She was near the door, is that it?

A   No - about in the - well, probably about in the middle of the store, I should judge.

Q   And you were at the gunrack? Is that the relative position, generally?

A   That's right.

Q   You - just to check on your memory now - regarding your recollection - the cash register, did you put that in the truck before or after you put Bernice into the truck?

A   I believe that had to be after.

190

Q   Do you recall your telling me yesterday that robbery was not your motive but

that you were intrigued by the mechanism of the cash register and that you operated it

when you got back to the shed?

A   That's right.

Q   And I believe you on that, because I know that you are not a robber. Do you

remember now whether or not you had any ammunition, even one shell, one cartridge in

your pocket when you entered the premises?

A   I must have, that's the only --

Q   Do you think it was there by design, I mean by design or accident, which do you

think it was?

A   Well, it had to be by accident.

Q   In regards to Bernice - you've told me that you remember definitely of taking

her life, is that correct?

A   Yes.

Q   You told that to me at the jail. What was your motive or reason for taking

her life?

A   What we talked about is the only logical reason -

Q   Like Mary Hogan, as you explained?

A   That's right. It had to be something like that to make that compulsion.

Q   I think you know what we do, Eddie. Let us resume and conclude the examination

and I think you can be on your way home very shortly. Are you intrigued by the machine

also?

A   That's right.

Q   Before you leave, you had mentioned to me that you would like to look at the

191

tracing. I'll be more than glad to show them to you.

A   That is _real_ interesting. And I believe my lawyer would want a report on that.

Q   Oh, yes, you'll get it. That, under the circumstances, any lawyer defending a
client would -- be he the district attorney, the district attorney, of course, is the
person that will get our information. We cannot release it to anyone else other than the
district attorney and the sheriff. The district attorney then will decide - be the sole
judge as to just how much he can make available. In view of what you have told about
Mary Hogan and Bernice Worden, do you recognize, or do you have any opinion, your
personal opinion based on your own personal knowledge as to whether or not this - these
two incidences or the individual incidents, acts that you accomplished, you feel that
it was right or wrong, what you did?

Well, now, and probably before when my mind was clear, that was wrong.

Do you feel at this time -

That's right - wrong.

That it was wrong? Do you feel that you knew, we, you, I, anyone else does not
possess the authority to take a person's life?

That's right. That's why this state, you know, changed that, the death penalty
to -

You see, I'm not a native of the state. I orginally came from Chicago along with
my brother. We've been here, working at this laboratory since/1950. What were you going
to tell me, you apparently have some knowledge about the law, you mentioned something
about the death penalty?

Well, I believe that was one factor about what having just imprisonment in this
state, because one factor was that it also gave a chance if a person was innocent,

192

unjustly accused – it would also give a chance for that to come out. But also, I

believe, in those that wanted that changed, was that nobody should take another's life.

Q   You still have that personal opinion?

A   That's right.   Unless it would be in self-defense or something, you know,

then, of course, that –

Q   Based on, and this is not a courtroom and you know that I am not a lawyer, I'm

not a judge, based on what you have described to us, based on what you have told me in

your recognition of knowing the difference between right and wrong, do you know

the difference between right and wrong?

A   I do now.

Q   Do you feel that a person who knows the difference between right and wrong

must acknowledge whether or not he has committed, or whether or not he is innocent

or guilty of an offense after the evidence is heard? Do you feel that the laws of

this state, basedon what knowledge you may possess, or the laws of the land, the

United States, are fair when, after a very careful analysis of the evidence or the

testimony of everyone concerned in the investigation, reveals that a person has been

found to be – beyond any reasonable doubt – to be the person, let's say, that's

responsible for what occurred. What is your opinion as to whether or not some form

of confinement which might include medical attention, if required, because of any

physical or mental condition,do you feel that that is – do you feel that it is or

is not the just thing to be done?

A   To my way of thinking and probably you think the same and probably a lot of

others, that in 9 cases out of 10, and maybe in all cases, it should be treatment,

because a person that commits a crime, there is something wrong there that may be

cured.

10

193

Q   Do you put yourself in that category?

A   That's right.

Q   And you are aware of the fact that you committed these offenses? I don't like

the word crime, let's refer to them as offenses. Do you recognize whether or not what

you did was right or wrong in the case of Bernice Worden or Mary Hogan?

A   I think I know just how you mean that. I do now.

Q   Did you know at the --

A   At the time, no.

Q   Can you explain to me why you feel that you didn't know at the time? - That

it was wrong? Not during the commission, Eddie, no I don't mean that but after -

either shortly after or days afterwards.

A   Yes, that would come to me that I was wrong. That's right.

Q   Was it a matter of minutes or days or ---

A   Well, sometimes, Like I told you, at the cemetery, it would be oh, minutes

                                            get to it.
about, as it doesn't take too long to ~~harexitxaommx~~ Sometimes, I wouldn't even get there.

Turn around, you know, and realize it and feel ashamed, and -

Q   In the case of Mary Hogan, when did you first recognize that you did wrong?

Was it while you were still on the premises with her, at her place?

A   Well, not too well, I believe that was about when I got home. Then I came to,

you know, and it didn't seem possible.

Q   Whereabouts in, I use the expression dressing out, or in the removal of the

fresh flesh would you prepare it from the standpoint of preservation, preparing it for

preservation, I mean, you said that you air dried them.

A   That's right.

Q   Would you place them in the shack, the shed, or in your attic where it was cold,

194

A   That's right, where, this so, like you'd say, well that wouldn't be in the winter

time, the ground would be froze. So that would just you know for natural preserving.

Q   When you disposed of Mary Hogan, do you recall whether or not you used anything

in the stove to help consume what you were burning?

A   I'm quite sure because I have for quite a few years, you know been using briquettes

or coal and wood.

Q   How about fuel or gasoline as an accelerant?

A   No, I don't believe I would have dared inside of the building, too highly in-

flammable. Maybe for starting the fire, you know –

Q   Is there anything else that we haven't discussed that you'd like to make known

to me before I draw these questions up?

A   Well, let's see. Well, I believe you mentioned that before, too.

Q   What was that?

A   – think the same as I do, that as a rule most, that everybody should have medical

attention and a chance.

Q   I agree, and I think I know definitely that the medical attention will be accom-

plished;when I speak of medical attention, you understand, it's regarding any mental

condition. The physical condition is secondary because it might be again we'll have to

tell Schley and Murty about having it checked. Would you care to go to the bathroom?

A   I believe I would.

Q   Why not let me get hold of Mr.Murty and Mr. Schley and you goto the bathroom

for a moment, and then you'll get a chance to walk about around.

A   Well, whatever you think. Indistinguishable. (Q) I think we can accomplish – and

then it will be over with. I think Mr. Murty or Mr. Schley are out –

195

Were you ever apprehensive, Eddie, when your neighbors or friends that you

invited or permitted to come into your house sat down on the chairs that they wouldn't

get suspicious of what you had upholstered the chairs with?

No, I don't, not to my knowledge.

Q.   Nobody has ever asked you, if this is --

A.   It might be a little that way, but lots of times, you know, it never entered

my mind they'd ever think of that. Sometimes, though, since you mentioned that, it

would seem natural, I probably did feel sometimes feel, you know, a little bit --

Q.   Conscious of --

A.   That's right.

Q.   Remember my remarks to you about people having extremely vivid imaginations?

And exaggerating the truth?

A.   That's right.

Q.   You recall my telling you yesterday as a result of your involvement in these

two specific offenses, namely, Bernice Worden and Mary Hogan, that the feeling had been

that you also were involved in these other matters, including Dick, Evelyn Hartley,

-- and this other little girl --

Mary Jean Weckler from Jefferson County - and it even extended as far as Chicago?

A.   That's right.

Q.   What would your answer be, Eddie, and again I wish to remind you that if the

questions are not clear to you as I have drawn them up or if you feel that they are

unfair for you to answer, please tell me so, so that I can rewrite them to your personal

satisfaction. Otherwise, if you can, try to give me your answer - Yes, No, or I don't

know. Would you have any difficulty, any reservation, you understand what I mean by

any reservation?

Q.   Would you have any difficulty in answering the question Have you now told me

the truth about what you had done to Bernice Worden?

A.   I think that's fair enough.

Q.   And what would you ---

A.   I'd say Yes.

Q.   Do you feel that you could answer the question - this other question - did

you shoot Bernice Worden?

A.   That would be Yes.

Q.   And the question Have you now told me the truth as to what you did to Mary

Hogan?

A.   That would be Yes.

Q.   And I will ask you the question and see if you can answer it Did you shoot

Mary Hogan? How will you answer that?

A.   Yes.

Q.   And I will ask you Mary Hogan and Bernice Worden are the only persons whose living

lives you took?

A.   That's right.

Q.   I will ask you Other than Mary Hogan and Bernice Worden, have you ever taken

the lives of any others?

A.   That would be No.

Q.   I would also ask you Did you have anything to do with the disappearance of

Evelyn Hartley?

A.   That's fair; that would be No.

197

Q.   You know that Evelyn Harltey is the girl from what location here in Wisconsin?

A.   LaCrosse.

Q.   Yes. Did you have an thing to do with the disappearance of Mary Jean Weckler, and who is Mary Jean Weckler?

A.   Well, as you said she's a 9 year old girl. The answer would be No. I guess that's the way that question was.

Q.   Yes, did you have anything at all to do with the disappearance of Mary Jean Weckler?

Z.A.   That would be No.

Q.   And how about Dick Travis?

A.   That would be No. I don't believe I remember reading about this Weckler girl.

         It happened either in '47 or '48. She was a young girl --

A.   Say, that wasn't the one they thought them two young fellows had threw in the river -- is that the one?

Q.   Um-m-m.

A.   Oh, that's right.

Q.   Two fellows from here in Madison.

A.   That's right, I remember that now. I didn't know the name. I guessthat one did confess that they had shot her, I guess, tied a stone to her and threw her off the bridge there.

         No, that was another case. Are you thinking about a case now in Milwaukee where --

A.   No, I think this was the case, where these same ones had shot the young fellow and threw him in. Is that the same case? With this Weckler girl?

A.   Yes.

198

A.   Well, that's the one.

Q.   Of course, there's a case also from Eau Claire similar.

A.   The way I remember in the paper, this one had confessed that they tied a rock
and then tied it around and threw her over by the same place.

Q.   You of course remember Evelyn Hartley, or Mary Jean Weckler have never been
found. I'll be right back.

A.   O.K.

          (Lapse of time)

Q.   How're you getting along, Eddie?

A.   Pretty good. – – – it might be interesting for you to watch that.

Q.   Whatcha gonna do?

          He wants
          ~~Hxwatms~~ to give just a short test here --

Q.   Probably won't allow it.

A.   That's probably -- (hard to understand) see you again tomorrow.

          (Interrogator returns)

Q.   All set. O.K. In other words, regarding Evelyn Hartley, Mary Jean Weckler
and Dick Travis, so that it will be all-inclusive, I mean, it will cover every possible
angle, so that from here on nobody can point the finger toward you and say We wonder.
See? We have re-drawn the questions. It will be Did you have anything to do with the
disappearance or death of Evelyn Hartley? Did you have anything to do with the disappearance or death of Mary Jean Weckler? Did you have anything to do with the disappearance or death of Dick Travis? And then I will also ask you, with your permission,
                     en
as an all-~~ɇ~~compassing question, Have you lied to any of my questions on this test?

A.   That would be No.

199

Grave Excavations Indicate Butcher Gein Told the Truth

WAUTOMA, Wis. (AP)—Dist. Atty. Earl Kileen says excavation of two graves convinces him that Edward Gein actually did raid cemeteries for parts of nine bodies found in his farm home.

Waushara County authorities Monday reopened two graves in the Plainfield Cemetery to check the story of the 51-year-old bachelor.

Gein, who is undergoing 30 days of mental observation, admitted killing two women and robbing the graves of nine other women.

He is charged with first-degree murder in the death Nov. 16 of Mrs. Bernice Worden, 58, a hardware store operator. He also admitted killing Mrs. Mary Hogan, a tavernkeeper, Dec. 9, 1954.

Authorities opened the graves of Mrs. Eleanore Adams and Mrs. Mabel Everson, both buried in 1951. Their names were on the list of women whose graves Gein said he looted.

Mrs. Adams' casket was empty. The other coffin also was empty, but Kileen said a few bones and a small prying bar were found in the dirt above the empty casket.

"As far as I am concerned, the opening of these two graves verifies Gein's story," Kileen said. "I won't open any more if I can help it."

He said any further excavations will be "a state matter," adding that if Wisconsin Atty. Gen. Stewart Honeck "believes that opening the others is necessary, we will open them all. This deal is too big for Waushara County."

Honeck entered the case upon orders from Gov. Vernon Thomson. The attorney general directed Charles Wilson, head of the state crime laboratory, to continue with all steps necessary to assure a complete investigation of the Gein case.

The governor asked Honeck to determine whether any crimes, other than the murder with which Gein is charged, had been committed by the quiet little handyman.

Ed Gein (Nicolas Castelaux)

Q.   Would you roll up your right sleeve, please, so that I can --

A.   If it wasn't for that - kinda tight like the other was, it would be a nice test,

you know, but it gets --

Q.   -- your arms, please. Is that too tight?

A.   Yes it is.

Q.   I'll loosen it up a bit.

A.   That's better, I think. There, I believe that's just about right.

Q.   We'll move this tube from under your elbow here, just relax and I'll --

X. Q.   As before, I'll ask you Isyour first name Edward? Is your last name Gein?

Do you live in Waushara County? Did you have breakfast this morning? Did you have a

cup of coffee with me while here?   (Just trying the lights.)

Q.   Is your first name Ed?

A.   Yes.

Q.   Your last name Gein?

A.   Yes.

Q.   Have you now told me the truth as to what you did to Bernice Worden?

A.   Yes.

Q.   Do you live in Waushara County?

A.   Yes.

Q.   Your first name, Edward?

A.   Yes.

Q.   Did you shoot Bernice Worden?

A.   Yes.

Q.   Did you have any breakfast this morning?

A.   Yes.

202

Q.   Have you now told me the truth as to what you did to Mary Hogan?

A.   Yes.

Q.   Did you have some coffee with me this morning?

A.   Yes.

Q.   Did you shoot Mary Hogan like you told me?

A.   Yes.

Q.   Your first name, Eddie?

A.   Yes.

Q.   Mary Hogan and Bernice Worden are the only living persons whose lives you

have ever taken?

A.   Yes.

Q.   Is your last name Gein?

A.   Yes.

Q.   Other than Mary Hogan and Bernice Worden, have you ever taken the lives

of any other human person?

A.   No.

Q.   Did you have anything to do with the disappearance or the death of Evelyn

Hartley?

A.   No.

Q.   Do you live in Waushara County?

A.   Yes.

Q.   Did you have anything to do with the disappearance or death of Mary Jean

Weckler?

A.   No.

Did you have anything to do with the disappearance or death of Dick Travis?

No.

Did you have some breakfast this morning?

Yes.

Have you lied to any of my questions on this particular test?

No.

That was the last question. Please remain still for a moment longer.

Now clench your fist. We'll take a short spell and, like yesterday, we'll repeat the

same set of questions and that will be it. You'll be glad and I'll be glad.

Then you can compare them and --

Yes.

That's real interesting.

on your boot
I like the color of your tire patch/-- Is it red, yellow and green? Is that

-- did that come from your tire patch kit?

Well, you see, I robbed a traffic cop - took his boots - what am I saying?

These belong to Dan Chase (?).

Oh, I see.   Have you ever owned (I have) a farm denim work jacket or work

coat?   The matching coat usually goes with denim big overalls.

Late years, no, but before that I have. I generally get these either unlined

or lined zipper jackets, what you call them - - - jacket, or something like that.

Yes. Now, these will be the same questions, Eddie, except I, with your

permission, will reverse the order on some. The questions will be the same but will not

come in the same order as I read to you earlier.

204

A.   What're you going to do about that bee in there?

Q.   That's the electric motor that drives the chart — — — — that drag on the paper.

It is annoying, I know.

A.   I know it. It don't bother me. It's like a little bee in there —kinda comical.

Q.   Just try to relax - just breathe naturally - if you need to cough or clear

your throat, do it during the test and don't hold it.   Is your first name Eddie?

A.   Yes.

Q.   ·Is your hast name Gein?

A.   Yes.

Q.   Other than Mary Hogan and Bernice Worden, are there any lives that you have

ever taken?

Q.   No.

Q.   Do you live in Waushara County?

A.   Yes.

Q.   Mary Hogan and Bernice Worden are the only living persons whose lives you

have taken?

A.   Yes.

Q.   Did you have some breakfast this morning?

A.   Yes.

Q.   Did you have anything to do with the disappearance or death of Evelyn Hartley?

A.   No.   I'll bet that shows up.

Q.   Did you have some coffee with me this morning?

A.   Yes.

Q.   Did you have anything to do with the disappearance or the death of Mary Jean

Weckler?

A.   No.

Q.   Did you have anything to do with the disappearance or death of Dick Travis?

A.   No.

Q.   Is your first name Edward?

A.   Yes.

Q.   Have you now told me the truth as to what you did to Bernice Worden?

A.   Yes.

Q.   Do you live in Waushara County?

A.   Yes.

                          like
Q.   Did you shoot Bernice Worden as you have told me?

       Yes.

Q.   Did you have some coffee with me today?

A.   Yes.

Q.   Have you now told me the truth as to what you did to Mary Hogan?

A.   Yes.

Q.   Did you shoot Mary Hogan like you have told me?

A.   Yes.

Q.   Is your last name Gein?

A.   Yes.

Q.   I am going to repeat a few of these, and that will be all, Ed. Relax.

Other than Mary Hogan and Bernice Worden, have you ever taken the lives of any other

persons?

       No.

Q.   Is your first name Ed?

A.   Yes.

Q.   Did you have anything to do with the disappearance or death of Evelyn Hartley?

A.   No.

Q.   Do you live in Waushara County?

A.   Yes.

Q.   Did you have anything to do with the disappearance or death of Mary Jean

Weckler?

A.   No.

Q.   Is your first name Eddie or Edward?

A.   Yes.

       Mary Hogan and Bernice Worden are the only living persons whose lives you

have ever taken?

A.   Yes.

Q.   Do you live in Waushara County?

A.   Yes.

Q.   Have you lied to any of my questions on this particular test?

A.   No.

Q.   That was the last question. Please do not stir for a moment longer.

Now clench your fist hard.

A.   This is kinda almost like your heartbeat, isn't it?

Q.   That's your breathing, but these little flutters are the heartbeat.

A.   I see. I notice some of them - -

Q.   (Someone else entered) You are through.

A.   Yah, we are.

A.   I'm glad.

Q.   Are you?

A.   -- telling things --

Q.   What did you say, I'm a little hard of hearing.

                                  deserves

A.   Don't you think that - - - ~~gives~~ a lot of credit for what he told us

without going through any more tests - -

Q.   I think it takes a lot of courage for the person to tell the truth.

                                                          we

That's right. And Eddie - I told him this morning I~~I~~ thinkthe world of

him for telling the truth. I admire you as a man for recognizing your responsibility

that you must tell the truth (Imean, you didn't ask him to if he didn't want to,

you know that). He could have just rebelled or just said I'm not going to say any-

thing else, I'm not going to talk any more.

Sure he could and made it awfully hard for us - - - -

If the Sheriff or Mr.Murty or if I or Herb are ever asked, we'll say,to

support the contention about your cooperative attitude on the part of extending

yourself on a voluntary basis to tell the truth, we'll be the first ones to champion

that fact.

Background conversation - unintelligble.

- - -

Q Eddie, this is Dr. Andrews, Director of the Diagnostic Center. Why don't you

sit down for a moment, Doctor? I would like for you to know, Doctor, that Eddie, from

the time we first met early last Sunday morning, prevailed upon me and anyone else that

had an opportunity ~~his~~ desired ~~(p)~~ that he immediate medical attention. Do you remember, Eddie,

when you told me specifically (unintelligble) (when you learned I was from the State Crime Laboratory) one of the first things that you asked me

complete
I'd like a lie detector test, to show that I don't have ~~xxxx(?)x~~balance. Remember that?

Well, I want to impress upon Dr. Andrews that you are most anxious and that you will be

most cooperative and, Eddie, the main thing as far as any help you can be given ----?

- - - -? We've discussed, Eddie, many very personal affairs and sometimes it was a

for us get
little hard/to ~~give~~/an answer, but ----? Now you're in the hands of -----? doctors and

I don't want you to withhold any thing, embarrassing or otherwise, because they are very

Understanding and they will - - - -? why this occurred. - - - -? Are there ~~Xaxxxxxx~~ any

Andrews
questions you'd like to ask ~~the~~ Doctor /before he goes back to his office?

  (Lots of talking - but not understandable.)

  You know the doctors are trained in this type of work and will be the first ones

encountered.
to recognize regarding the lapses of memory/ You know as a result of our conversation

just on the basis of maybe one word you've been able to refresh your memory. Can you

recall that? And then I know that as a result of conversations that I've had since I've

seen you last there were many things, and of course you were very tired and we're not

going to try to go into — there were many things which you told almost in detail that

you were asked to repeat again later on and you just went back into that loss of memor

memory
---- recollection. So with the aid of the doctors your ~~gradual~~ will gradually become

more and more refreshed. (Indistinguishable)

  Talking in background - nothing clear.

209

Q   Remember, Eddie, when I asked you last Sunday you became a little upset and

incensed when I suggested that maybe you received signals or voices, and I was

finally convinced that you were sincere when you told me that you never did hear

any voices or orders. That sometimes occurs in extreme cases of other types of

- - -. That was why I asked you that in the beginning before we became better

acquainted. On the other hand, Doctor, I am very much convinced that nobody else

will ------- my feeling about the matter that Eddie is not a thief. He has never

taken any money. As a matter of fact, it was suggested or inferred in this piece

from Portage County that this woman was known to possess large amounts of money.

I am satisfied that Eddie didn't touch a penny. He's honest after that fashion.

   (Gein talking but not understandable)

                              that

- - - - - respectful to a degree. I think you know, now, Eddie, that some -/a few

    ~~that~~ had been opened

of the graves/, and in one of them, we were told that, in one of them the ring of

the deceased was returned to the grave. So that if Eddie had entertained any

thought of being a thief he would never have returned a valuable gold ring. Can

                       Ganser

you think of anything else that you might like to ask Dr. ----? Or anything you

think he might advise you on that you might have some question about?

   (Gein talking but not understandable)

Q   Eddie, whenever you're ready, why you let me know and we'll get started.

Mr. Rrsberg and Mr. ∅∅∅∅/ ? want to go out for another coffee and the Dr.'s got

to get back to the diagnostic center.

   (We'll go on.)

Q   Fine. You'll be waiting out in front.

A.   (Gein) Sure appreciate it — your desire to help. (More talk) I was pretty well ∅∅∅--- - now that it's got to be treatments. /That electric treatment, first

The gave

they gave the spinal, they gave this electrical treatment yesterday, then they also

questioned me, you know.

Q   Do you feel a little woozy, as a result of the starting of the treatments?

A   That's right.

Q   Now, Eddie, any time you feel that you want to take a rest or you feel tired, you

just tell me, because we want to do this very slowly so that it won't be necessary to go

over this next week or next month. You know that everyone is most anxious for you to

complete your examinations with the doctors so the doctors will know what approach to use.

A   That's right.

Q   Now, I think as a result of our acquaintanceship, Eddie, that you know that

I am your friend.

A   That's right. I appreciate it.

Q   I appreciate the fact, also, that you told Mr. Belter, your attorney the fact

because I was told about what you had said to him. That you appreciated my efforts in

attempting to, and successfully in most instances, in refreshing your memory. Now, there

are some things that if we can, you and I, we'd like to clear up. Now, as an example,

when I asked you what you did with the remains of Mary Hogan, you explained to me that

with the exception of the portions of her body that you saved that you burned the rest

of it. Then/you left me, and as your memory became refreshed, then you were able to

recall that you had buried portions in the ground, I don't know if it was Mr. ------

or the Sheriff, I think that you showed them the various locations at the farm.

A   Let' s see, that was from Mrs. Worden, the blood. I guess they didn't find it.

I really shoulda went over there and showed 'em but they didn't have any rubbers on, the

211

Sheriff, he said, Gosh, you just point out to us. I told em as good as I could. You

see I had dug an addition to the toilet - outside toilet - and you know the earth was

filled up here and right next to it is where I buried that. And I told 'em

Q   Now, by burying that - what do you mean?

A   That's - oh - blood and things like that. That wasn't buried very deep and

I told 'em where it was, but maybe they did find it, but they told me that they hadn't

found it.

Q   WAs there any portions that you recall that could have been from her body?

A   No. That was all --

Q   Well, how about the case of Mary Hogan?

A   No, I don't believe I --- anything. I don't remember.

Q   You know now the majority of things from your home and the shed and car has

been brought here and I have had a chance to look at some of the things and, as an

example, you had a pink colored mask in the glove compartment of your car, remember that?

A   That's right. There was supposed to be a white one, too.

Q   Well, no, this is pink. There is a white braided rope that was in the glove

compartment, also. There was a house---- wrapped in green paper either from a drug

store or from some shop. Then there was a black leatherette bag with a slip/on it
                                                                        ng

and rubber gloves. Do you remember that? I have some of the things there and I'll

show 'em to you to see if you might be able to refresh your memory. I'm not going

to show you anything else, I mean, to upset you because I don't want to upset you and

there's no need to do it. But I don't know how much information you have received or

been told. There still is the finger of accusation, Eddie, being pointed at you

regarding the fact that of certain people are of the impression that you have killed

other living persons. And let us hope for your sake that that is something we can

212

settle here today. I have my own personal feelings and conclusions as well as the

faith that I have in you.

A   That's right. One thing, about the masks, that's a Hallowe'en mask. There

was 2 of them together, there was a white one and pink one together, and I don't know

what happened to the white one.

Q   (Excuse me for a moment, will you?)

A   Sure.

Q   Eddie, any time you want to use the Men's Room, or want any coffee or milk,

orange juice, you let me know.

A   Sure.

Q   Did you ever have any intentions, Eddie, of using this leatherette bag with

the sling on it for some use associated with what you have been involved in - the

rubber gloves -

A   I think so, on account of the way, I'm pretty sure that's been in my car

for I don't know how long. You see, most of these bodies --- I don't know, probably I

had it in my pick-up and put it in my car, I don't remember just - that's probably

the way it was. You know this embalming - you know that strong smell?

Q   Yes.

A   And I used the rubber gloves, you know, so I wouldn't get it all over my hands.

Q   You mean after you would remove the body?

A   That's right.

Q   Would the odor sometimes burn your eyes?

A   I'll say. I didn't want to get it on my hands.

Q   Were there ever any occasions, though I personally doubt it, where you found

213

that mold began to form on the face or the hands? You've had moldy meat –

A   Now that you mention it, there was one that one from the Spiritland cemetery.

That's right, when you mentioned that, that just came to me.

Q   Was that a man or a woman.

A   Woman. I think it was Beggs, or something.

Q   Beggs. How did you know that it was Mrs. Beggs – from the headstone or from –

A   That's right and I guess I probably seen it in the paper or was told about it.

Oh, you're right there, I'm pretty sure, the main thing is from the lot – you see there

was no headstone on the grave yet but it was that lot. I'm pretty sure it was Beggs.

Q   That mold is extremely dangerous, did you know about that?

A   No, I didn't.

Q   If you ever had a cut on your finger, if any of that mold entered that fresh cut

it would be a long, long time, if at all, that it would heal up because it prevents healing.

You know there are many molds that are used for healing purposes but then there are just as

many molds as there are poisonous mushrooms, you know. There were 4 gambels found in the

shed. Now, one fresh one was on Bernice. There was 2 very old ones, and then there was

another brand new one, remember my telling you, which was all fitted out with the twine and

wire and everything else. Just between you and myself, Eddie did you have any intentions

of anyone else?

A   No, I don't think so. That had been in my mind about this deer-hunting season.

They wanted me to go deer hunting – quite a few – Hank Worden, even.

Q   . So that one was for Bernice and the other one you had prepared you figured if you

were lucky enough to go deer hunting, is that it?

A   That's the way it had to be.

214

Q   Or did you, in fairness to yourself, prepare both of them for deer hunting? I want you to be frank with me, now.

A   I believe that, I could almost, you know I'm, like I said before, I can't swear to anything, but that's what I believe it was, and the old ones, if there was some found, they must be what Dad used.

Q   Yes, you told me that before, that one was for Dad. Do you think one of them could have been for Mary Hogan?

A   No, I don't remember using anything like that -

Q   On Mary Hogan.

A   That's right.

A   That must have been what Dad had used or something like that or made.

Q   In attempting to refresh your memory and based on what you told me previously, when did you first harbor or think about getting for yourself, getting Bernice? Was it on Thursday when you went to look at the rifles in that rack at her store? Or was it days previous?

A   I think - the closest I can get it is, I would just say that - I can't bring that up.

Q   Tell me as best you can and we'll see if we can't work it out.

A   On the spur of the moment. ———>

Q   That was on Saturday?

     Yes.

Q   Do you have any recollection, Eddie, of when you did make these 2 gambels up with the rope and the wire?

A   Oh, they must have been there at least a year or more. That new one, I wish I could - -

Q   I'll show 'em to you, if you'd like to see 'em.

A   That probably would help.

Q   And, this is something that we should have told Dr. Ganser, but unfortunately he had to get back to his office. But you speak of the spur of the moment, which is the same thing that you told me previously. Do you recall now what developed or transpired in your mind when that spur of the moment occurred, as to why you wanted Bernice? Was it because of the fact that you couldn't get any definite word from Frank on the previous evening that he was going deer hunting, because I know specifically he wouldn't purposely give you a definite answer as to whether or not he was going. As a result of that, did you feel unkindly towards him?

A   No, I don't --

Q   O.K. then. Eddie, on Saturday morning at this spur of the moment when you were at the rifle rack and Bernice was up in front talking with you but not facing you, what was the thought, what possessed you, that caused you to do what you did do?

A   I have figured out some of that, has come clear to me./ You know that a preacher I'll tell this first because it really was the beginning of it. He was a Baptist preacher from Wild Rose. He brought his Bible and he read quite a bit from the Bible and that helped a lot and then he left a little book, with, you know, passages taken out of the Bible and you know that cleared my mind up more than anything else. I was reading that and reading that --

Q   You have that with you now at the hospital?

A   That's right.

Q   You have it in your possession at the hospital?

A   That's right.

Q   Be sure to use that unless the doctors tell you not to to help refresh your memory.

A Gee, that helped me an awful lot, you know.

Q I believe you.

A So I could sleep decent and everything, you know, and that brought it out,
I remember about taking this rifle. First I asked permission and she said I could
look it over, and I took it out, you know, and worked the action. Then I worked
the action, you're quite a bit experienced with guns, see, this is that hammerless,
and after you get it cocked and everything, she's locked.

Q That's right.

A I tried to work the action and couldn't work the action.

Q There's a button/the side of the action where you could have released the
     on
action. It's purposely made that way, so you can unload it.

A Oh, I see, that's what I was wondering.

Q Had you, in the meantime, loaded it with that cartridge from your pocket?

A Yes, I had.

Q Did you have more than one cartridge in your pocket at the time, do you recall?

A I hardly think so because my overalls were hanging there, and if they looked
'em over they'd have found 'em.

  Eddie, do you recall whether or not you put the cartridge into the chamber
directly or into the magazine tube.

  Oh, I put it in the magazine tube.

  And then operated the action.

  That's right.

  At that time, at that particular moment when you dropped the cartridge into
the weapon, into the rifle, did you then know what your intentions were?

A   No, as far as I know now, I wanted to test the action and then unload it.

She was locked in there. I couldn't operate it at all.

Q   Then was when that spur of the moment developed?

Q   Yes, it had to be at that time. ————————→

Q   Well, Eddie, in view of what you did to Bernice, I mean you took her life,

what is your explanation as to why you wanted to take her life? Remember we were

talking about possession, having --

A   That's the only logical explanation there. ————————→

W: You had told me about a certain resemblance that Bernice had facially, physically,

age-wise and all in relation to your mother. Was it because of that reason or was

it because of the reason that you wanted to take her from Frank?

         Let's see. I'll explain that a little bit. It won't take long. You know

I was talking to these doctors at the hospital and maybe I never mentioned that to

you, but when I was thinking afterwards in my mind was a little bit clear, I thought
                                                    and

could it possibly be, well, I guess I did mention about that family that moved in,

you know, and that caused my mother's first stroke, about that dog-killing, and

I don't know this might not have anything to do, but you know this Bernice Worden

before she married she was a girl, they was telling me this. I didn't know about it

because I was, I doubt if we was up in this country yet. There was this Worden, the

one she married afterwards. He had another girl, he had a different girl, and the

way I understand it they was engaged and everything to be married and she was a real

nice girl, a dentist's daughter. And then, of course, you know how some men are, it

isn't so much the girl as if there is money in back in the family. Then he met

Mrs. Worden, whether she was after him, too, I couldn't say about that. I wouldn't

218

accuse anybody. But anyway he tried everything he could to get rid of this other girl -

Q   So that he wouldn't have to be obligated to marry her, is that it?

A   That's right. Holidays and everything, Christmas and everything, he sent cards to Bernice and to other girls and nothing to her. He was up in Plainfield seen with other girls.

Q   Did you know this of your own knowledge or did someone tell you -

A   This was told to me by the old timers. They knew all about it. It made this girl feel so bad that she killed herself. Her Dad, being a dentist, she could get this chlorofrom, and she took chloroform. They found her dead in bed.

Q   Did you ever have any conversation with her, I mean as a whild, when you were a young man, or did you just know her to see her walk down the street?

This was most all told to me.

Q   I see.   - - -

A   I don't want to say anything, you know. They said her tongue was almost completely bit right off, you know, ---- her teeth to keep herself from saying anything. Then of course he married her, Bernice Worden. Then after they, let's see, they had this -- I guess they just had that one boy. That's all the family, Frank. And then this Worden, the way I remember it, what brings it to my mind so clear, there's an old fellow was telling me Oh, that's so bad, too bad that this, I think it's leukemia, the blood --

Q   Yes, cancer of the blood, yes.

A   That's right. He was, you know, pitying him so, I said, Well, I don't know if he should really be pitied or not. Maybe it's a punishment -

Q   For what he did to that other woman that he was courting -

        That's right, to that girl.

Q   And jilted.

A   That's right. It kinda surprised him and I guess he started thinking about it, too. He's still living in Plainfield, the old fellow. I know he quieted right down. It gave him something to think about, you know. I told him about things, you know.

Q   As a result of what you had learned from this old fellow, did you sort of build up, say, a dislike or hatred for Bernice?

A   That's what kinda come in my mind when I was thinking. This woman there first started it, I thought, probably, got things started. ----- that my mother got the first stroke, and then this building up about Bernice and everything, and that isn't all, you see. After she married this Worden and he died, then there was two brothers, and she couldn't get this one brother, whether he died or married and moved away, I

220

couldn't say about that, but she said if I (supposed to have said this) can't get one

I'll get the other and it must have been true. This last one was married and had a wife

and I wouldn't say about children, but they seemed to be happy together, no trouble or

anything, and she broke up that family, so that there was a divorce. And then, of course

they went on a trip. She denied it always, that's what they've told me, I didn't talk

to her about it, but they've never been married, but there was something,/they ~~either~~ anyway

went out west on a nice big long trip around there. They should have been married to

go like that. Then when they came back it didn't take long, he was cooled off. It's

just like I see him yet, first when they was going together in Plainfield he was just

like walking on air, right on his tiptoes, like, you know. His hat blew off once, I

remember, when he was going to get in the car and Frank he ran and grabbed it. It

started rolling across the street. He brought it back to him. When they came back, oh,

probably a month, hardly a month, after that he walked just like an old man that's a

hundred years old, slumped down.

Q   What do you think occasioned, caused that?

A   That was/, they was breaking up, see, and getting over that excitement and

stuff like that. You know he was punished. He got a job somewhere south there. He

was either going or coming to work, big semi tipped over on his car and killed him and

flattened his car right out. So he was punished.

Q   You remember earlier you had explained you felt that there was a certain amount

of resemblance between Bernice and your mother. Was there any?

A   There was some.

Q   Was that a part of your analysis, also?

A   That's right. That all could be tied together.

221

Psychiatrists Complete Sanity Test of Ed Gein

Killer-Grave Robber Will Be Returned to Wautoma; Judge to Get Report Soon

Journal Special Correspondence

Waupun, Wis.—Ed Gein, confessed double slayer and grave robber, finished his mental tests Wednesday at central state hospital.

Dr. Edward Schubert, hospital superintendent, said the report on Gein should be in the hands of Circuit Judge Herbert L. Bunde of Wisconsin Rapids by Thursday or Friday.

Judge Bunde, who is holding court in Milwaukee this week, said he would study the report over the week end. He said it was likely that the Gein case would not be back in court before the first of the year because the judge has a full court schedule until after Jan. 1.

Judge Bunde said he would know more about Gein's court appearance after studying the medical report.

Schley Not Eager

At Wautoma Sheriff Art Schley of Waushara county said he was not eager to regain custody of the 51 year old Plainfield bachelor until after Christmas.

He said he would ask the hospital to keep Gein until Dec. 26. Dr. Schubert said he had no objections to that but said it would be necessary to have Judge Bunde extend the commitment order beyond the termination date, which is next Monday.

Dr. Schubert said that Gein had been examined every day since he was committed Nov. 23. The superintendent said that 10 or 12 persons—psychiatrists, psychologists, social workers and consulting physicians—had seen Gein at the hospital.

Dr. Schubert would say nothing about the report, but said Gein had been "a co-operative patient, no source of difficulty."

Summary to Be Given

Judge Bunde will rule on Gein's sanity based upon the medical report. Although the report will be voluminous. Dr. Schubert said, the judge would be given a summary on which he may base his decision.

If found to be insane, Gein will be re-committed. If sane, Judge Bunde will have to set a trial date.

Gein has been charged with first degree murder for killing and butchering Mrs. Bernice Worden, 58 year old Plainfield hardware store operator, on Nov. 16. Arraigned on that charge on Nov. 23, Gein pleaded insanity after confessing the crime.

He also has admitted the slaying of Mrs. Mary Hogan, 54, operator of a tavern in Portage county not far from Plainfield.

Gein said he murdered the two women because they resembled his dead mother, for whom he had an abnormal love. He said he robbed the graves while in a daze.

The Leather Was Stretched. (Roger Scholz)

Q   Well, tell me --

A   And this Hogan, Mrs. Hogan, ----(?), I was thinking about that. She was from Germany and my mother was from Germany. You see their faces - and everything, their face lines resembled ----

Q   Yes, Eddie you told me that you went as far as 4th grade in school, is that correct?

A   I went, well I was supposed to have went up to the 8th grade but that teacher, she was from kindergarten.

Q   Do you know how many years you did ga complete?

A   Well, I was,/I must have been in the 7th grade - that teacher - and then I
        I believe
was supposed to have been in the 8th and instead of that she went and put me down with the youngsters, so that I'd be in there, the next -----

Q   Did you have more than one teacher?

A   That's right.

Q   Do you remember some of their names?

A   One that comes quickly to me is Mrs. Hartford - Miss Hartford.

Q   Miss Hartford.

A   She was a young teacher, real nice teacher.

Q   Was she your first teacher?

A   No, that's the one that came to me first, and then there's Rena Salzer and let's see, I believe the first was Wallie Rathbone, but she wasn't, I guess, just one term, because I don't remember too well, I guess it was just one term. And then Rena Salter, she must have been quite a few terms. I worked real good with her. She was a good teacher, she wasn't really fair, but she was good.

Q   Do you remember, do you have any recollection when you were in ~~either~~ maybe 6th or 7th

grade and you were studying United States history or geography, especially history, do

you remember who the President of the United States had been then? Now, let's see,

you're 51 years of age -

A   That's right.

Q   And you were born in 1906.

A   That's right.

Q   So you probably went to school at the age of 6 or 7, is that ~~right?~~ correct?

A   ---- ---- we moved from LaCrosse to Juneau County and there was so far from

school that I didn't go that year and then we came up in this country, probably not

that year yet but the next year.

Q   Do you remember who our Presidents were during World War II?

A   Let's see - Wilson was in World War I. World War II would be Roosevelt and

Truman.

Q   And which of the two are living today?

A   Well, Truman is the only one.

Q   Have you heard any news about - what is our present President's name?

He's German, also, German origin.

A   Eisenhower.

Q   Have you heard what happened to him?

A   Yes, I seen that in the paper when we was coming up.

Q   Another heart attack.

A   Well, it said in there a mild stroke. I didn't - just the headlines.

Q   Do you know as a result of your own reading whether or not he has been a well or a sick man in the past?

A   Well, he has had heart attacks.

Q   In figuring out your taxes, you told me that your taxes, I recall, are roughly $140 a year. Am I correct?

A   Well, I think it was a little more - $157 or close to 60.

Q   If -- no doubt you will be probably asked and I don't want to.go into it, just for my own information, from, without a pencil and pad, what is the highest or the greatest amount of figures that you could be able to add up or subtract?

A   Just without pencil or paper?

Q   Yes.

A   Not too good.

Q   Well, if you had pencil and paper, what would it be - in the 100s, or 1000s, or could you subtract or add even in the millions?

A   Pretty fair, yes, with pencil and paper. (some noise)

Q   Put down 2 sets of figures, figures of the largest amount that you think that you could figure out. How about writing ~~40,000~~ 34,976 - now subtract 21,631. Now,let's see what you come up with, subtract that please.

> −21,681
> 13,345

A   That would be 13,345. *(correct)*

Q   Now, I'll arrange -- as a matter of fact, I have some of the items in the adjoining room that I would like for you to look at, especially one, is the book your family medical book. Did your family actually have it, or did you come by it after the passing of your parents?

A   No. That was, I believe - I don't remember just exactly how they got that --

Q   We had the same thing -- - -(?) here, let me get it.

A   long ago

It almost seems like that was put in there as a marker, but what made me

                          is

kinda interested, see, in this that I worked for a neighbor sawing lumber, you know,

and I'm pretty sure -- well maybe not - I thought at first, but I guess it - either,

let's see, in chicken pox, how many, thus is there just one kind of chicken pox or

is there -

Q   No, I don't think so, we should have had Dr. Ganser here to answer some

of those questions. That's a question you can ask of the doctors at the hospital.

A   Yes sir, I could do that ---, anyway his children died of disease, and I

thought I'd never had it and the fellow that's working there he thought he'd never

had it so we went to the doctor and got shots for that. That's what kind a ----

my mind first, but it might not be what it was.

Q   Measles --

A   That's measles.

Q   Is this some of your typing?   What does it read on that -- ?

A   That is kinda comical, isn't that? No, I don't believe so.

Q   Did you do any typing?

A   Well, that's - - - ? on the back, isn't it?

Q   Yes. You have an Oliver typewriter -

A   That's right.

Q   Did you ever permit any of the neighbors to use the machine or to -

A   - - - ? that's right. A neighbor that was across, he used the machine

a lot.

Q   Who was that?

Q   Now, this is just as it was found, Eddie. I would like for you to explain

to me, if you can, from your memory the reason for some of these inserts, what the

particular data meant to you.

A   I think that most of them was put in by either my brother, or, probably that

was mostly my brother. You see, Dad (did I mention that before to you?) he had,

well, it was trench mouth first from part of a tooth that hadn't been pulled, what

they figured anyway, the hospital, and this doctor we had, why he didn't amount to

anything, didn't know anything, I guess, and then that being all the time there and

that irritation, that started cancer underneath.

Q   Is that so?

A   And that's why this book was used a lot and probably certain places marked,

see? That's right, you see he had cancer of the jaw. I don't remember which side

it was now exactly, it was on a back tooth. But that isn't really what killed him.

That was leakage of the heart, and I guess they drawed the fluid three or four

times, this seems just like it, that's probably what that was, where it shows here

the teeth and jawbone.

Q   Is this your writing?

A   No, that's my brother's. Let's open it up and see once. That's right.

You see, he wanted to build a house on my 80 that I sold afterwards, you see that's

the outlines of the house. I guess there's some of his figurings on there, too.

This, I guess, he probably used that as a marker. ~~Disease of~~ the gums. Well,

let's see this - Philipsborn -

Q   That was addressed to your Dad, and I think this is some mail order house.

Yes, that's what it is, it was just used as a marker. This is many, many years dd.

228

A   That was a Wilson family, and his name was Charles Wilson, he was over there,

he used that a lot. This probably is just, oh, I see what that is -- oh, this is --

Q   It's a limerick.
I was certainly pleased with the last line that you sent in for for the

limerick.

A   That must be what that was for, see, that's that last line. First time, I

believe, I saw that - - - - ? Must be she slipped the flowers - - - -?

Q   - - - - various diseases of - - - mostly no painful menstruation, of erysipelas,

heartburn, inflammation of the bladder.   Why did you have those 2 bladders - in the

form of little bones?

A   Those weren't bladders.

Q   They weren't? What were they?

A   Let's see.

Q   They looked like intestine to me.

A   No, they're breasts.

Q   They're breasts?

A   That's right.

Q   the inner lining
You mean/the milk sacs within the breasts?

A   No, the outside.

Q   No.

A   You have 'em here?

Q   Yes.

A   Maybe if I get a chance --

A   All right, I'll show 'em to you.

Q   That's right. They were turned inside out - that's why it looks different.

The way they was dried.

Q   Here is another thing that I'd like to ask you about. This seems to be

well worn.

A   I noticed that -----? for years --

Q   I want to ask, Eddie, is ₤ there any possibility that you used any of this

material regarding the bodies? There's one here in particular. Can you recall

whether or not you had any noses, a mouth, and a couple of eyes --- the bodies that

you had ----

                                             I can straighten that out.

A   I think that I can explain that. That would be, I think/xhxxxxxxxxxxxxx

You see, you know when you found these, what you call 'em, masks, you notice there's

- -- -- --?

Q   Yes.

        Some that are not complete, that it's just from here?

Q   Yes.

A   You see, oh, I had that made out of one of these cardboard boxes and moths

got into it and if you'll look probably on some of them you can see the holes that

               ate.
the moths ᴇᴀᴛ. And that's where that was removed - see taken off.

Q   You have eyelids - the portion of that eye, you got 3 or 4 of those.

A   That's taken from where it was cut off, see?

Q   Was there any particular reason - was it because of the moths or some other

reason?

        That's right. - - - I thought I'd burned that - it must have been around

some place.

Q   How is your recollection on what you had told me previously that when you

would be in these dazes that you would put the hair and the scalp over your head, plus, as you refer to them, the vaginas?

A   I've been thinking about that, too. There now them doctors, you know, we

was talking quite a while in the hospital and whether that got started about me

taking these heads - you see I'd read stories about this where these head hunters they

take the heads and then, I think/- - - ~~Ixthinkxthatxtheyxcallxthat~~ a fetish, tree or something, what they call that, -- somewhere they

have a clearing that they can get in the jungle womewheres, and then they build a

house like, oh, it's something like a worshipping house or something like --

Q   A house of worship.

A   Yes - and they always try to have a tree right next to it in that clearing

and the ones that they've been fighting with or anything (you know they're cannibalistic)

and they dismember bodies and hang 'em all on the trees. I was just wondering if that

could have been probably the start of this here.

Q   Well, I know, but what I'd like for you to/re-answer or to correct your --

A   And these witch doctors would do that a lot. They had the hair, you know,

and everything over them. I'm so dizzy, you know, but that's what it is ------ you

might be right in what you said before, and they might be right. Well, youse all have

to get an idea and then youse can figure them out.

Q   You see, you had told me/originally, if you will recall, Eddie, that you more often wore

the scalps and the vaginas, do you remember that, you wore that combination more often

than you wore the face itself. Am I correct?

A   That's right. And like you probably noticed, like them others there complete,

I couldn't - -

Q   You couldn't put those on.

A   No.

231

Q   And then the o...er point I brought up and you gave me the answer to, and I'd like for you again to give me your answer since you've become gradually more relaxed, to refresh your memory also, did you tell me that as a result of wearing these scalps and the vaginas (in your own word, the vagina) that there was some connection, as far as you were concerned, regarding being a woman plus the sexual satisfaction?

A   Well, that I believe I would admit that there was a feeling like that.

Q   Do you recall your telling me also that as a result of the teachings of your mother regarding women in general that since you nursed your mother and looked after her in her last years after your dad passed away, that on many occasions prior to her illness and also during the time of her illness and after her death you would have preferred to be a woman rather than a man?

A   Well, I know I've thought of that a lot - you know, the difference between a man and a woman.

Q   Do you have any recollection of your telling me about considering the removal of your penis and your testicles?

A   Yes, that did come into my mind quite a few times when I was younger.

Q   Eddie, how did you remove the skull caps - that is the upper portion of the skull? What implement, what tool did you use?

A   A hacksaw.

Q   A hacksaw. Was that the hacksaw on top of the kitchen cabinet where you had the
plane?

A   I believe there was 2 up there. I don't remember just which one.

Q   Yes, there were 2, plus the hand plane. I also have - if I can get - the clothing here - it will help to refresh your memory.

232

A: Oh, that's right, that was what Mother made. That was one of our- I don't remember
if that was my brother's or mine.

Q   I used to wear dresses, too, so I've been told.

                                                    otherwise
A   I'm glad that you showed that to me because/I'd a never have - I'd have been
always puzzled over it.

Q   Then, this one here, do you remember -

A   That is my mother's.

Q   That is your mother's?

A   That's right.

Q   Eddie, what is your explanation for this bucket or pail?

A   Let's see, I'll try to get that straightened out. I think that was some kind
of container -

Q   Waste basket?

A   That's probably what it was, or something.

Q   What is it made of?

A   That is - that's human skin.

Q   That's human skin. Do you know from whom this came?

A   Let's see, I'm afraid I couldn't exactly say, but it seems that that is from
a leg, I believe.

Q   From a leg.

                                                    sewed in 2 places?
A   Or probably from 2, I don't know, you know, it's so — let's see,/is that --

Q   Don't handle it, Eddie - it's soiled, it's dirty. It's in 2 pieces.

A   Well, that could be probably from -

Q   The thighs -

A   Yes, or something like that.

233

Q   Is that from a living person or a person from the grave?

A   That's from a person from the grave.

Q   I'm going to leave the room for a moment, I want to make a phone call.

A   That little ———— ? that is from, let's see, that would be a Peinecker girl.

Q   Peinecker girl?

A   Yes, that's her dress. I don't remember just how, I think that was, you see

I took them to get their mother. That's the girl that I went with, you probably remember .

Q   Yes.

A   And then that was her little sister, and I think the windows were foggy, you

know how they'll get and that was late in the fall --

- - -

Q   Eddie, look at this, and I'll be back shortly.

(Lapse of time)

A   This I remember real well, too.

Q   Yes, I was quite curious, Eddie, to see that you were clipping articles

regarding missing persons and women that had been assaulted or beaten.

A   That's right. This here, I can explain this real good. You see it was in,

I don't know which one, this probably is the one I clipped first. Yes, this is the

first one here.

Q   "Woman found dead in ditch - Madison housewife apparently died of exposure

after beating."

A   Yes, that was clipped first, and this is the second clipping, I think, because,

and I'll always remember, and I don't know, maybe I haven't got any more, but this

fellow admitted, see, that cleared that up. I was always going to have a book for -

to put in odd things - sometimes a person could see a criminal or something, you know,

and have the clipping to refer back to.

Q   Did you have some particular desire, I mean you told me earlier as a

young man had considered seriously of being a doctor, studying medicine.

A   Yes, that's right.

Q   Well, did the thought ever occur to you that you would like to have been a

policeman or an investigator?

A   That's right, too. That's what a lot of this is, and this fellow, I believe,

I don't know if you remember it or not -

Q   No, I think that's before I came to Madison.

A   You see, he didn't get anything out of that.

Q   Now, you feel that that was right or wrong?

A   Wrong.

Q   Why was it wrong?

A   Because he beat her so that she couldn't take care of herself and left her in the
snow and everything to die. So he should have had some punishment because well, it was
deliberate, you see, he left her there to die. The money, too, on top of it.

Q   Well, getting back to that subject matter, Eddie, did you ever possess that
thought in the case of either Mary or Bernice?

A   Let's see.

Q   You saw them on the floor, after you knew that you had taken their lives.

A   That's right.

Q   Did you feel that you had some obligation to look for them thereafter, or did
you, as you had told me previously, that you wanted to possess them personally? Well,
that's something, if your memory is refreshed, that you tell the doctors about when you
                                                   try to
get back to the hospital Because I don't want to exhaust you on some of these things -

A   --- not too clear, that's right.

Q   Now, Eddie, this was the second gambel - are you still of the belief, Eddie, that
you made this one and the one that was found on Bernice, at least a year previously?
This looks fairly fresh.

A   That I doubt if it's been used for anything.

Q   I know that it hasn't.
     I know,
A   But I say that I doubt that that was with any intent to - there just was that
piece -

Q   This probably was a long pole at one time and you made two, is that possible,

236

you could have made 2 from one?

A   I doubt it because it was awful thin, and I think when that was made -- that

might have been some cut on it not too - I believe I did test a knife - cut some off on

of that. It probably would show on these ends.

Q   This one appears to be fresher.

A   That's right. But I decided that that was too thin to be used for anything

of any weight. It probably would be strong enough --

Q   Did you even consider that, I mean as far as Bernice was concerned?

A   No. Not at all.

Q   What is your explanation for this? These 2 bent nails with this baling rope

or binder twine?

A   Well, let's see. I remember making that.

Q   There's another set, of course.

A   Yes, that's about the same size, that was for, let's see, that was for

holding something.

Q   I know what it was used for, Eddie, but I prefer for you to tell me. Let

me tell you this much, Eddie, the same device - 2 bent nails and the cord - was used

in connection with Bernice. Does that help you any?

A   Oh, I see.

Q   This was an extra set.

A   It seems like it wants to come to me. I remember making that and bending

those - that was, let's see, there was 2 of them, wasn't there.

Q   Eddie, please remember to speak up as I'm a little hard of hearing.

A   That is the, that was made for - it's getting clearer now, for, say, for

237

holding a part of a body.

Q   Was it the lower portion of the body or did it have anything to do with the

upper portion of the body?

A   Because there's 2 hooks there – if it had been one hook –

Q   Since you bring up the subject of a body, would it be for underneath the armpits?

Did it have anything to do with the face or the head? As I say, Eddie, I know, but I

don't want to suggest –– I'll tell you one thing, it had something to do with the head.

See if that will help you any further, I don't want to tell you anything more about it.

A   Oh, I think I know now. You know, that's just like you said before, it's

something like –

Q   One key – one word –

A   One key – you know what made me think of that?

Q   What is it?

A   You know, when I made these masks, that's what I used, you know, to put right

in the ears here, you see, I stuffed them all out, it had to be stuffed –

Q   What did you use to stuff?

A   Well, most of them I used paper.

Q   Did you ever use any of the material from that old mattress?

A   No, I believe that was just used for kindling and stuff, you know, to make a

fire; that was paper and I believe I used sawdust once. But you know anywheres else

with this form, the head, you couldn't put it on the neck because that would pull to-

gether. So that was in the 2 ear openings and that would come up over the head so

that it would dry.

Q   All right now, Eddie, if you can, try to refresh your memory further because

238

this, a duplicate of what ‗ have shown you, was connected ‗th Bernice's head. I'll

tell you that now. And I also further know how it was used. Now Bernice's head you

had not prepared. You had just removed from the main portion of her body. Try to

refresh your memory as to how you used it on Bernice.

A   Well, figuring the way I used that before, I probably used that the same.

What would be - was there anything there to hang anything on?

Q   Yes, here, let me tell you this. Do you remember Bernice hanging by the gambel

through the tendons of her ankles? Do you remember that? You told me that you did.

A. Yes, first I didn't, but then afterwards it came to me.

¢ A.   You told me that at the jail.

¢Q   That's right. Then she was hanging and while her head was still a part of her

body, Eddie, you used these 2 bent nails and the rope. Now try to remember why you

had to use the bent nails and the rope. It had something to do with her head.

A   The 2 nails and that cord, or a rope?

Q   No, the cord, the same as that.

A   Was that to hold her head back, or something?

Q   ,   Well, it had something to do with removing her head from her body. Well, here,

let me tell this to you, because there are other things that I want to cover, and

again I remind you, as I have reminded you in past instances where we have been having

conversation, you know where a person is asked many questions and is told many things

there is that possibility sometimes of a person beginning to believe, that's right,

that actually they never occurred, but, under the circumstances, Eddie, Bernice had

both of the hooks in her ears when she was suspended in form of, her head down, the

2 hooks here, the Y, and you apparently stepped on the end of the rope. Does that

mean anything to you?

A   No, it doesn't. But it could be the way --

Q   Well, now here, maybe we can approach it in this manner. Why would you, while
                                                              of the nails
she is suspended from the chain hoist, why would you have the hook ends/in her ears

with an inverted V or a Y instead -- or have some heavy weight to pull down on the head?

It had something to do with the removal of her head from her body.

A   That would hold the body from swaying, or something?

Q   Would it stretch the neck? To make it easier?

A   That's right.

Q   Do you have any recollection?

A   No, I haven't.

Q   O.K. Fine. All right. Now, one other thing regarding the spare set. Did
                                                          on your hands
you entertain or possess the thought, Eddie, of having a spare set/(we might as well

face facts)

A   That's right.

Q   It was just by coincidence, probably, that Bernice was discovered. Probably

it never would have been detected; it's just one of those things.

A   And a good thing, too.

Q   Yes. We both agree on that. Did you possess any thought for the future to

have these spare parts on hand in the event you sought to get another living woman

or to remove some one else, another woman, from a grave?

A   I think that was the main thing why them were made - was as I used, as of

course, instead of using the others, the way 1 remember I used shingle nails. But they

was so small they'd slip out all the time, once in a while, you know.

Q   From the ears you mean?

A   Yes - and this being bigger it would come up higher and there would be no
240

danger of slipping out. I remember quite a few of them was ---- the same way.

Q   Do you have any recollection of doing that to Bernice at all? Of holding
her head so that the body wouldn't sway? Before you removed her head?

A   Not a bit, but it seems logical the way --

Q   Now, Eddie, what can you tell me about this bottle of formaldehyde solution?

A   That, as far as I remember, I bought that, I believe, in Hancock. It was
some drug store. That was used for, oh, squirrel tails.

Q   You told me, Eddie.

A   That's right. We --- a few of them away.

Q   On portions of Bernice, when I saw her, and on some of these other things
that you had at home, there still is the presence or residue of salt. It could have
been a mixture of salt and water, or it could have been straight salt.

A   That was only on one or two, wasn't it?

Q   Yes, plus Bernice. Now it was on Bernice's face and it was on Bernice's
vagina.

A   On the vagina
        xoxox I did, you know, sprinkle a little salt.

Q   You sprinkled the salt?

A   But the face, I don't remember.

Q   Could you have washed, maybe, your hands in that bucket of water that you
told me about that you took from the house. Maybe there was some grains of salt
that didn't dissolve and when you washed her off it could have been on the others,
other portions?

A   One thing I want to ask you, was the face washed?

Q   No. See the body was washed, but not her face.

241

A I was right there, I couldn't remember that at all.

Q You remember my telling you on Sunday, and I levelled with you right there and then, because there were some occasions, Eddie, when you doubted my word in the beginning, and I felt under the circumstances that I'd better reveal all to you, that I did not have a complete opportunity to observe and make a search of your home because it was so dark. Then I think after we understood each other, then there was a closer relationship between you and myself.

A That's right.

Q So I agree now, I mean, I know that within the past couple days that Bernice's head was not washed. Here is the other thing that you were vague on. You probably have already been asked this by the doctors at the hospital. No matter how embarrassing it might be to you --

A It's for the best of all.

Q That's right. Do you recall attempting to, or actually having intercourse with Bernice after you brought her from her place?

A I believe I did try, but without success.

Q Did you have an erection? Remember my definition or explanation of an erection? Where your penis gets hard.

A I doubt if it was complete.

Q Do you remember having as you know with the vagina, here's the thing I want to bring to your attention, even though you did salt it and all, and we have many things to examine here, you know that as a result of - and that was one of the things that I got off on the wrong foot with you - I asked you that very embarrassing question. First of all, you told me that you had never experienced intercourse with a woman - a living woman.

A That's right.

242

Q   Then I asked you the question whether or not you had masturbated and you were a little upset by that. But finally you answered the question. As you know, there is that glycerin-like or sticky-like fluid that comes from the penis. Now, in the event you were successful in having an ejaculation, where the semen or fluid comes from your penis, if there is any of that present on Bernice's vagina, either inside or outside, it will be found here at the laboratory. Do you recall, Eddie, whether or not you did have an ejaculation?

A   No.

Q   You don't think so. Was it that you couldn't accomplish a penetration or is it because your penis wasn't hard enough?

A   Well, I think the main thing was my mind. You see, you have to have it in your mind or else —

Q   You mean the sex, to get —

A   That's right.

Q   Did you then masturbate afterwards?

A   No, I don't think so.

Q   I'm trying to keep track of these things you tell me, sometimes it's a little difficult.

A   It is.

Q   What was your answer to sex intercourse with Mary Hogan?

A   None at all.

Q   None at all, eh? While I leave the room for a moment, I'd like to check —

(Not understandable)

Q   Oh, yes, tell me about that typewritten note.

243

'Butcher' Sent to Waupun

Order Ghoul Graves Opened

Story
on
Page 3

Gein takes a break. (Lou Rusconi)

A   That - I won't say for sure, but it is - Robert Hill. That is a young fellow

that - from Hill's store. He saw my typewriter once there and, now whether his little

brother was along or not, because he was lots of times, and they just typed that, you know.

(Not understandable) so mixed up.

Q   The reason that our eyebrows were raised a bit was something about Tony, and

then Go get her. - - - - Did you ever type any letters or ~~mexx~~ orders/ we'll say to ---- Sears, Roebuck

or Montgomery Ward or Aldens or Spiegels, where you'd use the machine?

A   Yes.

Q   What particular significance, if any, is there in that?

A   There should be one of those. ?

Q   Why not go thru this and I'll be back shortly?

)   (Lapse of time)

E.G.   That's ~~axxixx~~ the La Cross case.

Q   Exactly, and that is why, regardless of what you and I at this particular

point know, the people still insist because, basically you being from LaCrosse, that you

are the person

A   No, that I can say positively

Q   The other thing, Eddie, that has been brought up, first they disbelieved

that you stole from the graves. The sexton at Plainfield, of course, must have a very,

very red face because he said it could never happen. Now, of course, everybody agrees

)

that it did happen. But the point that they bring up now is they are inclined to believe

when I say, I mean people generally including some of the investigators that there is that

possibility that you could have had an accomplice, someone who you

A   No.

246

Q   Tell me, why couldn't you, or why wouldn't you have an accomplice?

A   Well, there's two ways -- when this oh say feeling would come on me when I had

built up you know and say just like that was unpredictable. That's one thing. And another

ingif I'd
that/had any sense at all --- well, I couldn't have had too much or I wouldn't have done it ---

is that if there's two why --- this is my reasoning now -- that the matter is - - -

Q   Let me, shall I go on - if more than one person knows the secret it is no

longer a secret, is that what you wanted to say?

A   You're right.

Q   That's my feeling in the matter also. That/would never have exposed yourself

to that element.

A   That's right.

Q   Getting back to the Hartley clippings and your explanation to me about your

interest, initially wanting to study medicine and maybe being an investigator, what is

your explanation for these articles concerning the Hartley case and these other crimes?

A   I guess that's natural. I kinda was interested in my home town, and I kinda

was interested --

Q   Have you ever worn tennis shoes? I've asked you that question before.

A   Well, when I was little I'm pretty sure I did, and the only time I wore

tennis shoes is, I don't know if they're still there or if I burned them up, but there was

a pair that Mother had used. When I was shingling on the roof they're better on the roof.

Of course, it was rough on the roof but it was these asphalt shingles and I wore one side

right off. I believe this here --

Q   Do you remember whether or not they were white tops or black tops - I mean

those that you used that your mother had worn originally?

A   They were brown.

Q   They were brown.

A   Tan.

Q   Tan. Do you remember whether or not they actually were women's gym shoes or were they men's shoes that maybe your brother owned and that your mother wore on occasions?

A   Of course, these here I guess were just split down this way and then this way. It seems to me these were kinda folded over here, more you know, they came down here --

Q   I see, yes.

A   Different than these. And the cap - I think there was a toe here, but that come over the -- let's see - well I couldn't - I wouldn't say - but I believe why I kept quite a few of these clippings here -

Q   How about this girl here?

A   Is because I always was suspicious of - that I'd kinda like to -

Q   Enclosed find B Books. What was that bank books?

A   That must be.

Q   Well, that's not too important. How about this particular photograph of that girl?

A   Let's see, what's her name here -- I believe that was just cut out that way.

Q   Was it because of the fact that portions of her body were exposed?

A   Either that or just cut out, I think it was more just cut out on account of she was that missing -- there should be more.

Q   There probably is. How about this particular map which I think is from the Chicago Tribune. What does that mean to you?

A   That, I cut that out just to get straight in my own mind just about how that location lay there, you know, that it said in the paper that there was a book, you know, found in the harbor there about that. I cut that out and --

Q   What case was that, do you remember? There were --

A   This is that last case. The Anderson girl --

Q   The Anderson girl, or is it the three boys that were found in the Forest Preserve? Remember what happened to the Anderson girl from what you have read?

A   Well,

Q   How did they find her?

A   You see, her body was found in them drums. They showed it to me there, the drums.

Q   The Chicago detectives did, eh?

A   That's right. And this was taken, you know, for - why I took this out kinda you know just to see how far it had to be - everything was kinda interesting.

Q   My recollection is that --

A   That's from back when I wanted to be a detective and stuff like that.

Q   Here was your dad's grave.

A   That's right.

Q   Who's ring is that?

A   That is, I believe, one of my uncle's. I wore that once in a while and
I guess I wore it when I was cutting wood once and you notice she's bent there where
I hooked into that.

Q   Let me get some of this stuff out of —

A   Kind of a —

Q   I think the initial is - it could be a G. I don't know.

A   It might have been my father's, because his name was George. This here
I was kinda wondering about because this uncle took this girl, I believe, yah, it says
here, and I was always interested if he wasn't mixed into it a little bit.

Q   I thought probably for —

A   This - I wished that I'd a had more of that and -

Q   This religious -

A   That's right. That would help to keep a person straight.

Q   For the purpose, Eddie, of a little change, would you be agreeable at this
time, before we have lunch, to go on a bit further with the lie detector test? You
remember my telling you about picking the number and you picked No. 8 and I told you
that your conscience was so strong that it even showed in pen and ink on the chart
the other number that you were thinking about before you wrote No. 8. You remember I
I told you.

A   It sure was right.

Q   We'll go through the same thing and I don't want you to pick 8 again, but

tell you anything about it because I didn't know anything about it other than the fact

that it was a girl's dress and about that big. You began asking whether or not it was

cotton. I thought that it could be. The color, I couldn't tell you what it was or

anything. And you feel that these 2 pieces of tissues or intestines which I had used

the words for that were ball-shaped and you think that they are reversed breasts?

A   That's right.

Q   Do you remember who you might have gotten them from? Were they from Mary?

A   I think you're right, as far as I remember.

Q   That's not too important. I notice that one of the vaginas was painted in

aluminum or silver paint. I think you had given Allen (you know Allen) an explanation

but I would prefer to hear it from you as to why you had painted some of these things

— and especially this particular vagina — with silver or aluminum paint.

A   That was because, I don't know whether it wasn't embalmed as most of them

do or something like that and it was getting a greenish color.

Q   Beginning to decay?

A   Yes — and I put that paint over it to see if that would preserve and stop it

Q   The first thought that occurred to some of the investigators was that it

came from a small child or a young girl.

A   No, it wasn't that.

Q   And of course along with the other rumors which sometimes are getting very

strong at thisstage of the game, some of the investigators from up around your area

still feel that you're responsible for the disappearance and death of Dick Travis.

A   That's right. What I should have done probably was keep my mouth shut,

but I tried to help and still I get it in the heck. I didn't have not a bit to do

251

Q   Would you care for another cup of coffee while I'm drawing up these questions?

Or a glass of milk, or a little orange juice?

                        it'll be all right
A   I think/it won't take you long to draw those questions up .

(No. No.
(
(
Q   (Or would you care for a glass of water?

A   No, maybe I'd better not. I'm starting to feel better now.

Q   You are?

A   That's right and my headache is starting to go. Whether that's the use of my

mind or just sitting relaxed here or something. I don't know. I'm afraid if I'd drink

water or something it might kinda bring it back on again. That lunch maybe helped too

I think.

Q   I imagine you must have had a very early breakfast this morning.

A   That's right.

Q   What time do you ordinarily get up at home?

A   Well, when I was to home it's according like saying this when it gets so late

dark, you know, why I stay in bed quite late.

Q   Seven, eight, nine o'clock?

A   That's right. I get up when it's daylight, you know, so that I can see

without using any lights.

Q   Yes. Well, can you think of anything else that your memory might have become

refreshed about since we've seen some of these things.

A   I think it's very -- know now -- well, we've got a lot of that, I guess most of

that, cleared up. The main thing what had me mixed up and kinda dizzy was that little dress.

Q   Remember that was the first thing I asked you about on Sunday, and I couldn't

252

any number between 3 and 7. We'll go through that and then I will draw a series of questions. That is primarily for your selfish sake and for mine. And this set of questions will run and be based on the same principle as the number test. You remember my explanation about the peak of tension, the way your conscience builds up to a peak and then the relief that occurs. In this peak of tension test, after we get through with the number test, I'll ask you Is your first name Eddie? Your last name Gein? And by the way, there are these questions that are brought up about the correct pronounciation - some people say it's Gien and others say it's Gein. What is it? Xeitxxxxxxxxxxxxxxxxxxxxxxxxxxxx

A   Well, I always called it Gien -

Q   And Did you live in Waushara County? or Do you live in Waushara County? And then I'll ask you Did you take the life of at least one living person? And what will your answer be to that?

A   Well, that would be Yes.

Q   Did you take the life of at least two living persons?

A   Yes.

Q   And then I will continue - Did you take the life of at least three living persons?

A   That would be No.

Q   And see, now could run that up to about 15. You know my feelings about you from your last contact with me and even today, but for the purposes of the record, I want to conduct that examination so that for once and for all we can put an end to that. And then we'll have lunch. Then we may go over a few more of these exhibits and a few more tests, and I think that by mid-afternoon -

A   We'll have everything about done. That's right.

253

with that.

Q   As I recall, you volunteered the information that you remembered him as a school boy and he drew up his fists once and since then --

A   I never seen him, I don't know --

Q   Now regarding your remark, Eddie, that you should have kept your mouth shut, please, now that you are in the hands of very competent and understanding people, - I speak now of the doctors at the hospital -- under no circumstances keep your mouth shut.

A   That's what I thought. I wanted to explain about that odor, you see, that's what started the whole thing. I wouldn't have said anything, there'd have been no mention. Well, there could have been --

Q   Yes, under the circumstances, Eddie, I beg of you, when you have further conversations with the doctors, please don't wait for them to ask the questions. You tell them as the thought comes to your mind, whether or not it be in one breath you are talking about Dick Travis and in the next breath you are talking about Mrs. Adams and in the next breath about Bernice. Because their minds are trained just like a phonograph record or a tape recorder - they can absorb it like a sponge and then, later on, after the conversation or interview is ~~completed~~ concluded, they themselves will separate these issues and put them together. So as the words flow out of your mouth, let them flow, and don't conceal anything.

A   I think I've got them pretty good convinced, anyway -- I hope so.

Q   ~~Perhaps~~ Tell me, also, how many doctors have you had conversation with?

A   In the hospital, you mean?

Q   Yes.

A   Let's see. Well, the main is just two. There was one first, but this last

254

time was two. There was one first.

Q   Is there any reservation (you understand the word reservation?) - is there any
feeling in your own mind that either one or both do not have what you would consider
complete faith and understanding? Do you feel that both of these doctors are very patient
and very understanding? Or would you prefer to have conversation with one rather than the
other?

A   I think they're about as good/ as could — try to understand -- I/ kinda think they're all right.

Q   Well, in the event that you might -- and sometimes it occurs, sometimes a
person gets up on the wrong side of the bed, that happens to me -- if you feel that in
your future conversations with any of the staff there -- maybe there'll be one out of 15
doctors that you will talk to -- if you feel that any of them don't understand your
problem, please explain that to at least one of the doctors that you have extreme confi-
dence in, because it's just one incident of that sort where you do not have complete
faith or trust in one individual might be the complete disruption of your medical attention.

A   That's right. I think as far as I've talked with 'em so far, they seem --
I think they're trying to get at the bottom of it, too, trying to give me help, because
that's what they're there for --

Q   That's right. You understand, also, Eddie, that in these professions, and
especially in the state service, a doctor that works for the state, or people in our
position do not, we're not paid as well as a person in private practice. So you can
come to only one conclusion as a result of the people that you come in contact with here
at the laboratory and at the hospital. They're there because of a sincere personal
motive in wanting to help people. They're not there because -- they could go out in

255

private practice and make 10 times what they're being paid. They're there because they want to help, and you must remember that, and I think you do.

A   That's right, and there wouldn't be no personal gain, otherwise you know they wouldn't -- it would be more to their advantage to get things cleared up than try to get everything mixed up.

Q   Let me wash my hands of some of this dust and dirt and then I'll come back here and we'll draw the questions up. Then, after we get through with these two tests, then we'll have a little something to eat. If you think -- you can wait here --

A   I'll go to the rest room.

Q   They're out in the hall waiting, anyway.

(Lapse of time)

Q   Remember when you were here last, Eddie, I showed you that card? After consideration you picked No. 8.

A   First No. 5 -- and that made it a little too easy, so I picked No. 8, and it showed up both of 'em.

Q   There is no need of my repeating, but I don't know what number you are going to pick this time, but it will not be 1, it will not be 2, it will not be 8, it will 9, or 10. Any other number of your choice. When you write it, hold the sheet of paper as you did the last time, put it under the block and let me know so that I can turn around.

A   All right.

Q   Roll up your right sleeve, please. I'll bet that you've had your blood pressure taken on numerous instances at the hospital now, -- on every test.

A   That's right. You know I only wish that we could have become acquainted, you know, in different circumstances.

256

Q   Well, I would love very much if you are agreeable, and I think we can make

the necessary arrangements, I would like during your time of treatment, whether or not

it would be for a period of weeks or months or even a year, if you'd like I'd like to

come and visit you on occasion.

A   I would like that.

Q   Because I think of all the people who have used investigation up to this time,

that you and I have become intimate friends. Now, of course, you will gain other friends

at the hospital amongst the staff there because they, too, will have very close relation-

ship with you. Now, Eddie, as before, I'll pump the cuff up to determine the proper

pressure for the pen and ink tracing and then I'll release the cuff, and then we'll go

through Did you write No. 1, 2, 3, 4, 5, 6, 7, 8, 9 and 10? Do you remember you will

answer No to every one of them. And during the test you will remember that every time

the cuff is pumped up you will remain as relaxed as possible and further if you have to

cough, or sneeze, or clear your throat, please do it, I mean don't withhold it. And

during the time that the cuff is pumped up, rest your hands just comfortably with your

fingers extended but not stiff. Talking about -- at this stage of the game -- of

visiting you, Eddie, provided it meets with the approval of the hospital, what would

you like, would you like, say, provided it's permitted -- oranges or candy or chewing

gum or things of that sort - cookies, what brand of chewing gum do you like?

Well, let's see, there's - -

Q   Spearmint, Beechnut, Juicy Fruit?

A   I wonder if you can get any of this -- oh -- what you call that - Pepsin?

Q   Dr. Beeman's Pepsin gum?

A   That's right. I'd like that very much.

257

Q   Do you like candy, also? Chocolates or creams?

A   That's right. Anything like that.

Q   And you told me that you liked fruit juices. Do you like fresh oranges, also, apples?

A   That's right.

Q   All right then we'll get on with this first number test. You understand you'll answer No to all of these questions. Did you write No. 2?

A   No.

Q   Your conscience still is ticking away on all eight, strong as ever. Hold that in your hands. This will refresh your memory. This is your breathing pattern and again this is the blood pressure and pulse, and this is where I recorded your blood pressure to determine the proper recording, and this is where we began the test. Now, again reminding you that it's building up, to the peak getting to the crest, and then a dropping off. Notice how apparent it is at the crest. I mean, even though your number choice of last week still is pronounced here in No. 8, your other highest peak is reached at this point here which was your written number as you see it there. 1,2,3,4,5 - notice at 6 here the high point?

A   That's right. It comes right up there -

Q   So now let us go on with this other short test, then we'll make arrangements for lunch.

A   You know, you mentioned before that there was - you can see it in there - like my heart isn't just the way it should be?

Q   No, I had mentioned on another occasion that your heartbeat was also shown or reflected in your breathing.

258

A   You know, I probably misunderstood, but I was just going to mention to you

you know, they had an x-ray of my chest, and my heart was enlarged, quite enlarged, so

I was just thinking, you know -

Q   First time you -- that was when they told you at the hospital?

A   That's right. - - - - In this hospital here they hadn't had the chest x-ray

developed yet.

Q   I see. I might add, also, Eddie, that your other number that you had con-

sidered before 6 is also on the record.

A   It sure is good.

Q   Now, reminding you that on this test you may answer Yes, No, or I don't know.

I'll ask you Is your first name Edward? Your last name Gien? And then I'll ask you

and will you please give me your answers now - Have you taken the life of one living

person?

A   Yes.

Q   Have you taken the life of 2 living persons?

a   Yes.

Q   Have you taken the life of 3 living persons?

A   No.

Q   Have you taken the life of 4 living persons?

A   No.

Q   5 living persons?

A   No.

Q   6?

A   No.

Q   7 living persons?

A   No.

Q   8?

A   No.

Q   9?

A   No.

Q   12 living persons?

A   No.

Q   20 living persons?

A   No.

                    I began to read from   then
Q   Just to refresh, again-it-will-be-from one to 10,/to 12, and 20.   That

would be 1,2,3,4,5,6,7,8,9, 10,12 and 20.

A   That will go a little bit better, probably.

Q   You're doing very well, Eddie. Do you have a headache, or?

A   Yes, it was almost gone and now it's kinda coming again.   That must be

from that spinal, that's what –

Q   Otherwise, do you feel generally well? In the event you don't, we can call

Dr. Ganser's office. I know he can get one of his staff members here to check on you

if you're not feeling well.

A   I think part of what causes this is constipation.

Q   Oh, are you constipated now?

A   That's right.

Q   And I assume that they know this at the hospital.

A   I told them this morning. I was hoping they'd work through, and that may

                              260

have caused my headache, too. But I think we can go through with this all right.

Q   At any time you don't feel well enough you tell me, so --

A   I think we can make it.

Q   This is as much for you as it is for us.

A   That's right.

Q   Is your first name Edward?

A   Yes.

Q   Is your last name Gien?

A   Yes.

Q   Have you taken the life of one living person?

A   Yes.

Q   Have you taken the life of 2 living persons?

A   Yes.

Q   Have you taken the life of 3 living persons?

A   No.

Q   Have you taken the lives of 4 living persons?

A   No.

Q   Have you taken the lives of 5 living persons?

A   No.

Q   Have you taken the lives of 6 living persons?

A   No.

Q   Have you taken the lives of 7 living persons?

A   No.

Q   Have you taken the lives of 8 living persons?

No.

Q   Have you taken the lives of 9 living persons?

A   No.

Q   Have you taken the lives of 10 living persons?

A   No.

Q   Have you taken the lives of 12 living persons?

A   No.

Q   Have you taken the lives of 20 living persons?

A   No.

Q   Have you lied to any of my questions on this particular test?

A   No.

Q   That was the last question. Please remain still for a moment longer. Now clench your fist hard. Well, I believe we'll take time off now maybe for lunch and I imagine the gentlemen are waiting outside and we'll get you some food.

A   I wish I had felt better. Maybe it would have been clearer, but maybe it was all right.

Q   We'll see. During ~~Xuxuxxxxxxxxx~~lunch -

A   Maybe I'll feel better, because I started feeling better there before --

(Outside - He's going to take time out for lunch. He was getting a headache. I told him if he didn't feel well we could make arrangements either to go to the Diagnostic Center or send someone over if he didn't feel well or ~~just~~ we'll stop the examination.)

        - - -

(Arrangements for eating - in background)

E.G.   As I said before, I don't think of myself, because whichever way this turns out wy I've got you know desserts.   (Indistinguishable)

Well, that's usually what happens, Ed, it's not the victims themselves, it's the people that you leave behind that are caused the heartaches. So it's under that impression that we're trying to get this all straightened out, without hurting any more people. - - - -

Did you enjoy your lunch? What is your favorite pie?

Well, pumpkin pie is one of my favorites.

Is that so, what else?

The others are all good, but my real favorite is pumpkin.

Eddie, what - you had given Herb - you remember Herb, the Sheriff? - a list of the names of the graves that you thought that you had entered at Plainfield and
also the one at, what was the n̶e̶x̶t name of -

At Spiritland.

What were the names of - there would be Adams, and

Sparks.

Sparks. Everson?

Everson, that's right. And right next to this - -

Well, how about the one at Spiritland?

That was a Beggs.

Any other names that come to you?

Foster.

Foster ? this was at Plainfield?

263

No, at Hancock. That was the only one that was taken there, and only one

at Spiritland.

Plainfield, Hancock and Spiritland?

That's right.

Now, Adams, Sparks and Everson plus another person next to the Adams grave.

That's a kind of a/‑‑‑‑, I believe ‑ we'll let that go. Maybe it will

Norwegian

come to me.

Can you think of any others?

Gee, that night has come to me so clear, you know.

I'm sorry ‑‑‑ wear size 13.

Sherman.

We can go over these later ‑ and I've made up a few notes also ‑ a check list.

Do you remember how you removed the scalps or the flesh from the skulls? Did you use

a knife, a skinning knife, or what?

I believe I used, well it was a ‑ I'm pretty sure that's the way it was ‑

it was a long ‑ well I found that ‑ I think it was sort of ‑ just thinking ‑ I don't

know just exactly where it was, but ‑ it was a large bladed/knife.

pocket

A large bladed pocket knife.

I lost that.

You lost that. And we discussed this earlier during the day. What solutions,

or what did you do to preserve the flesh that remained, besides air drying, maybe used

salt, common house salt? Remember you told me about oil also ‑ ‑

Yes, that's right.

But preliminarily, what did you use?

As far as I know,/I believe only 2, as far as I can remember that salt was used.

like on them masks

264

E.G.   But the others were just natural embalming fluid.

Oh, I see. You didn't have to do anything further to them. What did you do with the lower portions of the skulls?

That I believe was burned.

Would you have buried any of them?

See, some was quite late in the fall, the ground was even froze some, but not too deep.

Is there any possibility, Eddie, that you could have buried some of these remains, either bones or flesh or tissue or whatever you want to call it, right on your own premises, around the house or the shed?

Not too close - it possibly could be, you know - it's kinda slipped my mind, now.

Would it be many feet, do you think?

I think it would be. But I don't really remember it. I think that most of it, as I remember now was burned.

What particular reason possessed you, Eddie, to keep the skullcaps - the bone - and not the lower portion of the - did you want to use them as containers or something?

I think you got the right idea there. I think that's taken from an old Norwegian style -

From your reading, you mean?

That's right. That shows that that has a lot to do with that.

Do you recall any instances where you actually could have put food in, that you personally consumed liquid or solids?

265

Horrors Of Charnel House Are Revealed By Sheriff

MADISON, Wis. (P) — The horrifying story of grave robbery and butchery by a 51-year-old bachelor exploded into still more horror yesterday when the sheriff of a neighboring county declared he recognized one of the skulls and faces found in a secluded farmhouse as that of a long missing woman.

And the director of the State Crime Laboratory refused to tell newsmen whether he had brought 10 heads to the lab for study "because there may be more than 10."

Charles Wilson, head of the laboratory, made his statement after Edward Gein was brought here for lie detector tests.

SHERIFF's BELIEF

Sheriff Herbert Wanserski of Portage County told newsmen here that, "I absolutely do not believe" that Gein gathered the assortment of skulls and grisly human remains from cemeteries near Gein's Waushara County home.

Wanserski, who said he took part in the investigation of Gein's activities since it was touched off by discovery of Mrs. Bernice Worden's eviscerated body on Gein's farm Saturday night, told newsmen:

"We have found the face and head of Mary Hogan among the objects in Gein's farm house."

Mrs. Hogan was a 54-year-old Portage County divorcee who disappeared in December, 1954, from the rural tavern she operated at Bancroft — some six miles from Gein's Plainfield farm.

Gein admitted butchering the 58-year-old Mrs. Worden Saturday after dragging her bloody corpse from the hardware store she operated in Plainfield.

However, he insisted during ex-

EDWARD GEIN

. . . sits in police car.

tensive questioning that he did not remember actually killing Mrs. Worden. He also insisted that he "didn't know anything" about Mrs. Hogan's disappearance.

'DAZE-LIKE'

Gein maintained, during nearly 30 hours of questioning, that the skulls and other human relics found in his house had been looted from graves "while I was in a daze-like."

He said the same daze affected him while he was talking to Mrs. Worden in her store Saturday morning, and that he thus did not remember killing her. But he described taking her body home and disemboweling and decapitating it because he "thought it was a deer."

A tight news blackout of the ghoulish details of objects found in Gein's cluttered and filthy living quarters was broken by Sheriff Wanserski. His account, which was given to newsmen at the crime laboratory here, piled horror on horror.

The heads found in the farmhouse, he said, had been skinned. The detached portion, he added made up "faces of a regular size, well preserved, with hair, ears, lips and nose."

HUMAN SKIN

Wanserski confirmed that other items fabricated of human skin were found.

Most bizarre of these, he said, was a vest-like garment fashioned from the torso of a woman.

Wanserski said he also examined a chair which had been upholstered in human skin.

Wansserski also said that other fragments of human anatomy were found tacked to the wall and stacked in boxes.

"The skulls were scattered around the place," he said.

So far, Gein has been charged only with armed robbery of Mrs. Worden. He is being held under $10,000 bond on that charge pending the issuance of a murder warrant. This would be held up. Waushara County authorities said, until the investigation is completed.

Gein and one of his heads. (Lou Rusconi)

The way that comes to my mind now, and that must have come automatically

in my mind, subconsciously - is these old songs the Norwegians used to sing and they were

supposed to have
used to have skulls for, what was that drink - mead, or whatever they had -

Yes, I know what you have reference to.

The drinks they used to have and stuff. That must have come into my mind that

I kept some of them. That's the only reason --

Do you have any recollection of actually --

But I never used them.

You never used them. Do you remember what you did with the clothes of Mrs.

Adams or Mrs. Everson?

I believe that those were about all burned because so many of them had been

in the grave, you know, and would be affected by some embalming fluid. I remember they

were spotted and stuff.

When you removed the flesh - the outer flesh and tissue from the bones - you

say that you think you used a long-bladed pocket knife.

Yes, I'm sure of that.

Would you do this in the same fashion as a farmer or a butcher separating the

flesh or the meat from bones, holding the piece, cutting a few slits, working down?

That's right. Of course, over the skull, as I remember, that comes quite easy.

Did you ever try peeling?

Just the lower part.

Because I noticed on some you apparently must have slipped with your knife,

especially under the chin.

No, it's not supposed to be. It's right here.

268

In the case of Bernice, I don't know how good your memory is at this time

regarding Bernice. As you know, other than the bullet hole in the back of her head,

there also was a bruise. Do you remember whether or not besides shooting her striking

her?

No.

Is there any possibility she could have bounced around in the truck?

It could have been that, or when she fell.

When she fell. Of course, I understand that there was -- see, I've never

been at the Worden store -- but I understand that where it is presumed that she fell

to the floor that there was nothing that could have caused that type of injury which

was suggestive of her being -- of a blow.

Of course, it's a cement floor. ―――――――

Oh, is that so? Oh, I didn't know that.

So it wouldn't take much of a blow on a solid cement floor.

We didn't go into this too deeply the last time you were here - what did

Henry die of? I read in the newspaper something about a fire?

That's right. There was no autopsy performed or anything like that, but it

was generally figured that it was kind of part suffocation and --

I see. Was he a fire fighter with many others or how did --

No. He wanted to burn a marsh that belonged to him. I didn't want to go,

but there's another thing that points to when your time is up - it's up. Because I

coaxed him and tried to keep him to home because we had that new team that we

bought on an auction and I wanted to try it out. But he just kept at me till I took

him there.

269

With the religious beliefs and everything else that you have, are you also a fatalist?

Well, I'm starting to get stronger in that.

In what - religion or fatalism?

In this, when your time is like up -

When your number comes up in the book, that's it, there's nothing you can do about it.

That's right.

How old was Henry when he passed away?

Well, you see that was in '44 and 5 years older than me.

Yes. And your mother was how old when she passed away?

Let's see. I believe she was 62.

And she passed away when?

That would be not quite '45, I guess - it was just a day or so, but you couldn't call it '45.

In December.

That's right.

And how old was your dad when he passed away?

65.

He was 65, and what year did he pass away?

That was 1940.

1940. Remember I showed you the pictures, the clippings that you had of the Hartley case. Did you ever have a jacket like that?

No, I don't think I ever bought one. These covert jackets - cossack style.

And the tennis shoes that you say that your mother wore - that you wore on occasions when you were roofing - do you have any recollection whether or not they were hand-me-downs, that somebody gave them to her or did she buy them for herself?

No, I really think though that they were a man's tennis shoe because she was you know, fleshy -

Do you remember about what size shoes she wore?

Let's see. It seems to me they was too small for me -

And you wear what size?

And I believe these are 7 or 7½. That's why I think they went to pieces too.

Well, do you think that your mother's feet were larger than yours?

No, they wasn't longer -

But maybe wider?

They might have been a little bit.

And you think they were of a brown or cinnamon color?

Yes, that's right, just about. Brown or cinnamon.

I asked you earlier about this pink mask. You said it was a Hallowe'en mask. And that there should have been a white mask with it, too. What was the reason that you possessed the masks in the car.

That - I guess they had been in there for years.

Did you ever use them to -- I don't know how much of this you have read from the papers, but you have been accused of - by some of the towns folks - of being a window-peeper. Is that true?

That is untrue.

I thought maybe you might have worn the mask as a window-peeper.

No.

That pink dress that I showed you. What family did that come from? You told me—

The Klimaker family.

The Klimaker family?

That's right. It's their youngest daughter, Catherine.

Catherine Klimaker. They gave that to you to wipe off your windshield and
the windows in the car.

That's right.

By the way, I found a pair of hair clippers. Was that?

Oh, that was the folks bought that.

The folks. And what is the explanation for the house brick that you had
in your car, that was wrapped in green paper?

That I don't - if that was taken - you see, there was this fellow, Russell
                                    of course
Eastland, he wanted to buy my farm, xm as I figured on stuff like what I had, if he
wanted to take possession quickly like he said, that I'd have to have some place to
move into, and there's a place at West Springfield, that belonged to an old fellow,
Lawrence Waits, he owned that, and he's on the - oh, what's that, I guess the State
or something -

State aid?

Or pension, you know, that's turned over, and he had that for sale. There
should be, I believe that's where it came from, there should be another one there with
cloth over. I didn't know what them was myself. I suppose them was for get 'em hot and
use 'em for bed warmers?

Well, that's a possibility, yes. Now these watches, there were 3 or 4 watches

272

and one wrist watch. Who were they ──

.I believe there's some bands there, probably, too. That was - the wrist watches

were mine and the others were, I believe, that's from LaCrosse.

The old pocket watches?

That's right.

And the ring that I showed you - you thought it was your uncle's ring.

Yes, either my dad's or uncle's.

And the women's shoes? Could they have been your mother's?

Yes, they must be -

Because Bernice's shoes, which were brown in color, and stockings which were

fitted in the shoes by yourself, were also in the kitchen and dining room, as you call it.

Kitchen, I believe.

In the kitchen. Did you plan because you had them in the kitchen on burning

them?

That probably was my ──

Remember the heart also that was in the bag? What did you tell me ──

That's the idea - the idea of burning - you see that was in that waste ──

I was wondering why, Eddie, you selected the heart to burn and the remainder

of the intestines remained in the box with the head. ⍰

That would be quite hard to burn when they're fresh.

And you thought that maybe because the heart was a solid mass ──

That's right.

How about the lungs?

Well, them was separated, it could have been afterwards ── this was too fresh .

ashes. Do you think that something could or should be found amongst those ashes?

I think there probably could be.

And what do you think might be amongst these ashes?

Well, bits of bone they can, you know,

Identify?

I have not
Identify. Of course, I'm not/studied in anything like that - just how bodies

are burned - if there'd be teeth or anything like that.

When I spoke to you of these two sections, that is the noses, the one mouth

and the eyes, what was your explanation as to why you removed 'em?

Because the moths got at them and larvae, I suppose you'd call it, had eaten

through them then when I cut it through that was the only part that was really left.

I see.

That's why this one was in a plastic bag.

You mean Mary Hogan's head?

Yes.

When, by your best recollection now, do you recall your first incident, who

was the first person that you removed from the grave?

As close as I can - it's quite hard -

It was Adams, Sparks, Sherman, Everson, Foster, Beggs -

I believe it was --- Adams.

Excuse me for a moment. Mr. Wilson's here. The reason for this delay, Eddie,

Mr.Wilson has been at the State Capitol and was having conversation with the various

authorities. Now Mr.Wilson advises me that the District Attorney from Adams County

has learned that a woman by the name of Mrs. Norris Diggles, do you know her?

Yes.

From Plainfield. Mrs. Diggles claims that shortly after the disappearance

of Dick Travis you met her in front of Worden's store and told her that you put Dick

either in the car or the truck.

She's wrong.

What reason would she have to say that? About you?

Either she heard somebody else say that and she's mistaken and got it mixed

up with me or -- I doubt that she'd do that apurpose. She'd have no reason to hate

me or me her.

Is she an elderly woman? Do you think she'd have a vivid imagination?

Well, I'd judge her high in the 30's - maybe 40 - that could be wrong.

I can't understand that, that she'd say that about me.

Well, people sometimes like to take advantage of the dituation.

I didn't think she was that kind. And I was thinking, you know, that cord

you asked about - that briaded cord? I seen that in the house myself. Now, whether

my brother braided that or if I braided it myself, and you know I've been fishing

and the neighbors went along, took along poles, and I've been using cords for tying

fish poles on and stuff. And that brick business, when you was gone I was thinking

of that. You said that one brick was wrapped with paper, wasn't it?

Yes. I'll have Mr. Halligan bring it down afterwards. As a matter of

fact, I made mention of that to him just a few minutes ago, asking him to look it

up and to bring it down. So I imagine he probably will go up for it later on and

he'll bring it down. I told him just to rap on the door when he finds it and bring it.

The other question that we would like for you to answer, if you can, you had told me

this morning that you do recall attempting to have intercourse with Bernice but

275

that you were not able to accomplish it because you didn't have an erection - I mean that your penis wasn't stiff.

Yes.

Do you recall under what circumstances you did that, I mean, had you removed her vagina at the time?

No.

She was still in one piece?

That's right.

Was that in the truck or was that in the shed, do you --

In the shed.

Was it down in that ground pit or was it up on the wooden floor?

It was up on top.

You also told me this morning regarding an incident wherein your mother and yourself went to this farm regarding the dog. What was the purpose of you and your mother going to this farm?

We went there, you know, there was a hay marsh on there and that was after - oh, probably three days after the killing frost - and that hay would be dead and dry -- I wanted to cut some of that hay for bedding, because that was better, you'd get fertilizer, you know, out of it, and stuff like that. I wish that I never would have taken her over there because that was the cause that brought on her stroke.

How many days after this incident of the --

The same day.

At home or there?

You see, we went home then when I seen that nothing else had happened. She

276

took the little girl in and everything seemed to be quiet.

Why was he beating the dog?

That's - he killed it. There were 6 or 7 dogs found under a brush pile, they told me. Of course, I couldn't swear to that, I didn't see it. They had been beaten to death with a club.

Were they pups, do you know, or newly born dogs?

They must be, you know, ones that people wanted to give away like that. He must have just got 'em to kill or something.

Did you attempt to stop him or persuade him to stop?

No, that is quite a ways from where we were, you see.

That was in 1944. Or was it 1943?

That probably was in '43.

You say your mother passed away in December of '44. Almost the end of the year.

That's right. Just about that.

Q   - - - a woman of bad reputation?

A   Well - -

Q   She sold her body?

A   No, I didn't mention anything like that that I - - not to my knowledge.

Q   Was she a wicked woman from the standpoint of consorting with other men?

A   Well the only thing that they said, this woman in Bancroft in that tavern where we stopped that time, she said she was a tough woman. She said a woman had to be tough, she says, to run a tavern alone that way. That's all . . .

Q   When you left your house, rather, when you went to Mary Hogan's tavern on this particular day that she lost her life, did you have that in mind before you came to Mary's, or did that . . .

A   No, that was like a . . .

Q   Spontaneous - on the spot?

A   That's right.

Q   Do you recall whether or not you attempted -- you say you are little hazy about - - did you attempt to have intercourse with her?

A   No, of course I couldn't swear to it, but I don't believe so.

Q   When you say you don't believe so, why should the balance be on the . . . that you didn't?

A   Because the same - - what I base my opinion on is the same as with Mrs. Worden. And it would be worse being the first than the second, you know, because with Mrs. Worden I couldn't either.

Q   But you did try, I mean with Bernice?

A   That's right. My mind wasn't in it, you know - - -

Q   Now we'll go on with these tests. You remember my explaining to you about the

principle of this peak of tension test? That's where I ask you Did you take one

living life? You answered Yes. Did you take the living life of 2 persons? And so on.

Now let me show you this particular letter . . . Now the explanation is for you to

give, because I can find out by subsequent examination. Now, Eddie, this is where

I ask you Is your first name Eddie? and Is your last name Gein? Have you taken the

life of one living person? Yes. Have you taken the life of 2 living persons? Yes.

Then I ask you Have you taken the life of 3 living persons? And it doesn't begin to

come down until I ask you Have you taken the life of 4 living persons? . . . leaves

one question at this time Is there any remote possibility that there is more than two?

A   No.

Q   You're sure in your own mind?

A   That's right.

Q   Because then I ask you here Have you lied to any of the questions on this test?

And there was a reaction there.

A   That I guess is — I noticed — I think it was twice. I noticed that myself

in my nervous system — that's probably what showed on there - -

Q   Well, we'll repeat this one later on, because as you know from your last

visit here, we run everything in sets or in pairs. We'll put this away.

A   I'm sure of that, you know, so that was - - -

Q   Now to many of my questions you answer I'm not sure or I don't know on some of

these other issues, but is there any reservation or hesitation or doubt in your

mind from the standpoint of taking the lives of more than 2 persons?

A   No, there is no doubt to that, because I would have come to and realized   .

279

enough to know if there was more than 2.

Q   There'd be no reason to conceal the fact that you have admitted to 2, plus these graves.

A   That's right.

Q   Have you been able to refresh your memory any, Eddie, on the graves and these locations? You have given me the names and I'll repeat 'em again: Mrs Adams, Sparks, Mrs Sherman, Mrs Everson, plus this Norwegian woman, which makes a total of 1,2,3,4, 5 from Plainfield. How many are there, that you know of without trying to remember the names, of bodies from Plainfield? I know that you've given this information to others, but I don't have it.

A   I see it. That darn headache makes it . . .

Q   Is it becoming, your headache, is it progressively getting worse?

A   No, it's about the same but that might be that — my mind —

Q   Another thing that I'd like to ask you, Eddie, and you may agree or you may refuse. Would you be willing, provided the doctors approve also, after they are through with their examinations, and when you are rested, and that's a good place to get a rest, would you be agreeable for coming for a final interview with me here?

A   Yes, I think so. I know you're fair and square.

Q   That's right. Eddie, we are receiving telegrams, special delivery letters, and everything else regarding missing persons, and we want to make sure, to satisfy everyone, that after your memory has become refreshed to the nth degree, which might occur tomorrow, maybe a month from now, that you can fill us in on these little details. I know that it's very trying and difficult for you to try to remember

280

all these things that we'd like to know. So, if your doctors approve, later on, a month from now or whenever it is, 2 months from now, I invite you and ask you whether or not you would be agreeable for a final interview.

A   I think so. If this second test should - - -

Q   We'll take care of that today, Eddie. I don't want to prolong this too much more today, so that you can get back in the routine and examining your examinations and get rested at the hospital.

A   That's right. And if this test comes out like it should, and I believe it will because it seemed to be good before, and everything, so if that comes out good, I can't see no reason why I should refuse to - - -

Q   That's right. The reason that I ask this of you, Eddie, it's a long delayed slow process of examining all of the exhibits, and questions will come up that we would like to get an answer to and I think that that can be accomplished if you're agreeable at a much later date. Now, getting back to the Plainfield cemetery- - -

A   I can tell you a little bit more after this other test, too, I think it will- -

Q   Well, can't you tell me now?

A   Well, if these tests should show that I'd be guilty of something that I know I'm not - -

Q   No, the machine will not show that. If you can explain to me now, what was it that you wanted to tell me? I mean you mentioned it . . .

A   It's just like kind of a nervous reaction, you know, kind of a spasm, couple of times. Could I mention that when it happens to me?

Q   Please, yes. When that happens, you just say The spasm, and that's all you have to say. Then what I'll do, I'll ask Is your first name Eddie? Is your last name Gein? And then I'll repeat the question that occurred during the spasm. Just say "spasm" or if there's any other word that you'd like to use to identify it as such.

Eddie, even if you can't remember the names, I say that I know that you've

given me names of others . .

A   Bergstrom is the name of . . .

Q   Of the Norwegian - Bergstrom. I see. Would you know how many bodies you

removed from the Plainfield cemetery? There's Adams, There's Bergstrom, there's

Sparks, there is Sherman, there is Everson, which makes a total of 5 at Plainfield.

Is that that correct? Are there any more?

A·   There's more.

Q   There's more.

A   Because, youse would add, let's see, that would be 9, wouldn't it, that --

Q   No, the names that I have just read - -

A   Ya, I know, but I mean them masks, -- was 9. Say, I believe I got all of 'em.

Maybe there's one that I couldn't think of there to the sheriff's office. There's

8 or 9 I've got.

Q   And there was a Mrs. Foster, at Hancock.

A   That's right.

Q   And Mrs. Beggs, at Spiritland.

A   That's right.

Q.   Only one at Spiritland and only one at Hancock.

A   That's right.

Q   And you think maybe 9 at -- a total of 9 at Plainfield?

A   Well, that would be, let's see --

Q   These names that ou've just given me total 1,2,3,4,5,6, 7.   ou know,

282

Eddie, here is this brick. Why don't you open it up, you haven't got to see what is

inside.

A   I'm pretty sure I can explain. Of course, I can't give you a full explanation

but I think this was a test. You see, the place that I told you about - that Ornswick's

place? You know, I had a chance to sell my place. Well, I anyway hoped I had a chance.

And I was looking around for a place, you know, for to take my furniture if I couldn't

make an auction quick -- he wanted to move in right away, he said. And I looked at

that place and upstairs is a brick, well I figure it is anyway this type wrapped up

in cloth, though, instead of in paper.

Q   We have another brick there - I don't think so - the one we had didn't have

cloth on it --

A   I didn't take it. I don't believe I took it. But that's up in that building.

Probably is still there. It should be. And my idea was, like I mentioned to you,

that if that was used for a foot warmer, or something like that, and this was an

experiment to see if it would hold heat. You know, paper is an insulator. . . .

Of course, another fellow has the house now , it might be locked up. Johnson, I

believe bought the place.

Q   Where was that place?

A   That's West Plainfield. It was Lawrence Waite's place. That was upstairs

in that kind of a room - attic up there. Of course, I think, it was all sewed up

so I didn't open it. But the heft and everything.

Q   Did you go to that place much, I mean . . .

A   No, I believe I was only there twice. The first time when I seen that, say,

that's right, when I seen that this Hill boy was along and he looked at it, too,

283

and wondered what it was. Because you see I didn't hardly like to go alone unless

somebody was with me, or else I'd be snooping and stuff like that, you know. And

the second time, that was when I thought probably he was - - - going to get the - -

- he said he was sure he could get the money again and I just glanced through there

once quick, you know. I took a flashlight along because there was a little basement

door, just a hole dug, like, you know, so I could see what kind of a - - place it

wasunderneath there. So I was there twice. And I looked the barn and stuff over

what I didn't do that other time - - but that should be there unless - -

Q   Yes. Thanks, Mr. - - -?   . . . . . This black metal box, Eddie, that was

found under your bed. Where did that come from?

A   That was, I believe, - - - - or not, it probably should be, I think, inside

the cover, a gun box, I believe.

Q   Would you like to see - - what I'm getting at - -

A   That was what the folks had when they was in the store business. They got it

somewhere.

Q   What kind of business were they in?

A   They were in - well, sort of a butcher shop and grocery.

Q   General store, I see. Was that in Plainfield?

A   No, that was in LaCrosse.

Q   The suspicion was that maybe that metal box came from Mary Hogan's.

A .   No.

Q   That is not? Do you have any recollection at all of taking any money from

Mary Hogan's?

A   Not any - not any recollection, I don't.

Q   Could you have?

A   No, I wouldn't - you see -- I wouldn't have ha ime for anything like that.

Q   You're quite sure?

A   Yes.

Q   Of all the faces, or masks, or whatever you want to call them, full heads, you know, the entire head just with the bone or skull removed, there is one with blonde, comparatively blonde or light hair and light complexion. Do you know who that is?

A   That would be the one from Spiritland.

Q   That would be Mrs. Beggs?

A   Well, that was on the Beggs' lot, now whether that was her real name or not . .

Q   I think in your conversation, I think it was with Herb the Sheriff, or Mr. Haka the District Attorney, you had mentioned some name like Schaefer. Do you recall?

A   Oh, they asked me if I knew some Schaefer down from that part of the country or something like that, and the only Schaefer I know, and I don't even know him much, that's the one up in Plainfield. He goes with a cane.

Q   He goes with a person by the name of Cane, or he uses a cane?

A   No, he uses a cane.

Q   Is he an elderly person?

A   Yes, he's getting a pension, I believe.

Q   Was he a farmer, or what was his trade?

A   I couldn't say to that.

Q   Do you know his first name?

A   Fred, I believe.

Q   Does he have any children that you knw of?

A   His wife, there. She's quite a short, chunky woman. Fred Schaefer, that's right. Otherwise I don't know him, I've just seen him. When they mentioned

Schaefer, I thought it was him first, and I asked you if he carried a cane.

Q   You think that the black metal box definitely was your parents'.

A   Yes, I know that. They kept things in it - I kept it on, I cleaned it out sometimes. There might be even some yet in there.

Q   Do you recall any ~~incident~~ reason, you have given me the answer earlier, as to why you wouldn't have ~~asked for help~~ had help or sought any/assistance from others. But the same old doubt rises in everyone's mind in your community and elsewhere, how could a small frail person like you do these things? I mean how long have you had this hernia of yours?

A   That came when I helped one of my neighbors, let's see, that would be about 4 years ago, I believe. I helped him hay. You know, I still can't understand why he'd do anything like that. They bought some of this alfalfa hay - it was too big in the first place, he shoulda known, and then he went and raked it. I told him Don't cut too much, because I had experience in cutting hay -- Oh, he said, it's growing so good now I'll cut it all down and then it will grow so much quicker. Then he got a rain on it, then he raked it with one of these horse-drawn dump rakes, and then he bunched it, it was tangled so, you know, and I thought of all the un-loading of that by hand. And then on top of it, I'm sure that that's where this started. Then I caught cold from that - like grip - and then the coughing made that worse.

Q   Do you recall/any in of these instances, Eddie, when you would remove the bodies from the graves - would you open the entire casket, or just one of the halves?

A   As a rule, I believe, just the half.

Q   And slip 'em out?

A   That's right.

286

Q   That would mean you wouldn't have to dig a large hole.

A   That's right.

Q   Was there difficulty in removing these cadavers or corpses?

A--   Well, I'd say fairly difficult, but --

Q   Would you drag them or were you able to carry them like a piece of timber?

A   Yes, the lighter ones.

Q   The lighter ones you'd carry like timber over your shoulder?

A   That's right.

Q   And the others, what would you do?

A   Carry them in my arms this way - or kinda hold --

Q   Did anyone ever surprise you close enough to cause you to become apprehensive

or frightened that they saw what you were doing?

A   No, I doubt that anybody saw what I was doing. Now that you mention it, a car

did come through the cemetery once when I was there, but whether they were just lovers,

or whatever they were --

Q   Did you hide?

A   I believe I was right down in the grave. They went by and they kept right on

going -- that's the only time --

Q   Getting back to Mary Hogan, when you, on the day that you took her life, what

was your motive for going there, do you recall?

A   Well, I came from Bancroft.

Q   Were you alone, or was someone with you.

A   I was alone. What time was that supposed to be, do you remember?

Q   1955, I believe, in December.

A   -- and that was supposed to be around 5 o'clock?

287

Q   Something like that - between a quarter to 4 and 5:30.

A   When I was out at Bancroft, I stopped, you know a girl had been killed,

thrown off of a horse, and there was a burial over in the Bluff cemetery, I think,

and I thought I was right there, you know, and I happened to think of this girl and

I thought I could get more information how she really was killed, but because I

hadn't got too much. She was just thrown off the horse.

Q   Had you at that time entertained any thought of getting her?

A   No, I didn't think of that then. I went over there and I was talking with them

and I seen the vault that they had for the girl. I believe the whole vault was there,

come to think of it. And that was another woman that I think was buried -- and this

one - -

A   And there was another shovel there and I helped him fill the grave of that

woman. That's why I was kinda asking about the time.

Q   And then from there you went to Mary's -- is that it?

A   That's right.

Q   Do you think that as a result of your action in assisting in the burial of

this girl -- did that in any way spark any idea in your mind about Mary?

A   I never thought of that. That could be. -- ------

Q   Had you thought about Mary on many occasions prior to that?

A   No, not too often.

Q   Let me give you this card. I'm going to leave the room for a moment and

while I'm away would you try to get the names of all of these women whose bodies

you've taken from the graves?

A   Let's see -- there's -- --

Q   Why not mark these down?

A   There's 5 from Plainfield. There should be 2 more.

Q   A total of 7.

A   That's 7, and these others, 8, 9, 10. Mrs. Hogan is 10. That's the full

amount.

Q   Maybe this will help you by writing it down. Write the word Plainfield first.

All right. Then the name Adams, then the name Bergstrom, then Sparks, then Sherman,

then Everson, then run a blue line across here so you can leave some space for two

more names. All right. Now mark this Hancock. Then under Hancock will be the

name Foster, then a line beneath that, and that will be Spiritland, and that's Beggs.

Now, while I'm absent from the room, if you will Eddie, try to concentrate -- --

289

Judge Rules Ed Gein Is Insane

By FLOYD GONYEA
Sentinel Staff Writer

WISCONSIN RAPIDS, ⁚ ⁚ 6—Circuit Judge Herbert Bunde ruled late Monday a⁚ ⁚ noon that Edward Gein, ⁚ fessed -slayer and grave robber is legally insane.

The judge ordered the 51-year-old Plainfield handyman committed for an indeterr ⁚⁚ ate term to the Central S ⁚ Hospital for the criminally sane at Waupun.

Judge Bunde said evide ⁚ presented to him showed t ⁚ Gein was chronically ment⁚ ill and probably never will released from the maxim ⁚ security hospital.

290

Gein is arrested. (Lou Rusconi)

A   Well, I can't exactly say this one's name, but if it's Johnson or it's

anyway, if anybody wanted to find out, she was Henry Woodward's mother, I believe.

His father was married twice, and this was his first wife. So the name I couldn't

exactly say just what it was.

Q   And the 7th one you can't think of?

A   And the 7th one - I could look at the mask - -

Q   I don't know if it would be desirable, until after what the doctors have

to suggest or recommend. Now does the name Elzida, or Elzada Abbott mean anything

to you? In relation, we'll say, to either Hancock or Spiritland?

A   I believe there's one -- around Spiritland, but I wouldn't say.

Q   Could the body that you removed from the Spiritland cemetery, which you say

was in the Beggs lot, could it be?

A   You're probably right there, you see there was no marker or anything. You

know a lot of cemeteries, the undertaker puts a little plate. There wasn't any-

thing like that - just a headstone. You're probably right that Abbott, Kinda --

Q   Now, in view of what Herb the Sheriff and what John Haka the District

Attorney, both from Stevens Point - they were wondering whether or not there was

some possibility that this man Schaefer that we speak of, with the cane, whether

or not he could have seen you at the tavern at the time you went in to see Mary

Hogan. Was he at the cemetery when you helped bury --

A   Let's see. It's a funny thing, too, but it couldn't have been this one,

I doubt, from Plainfield. I don't know if they have a car or not. I couldn't

say about that -- I've seen a car there -- whether it's theirs or not --

Q   You say you saw a car there, where, do you mean at Mary's?

A   No. At Plainfield where they live. But whether they could drive, or if it was their daughter's car - - -

Q   Do you have any recollection, Eddie, when you removed Mary from her place, was it dusk or was it dark?

A   Well, dusk I would say.

Q   So there is that possibility that you could have been observed?

A   That's true.

Q   Did you cover Mary in any way to conceal the fact that it was a person when you removed her from the tavern?

A   I believe I did. I think I had a blanket on the seat and I put that over her.

Q   And then carried her out that way. You had mentioned earlier to me, Eddie, that there were only 2 bodies that you recall you used the salt on; the others that you didn't because they were in a good state of preservation from being embalmed.

A   That's right.

Q   Now, one that you say you used the salt on was Mary.

A   I kinda think so.

Q   Who was the other one, do you know?

A   And the other was Adams.

Q   I understand that Mrs. Adams was buried in 1950 or '51. Do you remember?

A   No.

Q   Did you make any attempt at removing any portions of the bodies from graves or anything else prior to 1951? Do you remember what possessed you on this first occasion - in the case of Mrs. Adams - to enter the grave?

A   Let's see. For a minute there I thought I did have - but what could it be. What come in my mind there for a minute, I don't know if it's right or not, you see

293

her boy, George, borrowed $10 from me, and I think he told a lie when he borrowed it,

he said his aunt was sick and he needed that to go to see her. Now, I don't know

just exactly, if I'd wrote it down, just what time that was, anyway he never paid

it back. And whether that got that started off -- or

Q   You mean revenge or something --

A   That's right.

Q   Do you know, was he devoted to his mother?

A   Not too much, nor his dad, neither one of them. I should have talked a little

bit more with the sheriff there, with what had been the sheriff, because he'd been

called down to Adams's a couple times. He was drunk and beat his wife up, or something.

He made believe afterwards that he had a lot of affection for his wife . . . .

Q   Is there anything else that you can think of? Otherwise, maybe we can take

a short break. Would you care for a cup of coffee or a glass of milk?

A   Which can we have?

Q   Either, or orange juice. Which do you want?

A   Which do you think would be best for a bracer?

Q   For a bracer - coffee or tea.

A   Coffee.

Q   Would you care to have something with it - a piece of pumpkin pie or a

sandwich?

A   Pumpkin pie sounds good.

Q   O.K.   In the meantime, Eddie, if you want to here's a - - -

A   Let's see. There's 1,2,3,4,5,6 - there'd be just one more.

Q   If you think of any other notes, you just go ahead and mark them down

and we'll get you the coffee and pie. Just sit and relax. Do you want to go to

294

the men's room or later on?

A   Well, maybe I could do it right now.

Q   I saw them waiting out in the hallway. Let's take a break. Leave that right there and we'll have them take you to the men's room.

Q   -- on this sheet, if you want to add to this, Eddie. I assume now that you might want to add the name Elzida or Elzada, add it down here. The last name is Abbott. And then here would be mother of Henry Woodward. And you say that No. 7, you're quite sure is Plainfield, you don't remember or know, is that it?

A .   It kinda seems to me that I never noticed the marker.

Q   You recall that on previous occasions, Eddie, you told me/~~xxu~~ you used to watch the Hancock and Plainfield obituaries. Would No. 7 have come from a name or a burial in the obituary?

A   That could be.   If I could remember just the time of that, why then - -

Q   How many bodies from the graves?

A   That would be 9.

Q   And then there was Mary Hogan 10, and then there was Bernice 11. Now would it confuse you regarding these other bodies from caskets, where you removed only certain portions? Would you make an estimate of how many graves you think you might have opened in addition to the 9?

A   Let's see. I wouldn't have opened any more.

Q   Do you recall, and is it true that you told me there were many times when you got to the point of digging in, maybe evening opening up, but stopped right there?

A   That's right.

Q   Now, would you have any difficulty, Eddie, with the question "9 is the total

295

number of bodies that you have taken from the grave?"

A   Yes, that would be the total number of graves that I completely opened.

Q   And 2 is the total number of living persons whose lives you have taken?

A   That's right.

Q   Did you ever attempt to take the lives of any others?

A   No.

Q   Is that a firm answer?

A   That's right.

Q   - - I spoke to you -- on the chain with a tuft of hair? What is your recollection

on that? Remember I asked you whether or not you could have removed it from Mary Hogan?

A-   That's right. It doesn't _seem_ possible. It could be, but it doesn't seem

possible, because as I remember it, and it's quite strong that I remember, her skull

was burned, complete, it wasn't opened or anything. And I know that I have fired quite

a few of these bullets, and the only thing, this here one, the way that I remember, I

thought it looked a little better, you know, I had it on my key chain. ᵗˣᶜˣᵐᵘˣˣᵃˣ If I

could have had an empty shell to put it in, it'd keep, but I didn't think. Well,

that's the way I think it was.

Q   That's good enough. Do you recall the name of the sexton or the grave-digger

at Hancock that you helped?

A   That was over there by the Bluff Cemetery.

Q   Is that the name of the cemetery - the Bluff Cemetery?

A   Yes. They was burying that woman and then this girl was going to be buried later,

the vault was there for the girl.

Q   What did you do, did you help dig the grave or did you help bury her?

A   I helped fill the grave.

Q   Oh, she was buried, then, is that it?

A   That's right. This woman was buried already. And the girl wasn't buried yet -- -

Q   I know - I understand. You helped bury some person, other than this girl that was injured as a result of falling from a horse.

A   That's right. He told me about that. That's why I stopped there -- --

Q   Were you told that one of your pinchbars or crowbars was found, I think, in either the Adams or the Everson grave? Did you know that?

A   No.

Q   Do you think that happened by accident, that you forgot it, or do you think you just left it?

A   Well, it could be either way.

Q   Now these are the questions I've written up to this/point, Eddie. See if you can give me your answers, again reminding you that if the question is not clear or if there is any doubt in your mind, tell me, ~~tell~~ otherwise try to give me the answer. Yes, No, or I don't know. Is 9 the total number of bodies that you have removed from graves?

A   Yes.

Q   Is 2 the total number of living persons whose lives you have taken?

A   Yes.

Q   Did you take the lives of 2 women?

A   Yes.

Q   Did you ever take the lives of any young girls or very young women?

A   No.

Q   Did you ever take the lives of any men or boys?

A   No.

Q   Other than Spiritland, Plainfield and Hancock cemeteries, have you ever

taken any other bodies from any other cemeteries? That you haven't told me about?

A   No.

Q   Other than Mary Hogan and Bernice Worden, have you taken the lives of any

other living human beings?

A   No.

Q   Are those questions clear in your mind?

A   That's right.

Q   Now that the telephones are busy so that I can't use the phones, so we'll

go on with this test and when I get through with this one, I'll try again on

this phone call. There's the water.

A   No foam on it?

Q   No foam. Do you like beer?

A   No.

Q   ~~No,/I/don~~ No.

A   No, I don't care much for it. It's all right when it's hot. It's a little

better than water.

Q   Remember my asking you earlier, Eddie, about these 2 pieces of tissue that

look like balls, and you said they were breasts turned inside out and you thought

that maybe they could be Mary Hogan's?

A   I'm quite positive.

Q   For what reason did you possess them? Did you ever place them beneath a

corset or brassiere?

A   No, I don't believe I did - they wasn't really finished yet. I was --

298

Q   Was it your intention --

A   Well, kind of a remembrance, I believe - to remind me of her.

Q   A remembranc of her.   What were your intentions on completing - I mean what

did you plan on putting some decoration on 'em or something?

A   Yes, something like that.

Q   Why did you put the drum on the lips of some of the other heads?

A   That was to make a more natural look.

Q   I see.   And what was the reason for your putting rouge or lipstick on some?

A.   Well, that was from the lipstick - I used that wax to fill that in.

Q   I see.   Was it wax or was it lipstick?

A   Well, it was kind of a - real lipstick, but it was kinda almost like wax,

you know, heavy type.

Q   Did you get that at one of the drugstores or one of the stores?

A   Let's see.   I believe I found that in my car, that some girl had dropped.

Q   Of Mary Hogan, I mean, what was the thing that impressed you most about her?

Was it the breasts, and of course I know you had her head and her vagina.   Was she

a big chesty woman, full-bosomed woman?

A.   She was chunky.

Q   Now let me read these questions to you quickly again.   I'll ask you Your

first name is Edward?   Your last name Gein?   You live in Waushara County?   Did you

have dinner or lunch today?   Is 9 the total number of bodies you removed from graves?

Is 2 the total number of living persons whose lives you have taken?   Did you take

the lives of 2 women?   Did you ever take the lives of any young girl or very young

woman?   Did you ever take the life of any man or boy?   Other than the cemeteries at

299

Spiritland, Plainfield and Hancock, have you ever taken any other bodies from any other

cemetery that you haven't told me about? Other than Mary Hogan and Bernice Worden,

have you ever taken the lives of any other living human beings?

- - -

Now clench your fist hard, please. As before, Eddie, I'll also repeat this

same set of questions. Take a short break. And also a little earlier you had mentioned

that if youd get a spasm, either muscular or otherwise, if you'd speak the world out

)so that I couldmark it down. ----

One thing I mention here, I don't know if that makes any difference with the

machine or not, but you know the other time when I had a test I didn't know notice that,

but now I noticed right in my temples, you know ---

A throbbing?

Yes. Fast. And my heartbeat must be faster, too, than it was before.

Did you, when you went to bed last night, any of the nurses or doctors give

you anything to make you sleep?

That's right.

Was it more than -

A large capsule.

Do you remember what color it was?

Red, it was.

Were you able to go to sleep very quickly after you took that?

Well, I should judge about a half hour, probably.

Then did you sleep soundly from there on in?

Yes, for probably a long time - when you sleep time goes so fast. (Lapse of time)

You sce how that was they gave one of these, well you know what they are where you put

these electrodes - and this operator, he gave me that capsule, that was later - I guess

this was after
by the time I got back itxoxxx supper time and they had my lunch there, said they tried

to keep it warm for me. And he gave mh this capsule and he thought probably you know

301

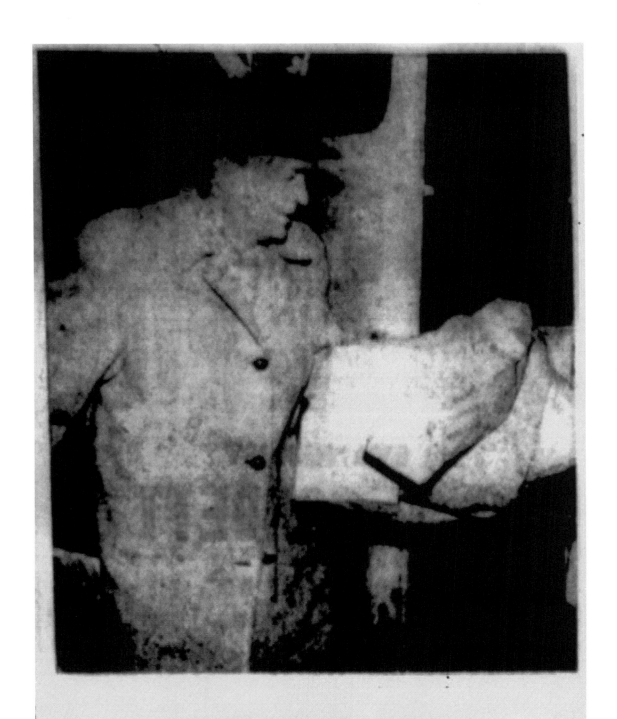

GRISLY HUMAN REMAINS

. . . in paper bags are taken into mobile unit of State Crime Laboratory by lab official.

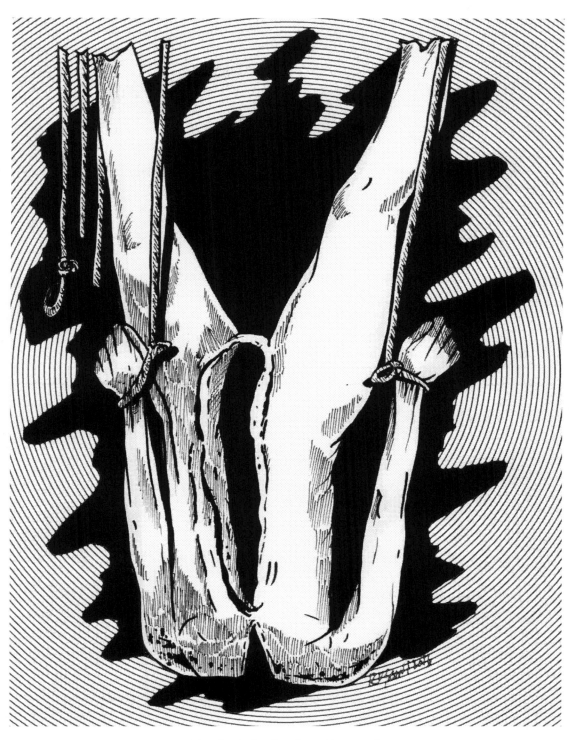

Worden's body. (Lou Rusconi)

thought I'd go to sleep, It never affected me at all.

Never affected?

No, it only affected me when you know when I was in bed. I never went to sleep before. I, of course, I didn't have no time so I probably slept for half the night without waking up.

Will you sit and relax while I sharpen this pencil and we'll go on with the same set of questions --

Compare 'em, that's right.

I don't know how this test will go. It might be all right, because my -- because it doesn't --

Do you feel well or do you feel ill?

Well, the only thing was that headache.

At this particular point, is it about the same, is it less, or has it worsened any?

My pulse doesn't seem to be just right, you know, just --

Rapid?

Yes, right in my temples.

At this particular moment, while you're seated and the test is not being accomplished, the cuff pressure is off, are your temples pounding now?

Yes.

Well, we'll take just a short breather and while we're doing that, I'll draw up another set of questions, Eddie, and I want to impress upon you that if at any time you feel - that you don't feel well, or that you note this condition that you've just explain ed to me, please tell me about it so that --

304

You can make allowance for it.

That's right.

I'd been noticing that. You know the other time when I had the test I didn't
- notice that anything like that.

You probably are becoming self-conscious of the fact, orxsomething --

Or something, because I notice it. And I think this, oh that spinal and
then that head test, probably that drug what they gave me, and everything combined
it's kinda --

Combination of all --

That's right.

Now, using your own words and your own definitions, to what area by
counties would you explain that you had operated in from the standpoint of taking
the lives plus taking the bodies from graves?

Waushara County would be the only one.

Well, how about Mary Hogan?

Let's see. Oh, that's right, she was in a different county. What come
in my mind was the state, you know. But let's see, that's Wood - no Portage County.

Now would your operations be limited only to Portage and Waushara Counties
or are they outside of either of these two counties?

No, they'd be the only ones. I believe. Let's see, where's this
Spiritland?

Let me find out. That was in Portage County.

Edward is becoming self-conscious of his heartbeat and this throbbing in
his temples.

How's the headache?

305

E.G.   Well, that's down in my neck now. I don't know --

Is it bad?

Well, as long as I'm sitting perfectly still it isn't so bad. Down here in my

shoulders and back right in here.

Before he got into bed last night he had a large red capsule.

They wanted to put me to sleep quick, but it didn't work right away. It

worked afterwards. (Time laps) Short I think I have gas pressure inside, too, because I ---

Caused by constipation?

That's right - because I just passed some.

I sent the young lady out for pepsin gum, which we can use after you leave.

This isn't going to take too much longer now. I'll write these questions up and will

read them to you and I think that will conclude today's examination. You heard me

ask you to give me in your own words what would be your own word, of your own choice,

to describe what you did to the bodies from the graves, to Bernice and to Mary Hogan?

What one word or combination of words would best define (like a definition) what you

did to them?

Let's see -

There is cut up, there's dissection --

Well, the others I can say cut up, but Mrs. Worden's wasn't completely cut up, so--

Well, you began to, anyway --

That's right.

Even though you began, would you consider that you did cut - make some cuts into

her. You removed her head.

That's right.

will
So ~~were~~ you agree on the word cutting up?

Yes, I believe that will be --

All right. And if there are any questions in your own mind when we add the nine bodies from the graves plus Bernice and Mary Hogan, make a total of 11, is that it?

That's right.

Now would you have any difficulty in answering the question Would 11 females be the total number of bodies that you cut up, like you had told me?

That -- question, that's right.

If there's anything you want changed you tell me.

That's all right.

And Bernice Worden and Mary Hogan are the only two ~~female~~ living females whose lives you had taken?

Yes.

And now I answered your question regarding where the Spiritland cemetery was and its in Portage County. Mary Hogan was in Portage County. Hancock is in Waushara is it not?

Yah.

And of course Plainfield is in Waushara. Now would you have any difficulty with the question Other than the 11 bodies (now that's dead and living) Other than the 11 bodies, are there any others that you haven't told me about?

That's -- question.

Other than the 11 bodies, are there any others that you haven't told me about? All of the 11 bodies came from either Portage or Waushara counties and that you have never taken any bodies living or dead from counties outside of Portage and Waushara counties? Do you think you can answer that?

Yes. I think so.

One other one Are you telling me the truth when you tell me that 2 is the

total number of human lives you have taken?   Now, let's go through these very quickly

again. Please give me your answers. Would 11 females be the total number of bodies

that you cut up like you have told me?

Yes.

Bernice Worden and Mary Hogan are the only two females whose lives you have

ever taken?

Yes.

Other than the 11 bodies, are there any other bodies that you haven't told

me about?

No.

All of the 11 bodies came from either Portage or Waushara counties?

Yes.

Have you ever taken any bodies, living or dead, from counties outside of

Portage or Waushara counties?

No.

Are you telling me the truth when you tell me that 2 is the total number of

human lives which you have taken?

Yes.

Then, of course, have you lied to any of the questions on this test?

No. Did my ------ kinda bother there?

Just a bit, I mean you seemed to be a little under tension or a little

apprehension. I don't know if it was some particular question or if there is something

308

about a question that is ⎯ ⎯ ⎯ ubt. But generally things ⎯ ⎯ ubstantially correct.

The other thing, like I told Mr. Wilson, is that I feel that some of this tension is due,

Eddie, to the fact that you are trying too hard to cooperate.

Say, that could be.

So, since this, I hope, for today this is the final test, try as much as you

can to relax, if you can, and I notice, as I say, that certain amount of tension —

because I think you are just trying too hard.

I loosened my belt a little bit, I thought maybe that would help.

Put these in your pocket. Oh, I'm sorry — Pepsin, Beechnut and 2 of Beemans.

You can use those while you're driving back.

I sure appreciate that.

It's all right. Let's put 'em up here — I'll put 'em with your jacket.

Let me make the necessary notations on the chart and then we'll begin this. Now just

try to relax. Let's hope that tomorrow, since tomorrow's Thanksgiving, that they serve

duck or turkey. They usually do, from what I've been told.

I'm going to have you take my blood pressure, too. There's something wrong

here, I don't feel like I should.

What seems to be your trouble at the moment?

It might be like you say — self-conscious or something. After this/goes up,
you know

the pressure here, by gee, you know I never noticed that. My pulse is faster and gee,

I can feel that and it just seems to shake me.

Now, Eddie, do you think that you can hold still for one more set as we

ordinarily do. If at any time you should feel faint or ill please tell me, because

this is not that important that we can't take time out to give you the necessary

attention.

309

Sometimes it feels a little bit better - then it will come on. I'll try to
help all I can. My pulse seems to be awful rapid. It shouldn't be that way - there's
something ---

Shall we make a go of it again, Eddie?

Yes.

Don't forget I remind you that in the event you become ill or faint, just say
the word.

I'll do that.

Under the circumstances, I feel that I cannot ask or expect any more.

E G   That's good.

E G   This arm has been bothering me, too. Tried to button my shirt, you know, and
I get my hand up here - -

Arthritis? Rheumatism? Eddie, we conducted this examination earlier and
I'll go over the questions again. The first name Edward; your last name Gein. Have
you taken the life of one living person? What is your answer?

Yes.

Have you taken the lives of 2 living persons?

Yes.

Have you taken the lives of 3 living persons?

No.

And then 4 living persons?

No.

5 living persons?

No.

6 living persons?

No.

7 living persons?

No.

8 living persons?

No.

9 living persons?

No.

10 living persons?

No.

12 living persons?

No.

20?

No.

Was that question humrous or something when I asked you if you'd taken the

lives of 20 living persons and you laughed?

Well, I gave a sigh --

Earlier, yes.

--- I couldn't help myself. You know, I kinda think I know what was

causing part of this.

What do you think it is?

You see, I was listening so strong to what you was saying that I didn't

breathe enough oxygen. My breathing was short and that's why these - kinda yawn

came - that gasp.

I feel that, as a result of the examination, you have become a little

self-conscious about the whole proceedings and you're just trying too hard. Now, let

me check your blood pressure and that will cover our examination for today, and I hope,

Eddie, that if it meets with the approval of the doctors at the hospital, whether or not

it be months from now, I would like very much for you to come back here so that - - -

(?) interview and inventory of things.

Oh, I got gas.

What did you have for lunch? I wonder if anything you ate could have caused

that.

Well, everything, like corn, you know, peas.

Now, in this instance, turn your hand around. That's it. We'll do this

3 times like we did the last time. Twice more. Once more. Other than your pulse

banging away like a trip hammer, there's no material difference in your blood pressure.

And as I say, I think we both agreed, this throbbing and your trying to lean over

backwards to help you and myself, has placed you under a certain amount of tension.

- - - -? Don't put your jacket on. It's a little warm in here, but you can wait

in the other room if you'd like to - - - - Would you like to go to the bathroom before

you leave?

- - -

Exhibition of Ed Gein Car Stirs Controversy in State

An old Ford once owned by Ed Gein, who gained notoriety last year after he confessed two gruesome killings and a series of grave robberies, has stirred up a storm of controversy in various parts of Wisconsin.

The 1949 model car, now being exhibited at Washington county's centennial fair, has been banned from appearing at a fair at Green Bay. And a Door county fair official said the car probably wouldn't be allowed there.

Harold Collins, village president at Plainfield, where Gein committed one murder, said: "It doesn't sound too good. There's bound to be reaction."

"There were a lot of people affected by Gein in Plainfield. I figured when the car was sold for more than it was worth that it would be used for something like this," Collins said.

"I don't know what we can do about it. It might open new wounds here."

The man in the middle of the controversy, Bunny Gibbons, concessionnaire of Rockford, Ill., was unperturbed by it all. He confirmed that he bought the car for $760 last March when Gein's property was auctioned. He used the fictitious name, "Cook Brothers, Wausau," at the time.

"People want to see this kind of thing," Gibbons said. He now is showing the car at 25c a look at the Slinger fair north of Milwaukee.

Gibbons said no one had complained yet about his showing the car. He said he planned to hit other fairs around Wisconsin and Minnesota.

Home, Property Of Ed Gein Goes On The Auction Block

PLAINFIELD, Wis. (AP) — Souvenir and bargain hunters 2,500 of them, swarmed over the farm of slayer and ghoul Ed Gein yesterday, buying anything offered on the auction block.

The 195-acre farm and the half-dozen ramshackle buildings were sold to Emden Schey and his partner Allen Little, Sun Prairie, Wis., real estate dealers, for $3,925.

Schey said they planned forestry plantings on the property of the little handyman who admitted slaying two women and the plundering of a dozen graves.

Gein is in a hospital for the criminal insane.

A Chicago man paid 25 cents for a rusty ax head. Other items that sold for cash included old chicken crates, lumber and wagon wheels.

Chet Scales, a junk dealer from Highland, Wis., paid $215 for the 1940 pickup truck Gein reportedly used to carry the bodies of the two women he killed. Scales said he would keep the truck as a souvenir.

Gein's 1949 two-door Ford sedan brought $740.

A damaged metal stool was sold for $14. A rusty manure spreader—apparently beyond any hope of repair—was sold for $36.

The old farmhouse in which Gein lived alone with his weird collection of graveyard souvenirs burned to the ground early this month during the height of a controversy over holding the auction on Palm Sunday. Authorities still are investigating the possibility of arson.

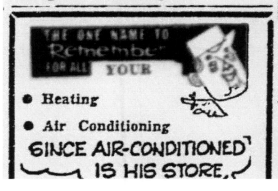

KEEP OUT
NO
TRESPASSING

By Order Waushara County Court

Any person Trespassing upon or Molesting the personal or real property of Edward Gein, without permission of the court, the Guardian or an authorized peace officer will be punished by law.

HARVEY POLZIN,
Guardian

Gein Seeks Release From Mental Ward

Special to The Sentinel

Wautoma, Wis. — Ed Gein, whose arrest 15 years ago set off a series of bizarre disclosures of slayings and grave robberies at Plainfield, has filed a petition with the Waushara County clerk of courts for a re-examination and a re-evaluation of his mental state.

Gein, 66, asks release from the Central State Hospital at Waupun, where he was committed in January, 1958, after he was found unable to stand trial on murder and armed robbery charges.

Gein was committed in connection with the macabre death of Mrs. Bernice Worden, 58, a widowed hardware store owner in Plainfield, who disappeared Nov. 16, 1957. Her body was discovered by Wood County sheriff's deputies at the Gein farm. It had been decapitated and dressed out like a deer carcass.

Authorities also found "death masks" made from skinned heads, skulls, human heads and chairs and lampshades fashioned from human skin in Gein's house. One of the death masks was identified as the face of Mrs. Mary Hogan, a Portage County tavernkeeper who disappeared three years earlier. Gein confessed to her slaying.

Gein at the time was quoted as telling authorities that he had robbed 10 graves after his mother died and that each was that of a woman.

The new petition for re-examination filed Feb. 27 and signed by Gein, states, "This patient has now fully recovered his mental health and is fully competent and there is no reason why he should remain in any hospital."

It further states " that a re-examination be made of this patient's mental condition for a determination that he is now fully recovered, sane and competent."

Psychiatrists who testified before Gein's commitment said that he had an unusually strong Oedipus complex, or feeling of attachment toward his mother. Before she died in 1945, Gein had nursed her following two paralytic strokes, strengthening the attachment, the doctors said.

He was diagnosed as schizophrenic by the psychiatrists.

In 1968, a panel of psychiatrists determined that Gein was competent to stand trial for the murder of Mrs. Worden. He was found guilty in her shooting death but under the two part trial was judged innocent by reason of legal insanity . Circuit Judge Robert Gollmar of Portage ordered that he be recommitted to the Central State Hospital.

Gollmar ordered two psychiatrists, Dr. George Arndt of Neenah and Dr. Leigh Roberts of the University of Wisconsin —Madison, to review the case and present findings to him.

Mr. Thomas Zander   August 27, 1976
Legal Assistance to Inmates Program
L607 Law School
Madison, Wisconsin. 53706

AUG 31 1976

Dear Mr. Zander:

I was informed by David Van Rens that if I requested help from
the Legal Assistance Program, you would come and see me.

I would very much like for you to come and see me, and discuss
my case and what I could do to get my release from Central State
Hospital.

I will be looking forward to seeing you soon.

                                        Yours Truly,
                                        Edward Gein
                                        Ed Gein

STATE OF WISCONSIN
DEPARTMENT OF HEALTH AND SOCIAL SERVICES
ORIGINAL CERTIFICATE OF DEATH

STATE FILING DATE
STATE DEATH **AUG** 9 84 0 17 7 71

LOCAL FILE NUMBER 1537

DECEDENT NAME First	Middle	Last	SEX	DATE OF DEATH
1. Edward		GEIN	☑ Male ☐ Female	July 26 1984

RACE Is a, White, Black, hispanic, American Indian, etc	AGE Last Birthday	UNDER 1 YEAR	UNDER 1 DAY	DATE OF BIRTH	COUNTY OF DEATH	INSIDE CITY OR VILLAGE LIMITS
4. White	5a. 77	5b. Mos	5c. Hours Min.	Month 8 Day 26 Year 06	7a. DANE	☒Yes ☐No

CITY, VILLAGE OR TOWNSHIP OF DEATH	HOSPITAL OR OTHER INSTITUTION~Name ☐Hospital ☐Nursing home ☒Other Instit.	IF HOSP OR INST
7c. MADISON	7d. Mendota Mental Health Institute	☐DOA ☐OP/Emer Rm ☒Inpatient

STATE OF BIRTH (if not in U.S.A., name country)	CITIZEN OF WHAT COUNTRY	MARITAL STATUS	SURVIVING SPOUSE (if wife, give maiden name)	WAS DECEDENT EVER IN U.S. ARMED FORCES?
8. Wisconsin	9. USA	10. ☐1 Married ☒4 Never Married ☐2 Separated ☐5 Widowed ☐3 Divorced	11. None	12. ☐Yes ☒No

SOCIAL SECURITY NUMBER	USUAL OCCUPATION(Give kind of work done during most of working life, even if retired)	KIND OF BUSINESS OR INDUSTRY
13. 388-28-8860	14a. Farming Labor	14b. Agri-Business

RESIDENCE-STATE	COUNTY	CITY, VILLAGE OR TOWNSHIP OF RESIDENCE	INSIDE CITY OR VILLAGE LIMITS	STREET AND NUMBER
15a. Wisconsin	15b. ~~Waushara~~ Dane	15c. ~~Plainfield~~ Madison	15d. ☒Yes ☐No	15e. 301 Troy Drive

FATHER-NAME First	Middle	Last	MOTHER-MAIDEN NAME First	Middle	Last
16. George		Gein	17. Augusta (nee Loehnke)		Gein

INFORMANT-NAME (Type or Print)	MAILING ADDRESS Street or R.F.D. No.	City or Village	State	Zip
18a. William N. Bolter	18b. P.O. Box 897	Wautoma, Wisconsin		54982

	CEMETERY OR CREMATORY NAME	LOCATION City or Village	State
19a. ☒1 Burial ☐4 Removal ☐2 Cremation ☐5 Other ☐3 Entombment	19b. Plainfield Village	19c. Plainfield, Wisconsin	

FUNERAL SERVICE LICENSEE Or Person Acting As Such	NAME OF FACILITY	ADDRESS OF FACILITY Street or R.F.D. No. City or Village	State	Zip
Signature 20a. William H. ___	20b. Gasperic F.H.	20c. P.O. Box 336 Plainfield, Wisc.		54966

21a. To the best of my knowledge, death occurred at the time, date and place and due to the cause(s) stated.

Signature and Title ▶ J. ___ Hansen MD

DATE SIGNED			HOUR OF DEATH	
21b. 7 26 1984			7:45 A M	
Month Day Year				

22a. On the basis of examination and/or investigation, in my opinion death occurred at the time, date and place and due to the cause(s) stated.

Signature and Title ▶

DATE SIGNED			HOUR OF DEATH	
22b. Month Day Year			22c.	

21d. NAME OF ATTENDING PHYSICIAN IF OTHER THAN CERTIFIER (Type or Print)

22d. PRONOUNCED DEAD Month Day Year   22e. PRONOUNCED DEAD (Hour) M

23. NAME AND ADDRESS OF CERTIFIER (PHYSICIAN, MEDICAL EXAMINER OR CORONER) (Type or Print)
Leonard Ganser MD 300 Troy Drive Madison, Wisconsin 53704

REGISTRAR 24a Signature ▶ Carol R. Mahnke	DATE RECEIVED BY REGISTRAR
	24b. JUL 30 1984 Month Day Year

25 PART I	IMMEDIATE CAUSE	(ENTER ONLY ONE CAUSE PER LINE FOR (a), (b), AND (c).)	Interval between onset and death
Conditions if any which gave rise to immediate Cause stating the underlying cause last	(a) Respiratory failure DUE TO, OR AS A CONSEQUENCE OF		
	(b) Carcinomatosis DUE TO, OR AS A CONSEQUENCE OF		
	(c) Carcinoma of Colon metastasis to Liver and lungs		

PART II	OTHER SIGNIFICANT CONDITIONS-Conditions contributing to death but not related to cause given in PART I (a)	AUTOPSY	WAS CASE REFERRED TO MEDICAL EXAMINER OR CORONER?
Schizophrenic Disorder Chronic Dementia		26. ☐Yes ☒No	27. ☐Yes ☒No

	DATE OF INJURY	HOUR OF INJURY	DESCRIBE HOW INJURY OCCURRED
☐1 Accident ☐4 ___ ☐2 Suicide ☐5 Pend. Invest. ☐3 Homicide	28b. Month Day Year	28c. M	28d.

INJURY AT WORK	PLACE OF INJURY-At home, farm, street, factory, office building, etc (Specify)	LOCATION Street or R.F.D. No.	City or Village	State
☐Yes ☐No	28f.	28g.		

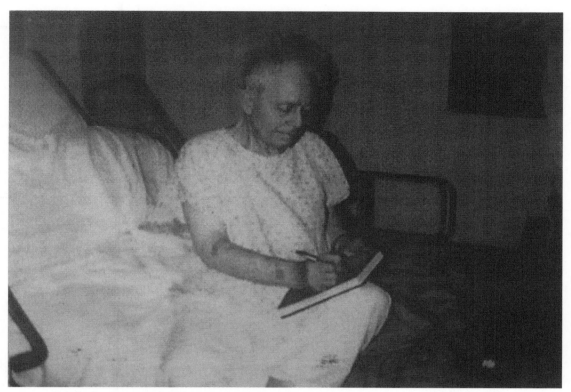

Ed Gein at Mendota Mental Health Institute. (Courtesy of Rick Staton.)

Ed Gein's tombstone.